CONTENTS

KT-572-385

WITHDRAWN

PREFACE

Stalin was one of the few individuals who made history rather than being just part of it. This is not to say that everything which happened in the Soviet Union during his lifetime was directly his responsibility, but simply that it is inconceivable to study the history of the twentieth century without a detailed examination of Stalin's contribution. That contribution, both to the domestic affairs of his country and to the international politics of the Cold War, extended well beyond his death. Indeed, it took more than a generation after 1953 for 'Stalinism', that collection of precepts and practices attached to his name, sometimes rightly and sometimes wrongly, to lose its grip on the Soviet Union and other areas of the world.

This book traces the history of the man and his influence. A broadly narrative approach is followed in the earlier chapters, interspersed with analyses of the sorts of questions which interest historians. The later chapters contain an analysis of what has become known as 'Stalinism'. Whether we like this appellation or not, it is important to see it as more than a term of political abuse, but rather as a critical tool aiding an understanding of what was going on during and after Stalin's lifetime. The final chapter is a historiographical survey. It has been included because it is an increasing and welcome practice amongst History students to study the historian as well as the subject, since there is no such thing as 'objective' history. It is my hope that, after reading this book, students may turn to some more detailed studies of Stalin, with a critical mind and an inclination to ask questions about even the most established interpretations.

Not every facet of Stalin's career can be analysed here in detail, and the differing lengths of chapters reflects perhaps my own interest in particular phases or aspects of the subject. I hope that I have been fair to the authors of the sources which I have quoted or to which I have referred, but the judgements are my own and are there to be challenged. The reader is at liberty to put his or her own interpretation on people and events.

Thanks are due to Julie Laver, for her willingness to discuss issues which sometimes appeared only important to me, and for being the sternest critic of my efforts.

John Laver

INTRODUCTION

'The death of the vanquished is necessary for the calm of the victors.' This comment by Ghengis Khan was marked in a book approvingly by Stalin some years before he came to power in the Soviet Union. It is tempting to regard such evidence as proof of the 'Man of Steel''s tyrannical and vindicative disposition, which led him to become probably the greatest mass murderer in history. Yet would this be a gross oversimplification of the truth? Stalin was more than a despot and a destroyer. The Russian state created in 1917 was a massive experiment: old political, social, economic and cultural certainties were challenged and often overturned. At the end of the 1920s the fledgling Soviet state was launched on the path to super power status, surviving in the process the trauma of economic dislocation, mass terror and devastation in total war. Stalin's name is inextricably linked with this process; and Stalinism is a political label which still excites strong feelings both within the states of the former USSR and the outside world.

Yet there is no agreement as to Stalin's short- or long-term significance. The 'crafty Georgian' is clearly an important figure in twentieth-century history. But exactly why? Why is the man and what he stood for, or what people think he stood for, still so important several decades after his death? At the most human level, he was responsible, directly or indirectly, for the deaths of over thirty million of his own subjects – and the word 'subject' is used very deliberately. Yet the survivors amongst those subjects wept on hearing the news of his death – even some of his victims still alive in the prison camps wept. The stern father of his people was not unloved.

In time critical views of Stalin began to be heard – views that very few would have dared express, even in private, during his lifetime. He could be blamed not just for personal excesses, but for grand policies that no longer seemed quite so praiseworthy. It was particularly convenient for those former colleagues who had implemented the policies to heap the blame for excesses and failures on to one man, rather than admit to faults in themselves or the system that had spawned them and raised them to positions of power and privilege.

By the late 1980s it was quite common in the Soviet Union to hear and see bitter denunciations of almost everything associated with Stalin's name. Yet in this painful process it could appear that the denouncers were attacking not just the rule of one man but the very foundation of the society which for years they had defended in an ideological battle with the Western democracies. Even President Gorbachev, later a stern critic of his predecessor, was moved to declare in February 1986 to a French journalist that 'Stalinism is a concept made up by opponents of communism and used on a large scale to smear the Soviet Union and socialism as a whole.' In view of pronouncements made by Gorbachev within months of this statement, one might doubt whether the view expressed in this interview reflected his true feelings, unless he was about to experience a sudden conversion on his own road to Damascus. But whatever the soul-searchings of Gorbachev and other prominent politicians, Stalin's legacy was to prove extraordinarily difficult to erase, both within and without the old Russian empire.

The arguments continue. How could such a 'grey blur' or evil genius come to power? Was he motivated by anything other than lust for power? How successful was Stalin's economic transformation of the USSR? Was it worth the cost? Does the Great Terror prove that Stalin was mad? Should he be praised or reviled for his record as a war leader, fighting the Nazi menace which some say he helped to power in Germany in the first place? Was Stalin responsible for the Cold War? Was Stalin actually a Communist? Does it matter? What exactly was Stalinism? If it can be identified, why did it take so long to kill off after its sell-by-date if it was so unpopular?

The body of Stalin once lay in state in a marble mausoleum alongside Lenin. Some time after Khrushchev's denunciation of Stalin in 1956, the remains were removed to a less conspicuous resting place near the Kremlin wall. Yet his ghost lingered on. Imitators clung to power in parts of Eastern Europe and Asia. Nostalgia was even in the air: after all, strong rulers deserved respect, and Stalin was the man who had won the war. But today there are few defenders.

The following chapters will attempt to address some important issues. What influences made Stalin the man he was? How and why did he come to power? Was he responsible for all the things usually attributed to him? What was his impact upon the USSR? Was there such a phenomenon as Stalinism?

These issues will be addressed, but also the opinions of other commentators and historians will be analysed. There is no single view of Stalin; but clearly the judgement of one of his outmanoeuvred contemporaries, Trotsky, that Stalin was a 'mediocrity', is absurdly simplistic if we are to begin to assess the importance of the man's public career. As a fellow Georgian wrote: 'Stalin was born to be two legends. They created one for him as a living god, flattered by everyone, glorified by everyone. After his death they created another legend, namely that he was Satan.' Saint or sinner, or does the truth lie somewhere between the two extremes?

1

THE MAKING OF A REVOLUTIONARY

Revolutionary leaders rarely come from working-class backgrounds. Some of the prominent Bolsheviks, Lenin included, grew up in middle-class families which were quite prosperous by contemporary Russian standards. The advantages of a good education opened their eyes to a range of literature. The revolutionary tracts of Karl Marx converted them to a political and economic philosophy which, they claimed, gave them a scientific analysis of society combined with a prophetic vision of the future. Their confidence was not shared by the majority of dis-possessed or poverty-stricken workers and peasants, who had their own practical concerns and had little time for organised politics. Thus it was that Lenin devoted much of his time to literary and practical attempts to 'raise the consciousness' of the working class.

Such attempts carried the danger of appearing patronising or élitist. This was less of a danger in the case of Stalin, who did not come from a privileged background, and was a provincial outsider (from Georgia) to boot. In many respects Stalin was to remain an outsider to the end of his life.

BIRTH AND CHILDHOOD

Joseph Djugashvili was born in the town of Gori, less than forty miles from the Georgian capital of Tiflis, or Tbilisi. This proximity was significant, because Tiflis was the centre of Georgian resistance to the Russification taking place throughout the Russian Empire in the last decades before the 1917 Revolution. Georgian intellectuals were attracted to nationalism as a weapon against this process. Not that the young Djugashvili came from an 'intellectual' background. His father was probably a serf, who later became a cobbler.

There are many rumours about Stalin's background. Most cannot be verified. We do know that there had already been three children born to Stalin's parents before his own birth, but none of them had survived infancy. More speculative is the story that Stalin's real father was actually a tsarist official, and there have also been claims that Stalin's real or adopted father was a small entrepreneur employing several men, rather than a poor cobbler.

Stalin's own recollections in later life were that his was a poor background, and a tough one, in which he frequently protected his beloved mother from the drunken beatings of his brutal father. There is little reason to doubt the essence of these recollections. They may partly account for Stalin's own emotional difficulties in later life: relationships with his own wives and children were not easy. Perhaps his physical characteristics also determined his personality: the young boy developed a withered arm from a childhood accident, and was scarred by smallpox. In later life evidence of the withered arm and the smallpox scars was carefully removed from photographs and paintings.

However, we do not have to rely on theories of psychological mal-adjustment, insecurity and a defensive vindictiveness in order to explain the adult Stalin. There were enough reasons in the Georgia of his childhood to turn many of his compatriots into rebels or revolutionaries. That Stalin was to emerge as the most prominent Georgian of his generation, from unpromising beginnings, suggests a skill and deter-mination only grudgingly admitted by many contemporaries and later historians. Some commentators, baffled by the rise to power of someone without the charisma of a Trotsky or the towering intellect of a Lenin, concluded that Stalin must simply have risen through the ranks unnoticed, almost as a historical accident. Such conclusions should not satisfy the conscientious investigator. There are enough clues about Stalin's early years to explain his later pre-eminence, without accepting notions of 'accidents'.

STALIN RADICAL

Education is usually a formative influence. It was certainly important in Stalin's case, but not for the reason sometimes supposed. The young Stalin was known as something of a loner, but a boy who was very competitive and accepted as friends those who would follow his dictates.

Stalin attended a church school between the ages of nine and fourteen. This was a source of conflict in the Djugashvili family, since his mother Yekaterina wished him to become a priest, but his father Vissarion wished him to learn the craft of shoemaking.

Despite the denigration of his intellectual ability by opponents later in life, the young Stalin proved to be an able pupil. He learned Russian, a foreign language, grudgingly, but his photographic memory enabled him to do well in examinations. Stalin graduated at the top of his class. By now his father was dead – whether the result of peaceful causes or involvement in a drunken brawl is not certain – and his mother was free to pursue her ambitions for the boy. Stalin won a scholarship, and spent his years between fifteen and twenty in the Theological Seminary at Tiflis. There was nothing particularly sinister in this: attempts to suggest that a theologically based education somehow accounts for Stalin's austere and dogged personality traits are akin to those theories that Hitler's experience of singing in a church choir determined the institutions of the Third Reich – fun to speculate on but not very sound

Stalin as a seminary student.

history. The importance of Stalin's experience in the Tiflis Seminary was basically twofold: it continued his education in the Russian language, which he always spoke with a heavy Georgian accent; and it brought him into contact with revolutionary politics.

At the Seminary Stalin lost his belief in God, and devoted much of his time to reading politics. Many of his books were confiscated by the teachers. Stalin was to complain of the 'jesuitical methods' of the authorities who spied on him and tried to indoctrinate him – the very methods which his regime was to employ nationwide many years later. Perhaps it was natural for students to resent the austere life of the Seminary. What we do know is that there were stirrings of proletarian unrest in Georgia in the late nineteenth century, as groups of workers eked out a hard existence in the oilfields, mines and railway workshops which were springing up. Strikes in Tiflis spread to the Seminary. In 1898 Stalin joined the 'Third Group', which became a branch of the new revolutionary Social Democratic Party. In Stalin's own words, uttered twenty eight years later, he 'became an apprentice in the art of revolution'. He ran study groups, similar to those run by Lenin in St. Petersburg. Stalin showed little patience with those who disagreed with his views. He was now attending political meetings outside the Seminary, as well as within it. Not surprisingly, Stalin was expelled from the Seminary in May 1899. His mother was distressed, but Stalin was committed at the age of twenty to a new and dangerous life.

THE ROAD TO MARXISM

At about this time Stalin became a socialist. At least, he began to study Lenin's journalism in *Iskra* (The Spark), and regurgitated Lenin's ideas for a Georgian revolutionary newspaper. In lighter moments he also wrote Georgian poetry. The real significance of this period was that it saw the conversion of Stalin from a Georgian nationalist into an international Marxist-Leninist, that is a socialist who put the struggle for socialist revolution before all nationalist and other considerations. In the Georgian newspaper *The Struggle*, Stalin argued for working-class leadership of the revolution, and he also translated Lenin's *Iskra* articles into Georgian. He adopted the alias 'Koba' in Batum. Koba was a Georgian folk hero who supposedly fought for Georgian peasants against oppressive landlords. Stalin was also arrested for the first time. Having organized street demonstrations and riots, and been elected in November 1901 to the Tiflis Social Democratic Committee, Stalin was now a wanted man. Certainly the secret police regarded him as important and dangerous.

Stalin's police file under the Tsarist regime.

In November 1903 Stalin exchanged a prison cell for exile in Siberia. In the meantime he had contracted his first marriage, although his wife, Yekaterina, was to die within a few years. A grief-stricken Stalin was to claim that all his feelings for humanity died with her. Whilst in prison he was elected to the All-Caucasian Federation: obviously his talents had already been noted.

Whilst in exile there took place the split in the Social Democratic Party which resulted in the formation of the Bolshevik and Menshevik factions. Stalin avoided the theoretical arguments, but escaped from exile to reappear in Tiflis in 1904. By the end of that year we may classify Stalin as a Bolshevik, in that he fully accepted Lenin's conception of the centrally organised, disciplined, professional Party.

CONTACTS WITH LENIN

The 1905 Revolution found Stalin still in the Caucasus. Events were bloody in the region. Tsarist Black Hundreds tried to divert hostility from the regime by fomenting unrest between local nationalities. Stalin, in contrast, argued for unity of the working class. He also had to contend with the Mensheviks, who were the majority among the Georgian Social Democrats.

Stalin's activities in this 'dress rehearsal for revolution' brought Stalin to Lenin's attention. In December 1905 the two men met for the first time at the Bolshevik National Congress in Finland. There is no reason to suppose that Lenin liked Stalin personally. However, the Bolsheviks were operating inside Russia as an illegal, underground organisation; and Lenin needed specialised, military-style sections within the Party organisation to carry out difficult, practical tasks, as a complement to the thinkers and intellectuals with whom Lenin was usually associated in these years. Lenin identified Stalin as having the organisational skills necessary to hold the Party together and win more support in a particular area of the old Russian Empire. Hence Lenin's interest in 'Koba'.

Unfortunately we possess few precise details of Stalin's underground activities in these years. The activities of Lenin and other Party intellectuals are well-documented in comparison. Stalin's work was illegal and secretive. He was given tasks in the Caucasus. He certainly planned bank raids, an important source of funds for the Bolsheviks, but he probably did not take part in them himself.

YEARS IN THE WILDERNESS

Life was still hard for Stalin, despite his promotion by Lenin. Travelling to London in 1907 for the London Conference of the Social Democrats, he found himself opposed by the Mensheviks. In 1908 he was deported, but escaped back to the Caucasus. He was in exile again during 1910 and 1911, and banned from the Caucasus. In 1912 Lenin proposed the absent Stalin for the Central Committee of the Party, and although the nomination was opposed, Lenin had him co-opted anyway. Lenin got Stalin, whom he described as a 'wonderful Georgian', to write a lengthy article on the Nationalities question for the Party journal. Stalin argued that the different nationalities had the right to independence, although their cause would be furthered by working within one political party.

The name 'Stalin' first appeared on this article. It was an apt alias, meaning 'man of steel'. Stalin displayed evidence of his toughness in prison, enduring beatings and other ill-treatment without a murmur.

Lenin sent Stalin to Vienna on Party business. But Stalin spent most of the years between 1913 and 1917 in prison and internal exile. Stories later appeared that Stalin was a police agent working for the tsarist regime. Infiltration of revolutionary groups was certainly a police tactic, and Stalin's often shadowy activities almost inevitably fuelled rumours; but the stories are probably groundless, since had Stalin really been an agent, he would have been of more value to the authorities at large, on the Central Committee, than locked up, with fewer contacts.

Along with most Bolsheviks, Stalin was taken by surprise by the Revolution of February 1917. The difference was, most prominent Bolsheviks had spent the three years of World War in foreign exile; Stalin had spent the War in Siberian exile. Soon after strikes and demonstrations on the streets of Petrograd had burgeoned into full-scale Revolution and the abdication of the Tsar, Stalin was released and travelled there. He was the first prominent Bolshevik to arrive.

REVOLUTIONARY CREDENTIALS

As yet Stalin was largely unknown outside Bolshevik circles. And yet he had already travelled a long way politically, and furthered his revolutionary education. Clearly Lenin had discovered organisational qualities in him which, combined with a dedication and willingness to endure personal sacrifice, the life of a professional revolutionary demanded. The fact that he was a non-Russian appeared to provide Lenin with a useful tool in spreading the Bolshevik message to the Nationalities. Later, Lenin was to regret this, but in the pre-war years he had deliberately groomed Stalin for advancement, and furthered his experience by sending him abroad. Stalin did not spend years abroad, unlike many of the emigré revolutionary intellectuals, but he was not as parochial as later commentators and opponents claimed.

And yet there were features of Stalin's character and experience that mark him out from the other names we associate with the Russian Revolution. Stalin was not an intellectual who delighted in theoretical debate. He positively despised the emigré intellectuals who lived in relative security abroad and spent many of their days arguing over theoretical niceties. He spent his formative revolutionary years in prison or the underground. He was quite prepared to criticise Lenin himself: the idea that he was an obsequious toady who only opposed the leader when Lenin was in his declining years was spread by opponents who were defeated in the struggle for power. Stalin's motivations were different in origin from the likes of Lenin and Trotsky. These men became revolutionaries partly through a sense of guilt at their own relatively privileged position in a harsh society, and discovered what they perceived as a scientific analysis of that society and how it could be changed. Stalin fought against people he regarded as his personal oppressors and despised revolutionaries whose motives he perceived of as primarily intellectual and theoretical rather than personal. Perhaps that is one reason why Stalin was so vindictive towards his prominent colleagues, once he had power. Perhaps he did have an inferiority complex: after all, he was an 'outsider', was no orator, and although he subscribed to Marxist dogma, he was no great writer or intellectual. Yet he had the quality of determination allied with administrative skill, despised or ignored by more famous colleagues, but crucially important to the growth of the Bolshevik movement. He also wanted power. Stalin understood the mechanics of power. Power involved far more than speech-making. Those who confused the substance of power with the image simply demonstrated their naivety, a mistake which was to prove literally fatal to them in the long run.

timeline	1879 December	Stalin born in Gori, Georgia
	1898	Social Democratic Party founded
		Stalin joined 'The Third Group' – an illegal Social Democratic group
	1905 January	Bloody Sunday and the start of the 1905 Revolution
		Stalin met Lenin in Finland
	1912	Stalin co-opted onto Central Committee of the Social Democratic Party
	1913	Stalin exiled to Siberia
	1917 February	Revolution and abdication of the Tsar

REVOLUTION AND CIVIL WAR

BETWEEN REVOLUTIONS

Stalin was thrust into the limelight immediately upon his arrival in Petrograd, on 12 March 1917. On that very day, the Russian Bureau of the Central Committee co-opted him as one of their number. The minutes of the meeting report, however, that 'in view of certain personal characteristics, the Bureau decided to give him only a consulting vote'. These characteristics were not spelt out, but it is likely that they were similar to the ones outlined by Lenin a few years later in his famous *Testament*. Stalin was considered a rough diamond, and yet he was too useful to dispense with.

Stalin certainly seized his opportunity. He immediately took over the editorship of *Pravda*, the Party newspaper. Until Lenin's return to Russia in April, Stalin ran the Party, helped by Kamenev. The line pursued by Stalin was very different from that of Lenin, who was seeking to find the means of returning home across a war-torn Europe. Stalin shared the enthusiasm of most revolutionaries for the unexpected revolution. The *Pravda* line was: support for the new Provisional Government, so long as its measures were in the interests of the Russian people. Co-operation with the Mensheviks was called for. Discipline in both the Army and the factories should be maintained. In putting forward these views Stalin and Kamenev were reflecting the majority opinion rather than forming it. After all, conventional Marxist thinking was that in a semi-feudal society like Russia, there could not be an immediate transition to socialism. The intermediate bourgeois stage was represented by the February Revolution and the Provisional Government. Lenin, not Stalin and Kamenev, was the exception in calling for an immediate transition to the socialist stage of revolution. Stalin was even prepared to argue the point with Lenin in print. Trotsky wrote that Stalin's conciliatory line in *Pravda*, when it was read in the factories, 'aroused utter dismay among our party members and our sympathisers, and caustic gratification among our opponents.' But these words were written from exile in 1932 by a somewhat embittered Trotsky, and Stalin's attitude in the early months of 1917 was by no means unique.

Nevertheless, Lenin's arrival at the Finland Station on 16 April 1917 was to fundamentally change the course of the Revolution. Not that the change of strategy outlined by Lenin in his 'April Theses' was accepted by his colleagues overnight. Lenin had to work hard to persuade them that his call for the immediate overthrow of the Provisional Government made sense. Nevertheless, his views did prevail, and when Stalin saw which way the wind was blowing, he came over to Lenin's side – whether from conviction or a desire to be on the winning side is unclear, although as has already been shown, Stalin had been prepared to argue with Lenin before, and there was no certainty in April 1917 that the Bolsheviks would prevail. At any rate, Stalin did keep the editorship of *Pravda*.

In April Stalin was also elected to the Central Committee of the Party, third only to Lenin and Zinoviev in number of votes. Previously he had only been a co-opted member. Yet Stalin's name does not figure prominently in the events of the summer and autumn which culminated in the Bolshevik coup of October. Stalin was an important figure, not only for his membership of the Petrograd Soviet and the Central Committee, and his editorship of the Party newspaper, but by virtue of the fact that from July, Lenin was in hiding in Finland, and other prominent Bolsheviks were under arrest following the disturbances of that month. He was very active in organisational matters and generally just keeping the Party's machine oiled. This was a vitally important task, and one to which Stalin was well suited, but it did not catch the eye in the way that a rhetorical flourish from a Lenin or Trotsky did. The Menshevik Sukhanov, who wrote one of the most detailed contemporary accounts of the year of revolutions, was entirely dismissive of Stalin:

> Among the Bolsheviks, beside Kamenev, there appeared in the Executive Committee of the Soviets in those days Stalin. During the time of his modest activity in the Executive Committee he gave me

the impression – and not only me – of a drab spot which would sometimes emit a dim and inconsequential light. There is really nothing more to be said about him.

What is harder to understand is why, for so long, historians themselves underplayed Stalin's role. The Trotskys of this world were quite prepared to pass on to Stalin what they regarded as the boring administrative work, whilst they made history. Since it was the administration, through the Party machine, that came to dominate the country, it might be said that power drifted into Stalin's hands. But he did not just wait for it to happen: with Sverdlov, Stalin was responsible for communication with the Party organisations which were springing up in the provinces. The personal contacts built up at this time were to serve Stalin well in the next decade.

During the July Days Stalin acted as the intermediary between the Central Committee and the Executive of the Petrograd Soviet. Perhaps he was able to operate openly because he had a reputation for moderation and conciliation within the Party, despite the supposed roughness of his character. Trotsky later wrote slightingly of Stalin in this period as a 'vulgar conciliationist and, moreover, during the most acute moments.' Stalin did vote in favour of the October coup. When Kamenev and Zinoviev, alone of the Central Committee, voted against the decision, and Lenin accused them of traitorous behaviour, Stalin defended Kamenev. A charitable interpretation might be that Stalin was trying to preserve unity in the Party in a spirit of conciliation. Trotsky claimed it was proof that Stalin was still under the influence of his 'Menshevik policy' of February 1917 – Menshevism was a charge later levelled against Trotsky by Stalin! What is beyond doubt is that Stalin was quite prepared to resurrect the accusation of treachery when Kamenev and Zinoviev were dragged through the mire of a show trial in 1936.

Stalin stayed at the helm of *Pravda* during the October Revolution. He was not involved in active operations, although a later generation of Soviet hagiographers was to exaggerate his role and create the myth of Stalin as Lenin's right-hand man during the 'ten days that shook the world.'

PROMOTION AFTER THE REVOLUTION

Immediately after the coup the Bolsheviks had to create a government from scratch. Stalin was one of seven members in the Politburo, and he was given the post of Commissar of Nationalities in the Soviet of People's Commissars, effectively the Cabinet. Stalin had built up a reputation for skilful handling of Nationalities issues, and skill was certainly called for: his task was to try to prevent the old Russian Empire breaking up. National groups were taking advantage of the chaos of revolution and military defeat to achieve self-determination. Lenin accepted their right to do so, but wished to persuade them otherwise – after all, national differences would become irrelevant in the new socialist order. But Stalin was to employ persuasive tactics of a more ruthless kind than Lenin had envisaged. In November 1917 Stalin joined Lenin, Trotsky and Sverdlov in an inner Cabinet, authorised by the Central Committee to decide 'all emergency questions'. He had already come a long way from organising bank raids in the Caucasus.

CIVIL WAR AND RIVALRY WITH TROTSKY

The most pressing problem facing the new regime was survival itself. 1918 witnessed the start of a bitter civil war, in which Left- and Right-wing opponents of the Bolsheviks battled together for its overthrow. The Whites were aided sporadically by troops and material from seventeen foreign nations, intent at first on bringing Russia back into the war against Germany, and then on destroying Bolshevism itself before it could cross their own borders. At the same time the Bolsheviks were attempting to implement the ruthless policy of War Communism, involving the nationalisation of industry and the requisitioning of grain from the peasantry, whilst a series of measures were decreed designed to create the world's first Socialist state.

What was Stalin's part in these events? The first essential task of the new regime was to make peace with the occupying Germans. Following the Armistice of November 1917, Trotsky had the difficult task of negotiating the Treaty of Brest-Litovsk with them. According to Trotsky, on this issue Stalin 'would vacillate, side-step and keep silent. At the last moment he would vote for Lenin's motion.' Stalin's position is characterised as 'muddled and impotent'. During the civil war, 'Stalin was opposed to the principles upon which the creation of the Red Army was based.'

Trotsky's attitude is understandable: Stalin came into direct conflict with him for the first time, chiefly on the issue of the role of professional military specialists in the civil war. Trotsky was prepared to employ anyone, even former tsarist officers, if it would help save the regime from its enemies. Stalin distrusted such men. Sent to Tsaritsyn on the Volga to arrange the delivery of food supplies, Stalin assumed full powers and clashed with Trotsky, the military supremo. Stalin was recalled to Moscow. The memory probably rankled. Stalin actually clashed with a number of military commanders as Party dogma often came up against military priorities. Stalin acted brusquely, and showed his contempt for 'experts'.

Stalin was in many ways representative of a new type of Bolshevik which came to prominence during the civil war. Ideological purity and rhetoric were less important than survival; administrative skills more vital than mastery of Marxist dialectic. A book by Trotsky, published in 1941, a year after the author's death, analysed Stalin's ascent to power. Stalin achieved power, wrote Trotsky, 'not with the aid of personal qualities, but with the aid of an impersonal machine. And it was not he who created the machine but the machine that created him.' Trotsky went on to state that, in order to take possession of this machine

> exceptional and special qualities were necessary, but they were not the qualities of the historic initiator, thinker, writer, or orator. The machine had grown out of ideas. Stalin's first qualification was a contemptuous attitude towards ideas.

Trotsky here betrayed the intellectual's arrogance and contempt for administrative skill, and his own lack of understanding of the mechanics of power – strange in a man who was not just an intellectual himself, but someone with a reputation in these years for action and ruthlessness. For Stalin's qualities were very much in demand in the Civil War period. True, there was a need for oratory and dashing leadership, to raise and sustain morale in a time of crisis. But there was an equal need for someone who could keep the Party machine going, who could rebuild the Party organisation in liberated regions and appoint loyal administrators. If, in the process, Stalin was able to amass personal power, that was the price of Lenin's system, born out of the years of struggle before the

Revolution when the Bolsheviks had been a conspiratorial, secretive political group. The Bolsheviks had needed hard-headed, single-minded operatives who could subordinate personal comforts to the needs of the movement. The Bolsheviks might be in power after 1917, but in these crisis years after the Revolution, the essential needs remained, and there had never been any commitment to the ideals of what Lenin called 'bourgeois democracy'. Stalin rose in the Party partly by luck and because he was underestimated by some, but also because his type was needed. Cometh the hour, cometh the man.

CENTRALISATION AND COERCION

Stalin was a political commissar during the brief Russo-Polish War. Tukhachevsky, the Soviet commander, complained about Stalin's lack of co-operation. But Stalin's interests were now elsewhere. He wanted to concentrate on his role as Commissar for Nationalities. Poland, Finland, Estonia, Latvia and Lithuania had already left the Soviet orbit, but other peoples throughout the territory of the old Empire were seeking self-determination. Stalin fought for centralism: that is, he resisted the attempts of the Nationalities to secede from the new socialist order, and even sought to bring the Ukraine back into the fold. Separatist movements in Azerbaijan and Armenia were defeated, and in 1921 Stalin sent the Red Army into Georgia to crush the Menshevik independent government there. Many, including Lenin, were to be shocked by Stalin's ruthlessness, but he succeeded in establishing the Russian-dominated Union of Soviet Socialist Republics, constituted in 1922.

Stalin's influence was evident elsewhere. The secret police, or Cheka, Lenin's 'sharp sword of the Revolution', was active in crushing suspected counter-revolutionaries. Stalin was involved with it from the start, being a member of several committees which supervised its activities. Stalin also ran the Workers' and Peasants' Inspectorate, which had a crucial importance in controlling the machinery of state, since it supervised the entire administrative machine. He was also a member of the Politburo and the Orgburo (Organisational Bureau). In Lenin's words, the Orgburo 'allocates forces, whilst the Politburo decides policy'. These were the instruments of one-party rule. Crucially, Stalin was the only member of all four interlocking bodies: the Central

Committee, the Politburo, the Orgburo and the Secretariat. The Secretariat controlled party appointments and therefore effectively controlled Party careers at all levels. It appointed the Party Secretaries, who in turn controlled the Party rank and file throughout the provinces. Strangely, the importance of the role of General Secretary was not appreciated at the time; and yet Stalin's appointment to the post in April 1922 was to make him the most powerful man in the Soviet Union. Perhaps it just seemed an unglamorous job.

THE RISE OF THE PARTY

How did Stalin build his influence? Soon after the Revolution local soviets lost their independence as their chairmen were appointed by Party secretaries, who were responsible to the rapidly expanding Central Committee apparatus. By 1922 the Central Committee had a personal record of every Party member. The local Party Secretary was a full-time official who regularly reported to the Central Committee and wrote secret monthly reports on the political situation in his province. Local disputes were resolved by control commissions set up by the Central Committee. Any local Party functionary showing signs of independence was removed. Local Party committees often welcomed guidance from the centre, and the virtues of discipline and unity seemed self-evident, particularly in the crisis years of 1918–21. Stalin was appointing his nominees to key positions, whilst at the highest levels he was preparing Politburo agendas.

It would be inaccurate to ascribe the growth of the one-Party, centralised state to Stalin, although this has often been done, particularly by apologists for Lenin who seek to make a clear distinction between the Leninist and Stalinist states. The basic pattern of the Party's administration had already been established before Stalin's appointment to the Party Secretaryship in 1922. The most enthusiastic centralisers were often to be found in the provinces, and it would have been impossible for Stalin and others in Moscow to have created a centralised Party machine without the wholehearted collaboration of many in the lower ranks of the Party in different regions of the country. Nevertheless there is no evidence that Stalin found the process distasteful, and he made effective use both of the idealism and the self-seeking desire for advancement found amongst Party members at all levels. By contrast, his rivals for power made errors of judgment and operated from a narrower basis of support. Zinoviev was head of the Petrograd Party organisation; Kamenev was his counterpart in Moscow. Trotsky coupled enormous public prestige with no Party base at all. Stalin had a finger in every Party pie, and he was helped by the ban on 'factionalism' imposed at the 1921 Congress. The one-Party state was already in place before Lenin's death in 1924. In fact, by the time of Lenin's first serious illness in 1922, Stalin was already the most powerful man in the Soviet Union, although nobody, possibly Stalin included, realised it at the time.

timeline	1917	March	Stalin's arrival in Petrograd
			Stalin became editor of *Pravda*.
		July	July Days. Stalin took over temporary leadership of the Bolsheviks
		October	Bolshevik coup
			Stalin appointed Commissar for Nationalities
	1918	July	Adoption of Stalin's Constitution for the Russian Soviet Federative Socialist Republic
	1919	March	Creation of Politburo and Secretariat, with Stalin as a member of both
		April	Stalin appointed as head of People's Commissariat of State Control, later the Workers' and Peasants' Inspectorate
	1921	February	Stalin supervised Soviet occupation of Georgia
		March	Stalin elected to Politburo and Orgburo of the Party's Central Committee
	1922	April	Stalin elected General Secretary of the Party

Points to consider

1) **How important was Stalin's contribution to the Bolshevik victory of October 1917?**
2) **How was it possible for Stalin to become 'the most powerful man in the Soviet Union by the time of Lenin's death'?**

THE RISE TO POWER

LENIN AND THE SUCCESSION

The struggle for influence and power in the Soviet State was under way well before Lenin's death in 1924. Stalin, as already indicated, had offended Lenin by his peremptory treatment of the independence movement in Georgia in 1921. The two men had also disagreed about the issue of foreign trade: Lenin wanted it conducted solely through the Commissariat of Foreign Trade, whilst Stalin felt this was impractical and argued for a relaxation of the monopoly. Stalin was not being perverse in this, but simply represented the views of many other pragmatists in the Party.

Lenin was certainly coming to regard Stalin as a brusque, rough individual. Yet Lenin himself was not squeamish about taking brutal measures when the security of the regime was at stake. Lenin belatedly concluded that Stalin was amassing too much personal power, but he had been happy to promote this rough diamond when it suited him and, if he was now to worry about Stalin resurrecting a tsarist-style bureaucracy, who was ultimately responsible for allowing this to happen?

Lenin had a long convalescence after his first stroke in 1922. Stalin was close at hand, having been given the task by the Central Committee of supervising Lenin's treatment. Lenin was unable to work, but he could think. His thoughts turned to the succession. Who had the authority and the personal qualities necessary to carry on his mission? Lenin committed his thoughts to his famous *Testament*, actually a collection of his musings, compiled between December 1922 and January 1923.

Lenin listed the qualities of several prominent Party figures. His comments on Stalin were unambiguous:

Comrade Stalin, having become General Secretary, has concentrated *unlimited authority* in his hands and I am not certain *whether he will always be capable of using that authority with sufficient caution.*

In the following month Lenin went further:

Stalin is too rude and this defect, although quite tolerable in our midst and in relations among us Communists, becomes intolerable in the post of General Secretary. That is why I suggest that comrades think of a way of removing Stalin from that post.

Lenin's comments on other individuals like Zinoviev, Trotsky and Kamenev, although less damning, reveal that he had serious doubts about any of them as potential successors. Perhaps Lenin desired a collective leadership as a compromise.

SURVIVAL AND CONSOLIDATION

Fortunately for Stalin, the *Testament* was not made public on Lenin's death in January 1924. Lenin had ordered that only his widow Krupskaya might publish it. The Central Committee was told the contents, and Stalin's fate was briefly in the balance. An outwardly calm but almost certainly inwardly agitated Stalin felt obliged to offer his resignation, but was saved this step by the desire of his colleagues, including those he was to send to their deaths in the 1930s, to present a united front to the outside world. The fateful document remained hidden away in the belief that this was for the good of the Party. This perception of an abstract good was to be used in the future in order to justify extraordinary measures against the most devoted and loyal old Party members. It was possible to persuade some committed Communists in the 1930s that even to go to their deaths would somehow benefit the Party. It is not known whether Stalin appreciated the paradox.

Stalin played a prominent role in Lenin's funeral. His principal rival, Trotsky, was absent from the proceedings, although this was not, as is often claimed, because Stalin misinformed him about the date. Other leading Communists were present in Moscow for the funeral rites, but Stalin stole a march on them by his prominent role in the proceedings.

On 26 January 1924 Stalin delivered a speech of great significance at the Congress of Soviets:

> In leaving us, Comrade Lenin commended us to hold high and pure the great calling of Party Member. We swear to thee, Comrade Lenin, to honour thy command. In leaving us, Comrade Lenin commanded us to keep the unity of our Party as the apple of our eye. We swear to thee, Comrade Lenin, to honour thy command.
>
> In leaving us, Comrade Lenin ordered us to maintain and strengthen the dictatorship of the proletariat. We swear to thee, Comrade Lenin, to exert our full strength in honouring thy command.
>
> In leaving us, Comrade Lenin ordered us to strengthen with all our might the union of workers and peasants. We swear to thee, Comrade Lenin, to honour thy command . . .

The oration continued, and the solemn rendering of vows, as if part of a religious ceremony, appealing to the faithful who could not easily take on board the fact of Lenin's death. Was this an adroit political move by Stalin to inherit Lenin's mantle, or was it simply the unconscious influence of his boyhood training in the Tiflis Seminary? Surely Stalin was well aware of the advantage of constantly associating himself with Lenin's name, the beginning of a skilful process culminating in the propaganda of the 1930s which portrayed Stalin as Lenin's confidant and right-hand man even at the time of the Revolution? Stalin certainly did not display the mediocrity with which he was later labelled by unsuccessful rivals. Stalin's *Foundations of Leninism* and *Problems of Leninism*, published in 1924 and based upon lectures he delivered at the Higher Party School, are little more than codifications of Lenin's ideas – but they did meet the needs of many ordinary Party members. Stalin gave them a creed. By building on the Lenin myth and by establishing himself as the guardian and interpreter of that myth, Stalin immeasurably strengthened his own credentials. His opponents had to steer a careful path to avoid the taint of anti-Leninism in their disputes with him. Stalin's rivals frequently fell into the trap, and were also in danger of committing the sin of 'factionalism', outlawed at the 1921 Party Congress.

Nevertheless, Stalin's position was by no means secure in 1924. Had the *Testament* been widely circulated, his career could have been over.

Stalin did demonstrate political skills, but he was aided by the mutual antagonism of, on the one hand, Trotsky, and on the other, Kamenev and Zinoviev. Fortunately for Stalin, they also had skeletons in their closets which diminished the effects of their attacks on Stalin. Stalin yet again appeared as the man of the centre, cautious and responsible, as more brilliant minds poured out their vitriol on each other in print. Stalin's own pragmatism was at a premium in these years, when confusion and uncertainties still existed, even if the very survival of Bolshevism seemed more secure than in the Civil War years. Stalin had proved that he could apply brutal methods when required. Now new situations had to be addressed. Workers' councils had proved incapable of running the factories; the Party lacked influence in the countryside; world revolution was not on the horizon. A new bureaucratic class was growing up to meet the demands of government. Stalin could identify with this class, made up of men and women (mostly the former), who were anxious for work and influence, whether ideologically motivated or not, and who were not particularly interested in the outside world. Such bureaucrats did not share the concerns of the older generation of cosmopolitan emigré Bolsheviks, who were seen as lacking the ruthless, single-minded devotion to administration and management. Stalin was more in line with the bureaucrats' way of thinking, and they with his.

ARGUMENTS ABOUT POLICY

Stalin did not challenge the intellectual establishment in one go: but he did not have to, since the intellectuals fell out amongst themselves in the Party debates of the 1920s. During those debates, Stalin promoted protegés like Kirov; these in turn were to be replaced in the 1930s by more intellectually limited but more ruthless operators like Yezhov. Stalin brought in his supporters from the provinces to outvote the more sophisticated intellectuals like Zinoviev and Kamenev in the crucial debates. Trotsky was easier meat, because although ruthless himself, he lacked any sort of Party base and therefore had no support when and where it counted. Trotsky had not assiduously cultivated the support of loyal functionaries as Stalin had.

Stalin soon developed the confidence to add his voice to the ideological arguments. There was considerable debate in the Soviet Union in the 1920s about the future economic direction of the country and the prospects for socialism. Lenin had introduced the New Economic Policy (NEP) in 1921 in order to appease the peasantry and to restore the shattered Soviet economy. Typically, he had then produced a theoretical justification for the policy on the lines that a mixed economy was a necessary halfway house between the overthrow of feudalism and the advent of socialism. Nevertheless, the semi-market economy of the 1920s troubled many ideologically committed Communists. As Marxists they all agreed that for both practical and ideological reasons socialism had to be built in the USSR, and that socialism could only take root in an industrialised nation. Therefore industrialisation was the key. But how should industrialisation be introduced, and, equally important, how should it be paid for? And, meanwhile, what about the USSR's isolated position in the world?

Trotsky argued in the mid-1920s for world revolution. In his view, the Soviets should devote their main effort to promoting Communist revolutions elsewhere, in order to end Russia's isolation and overthrow unfriendly capitalist governments. The long-term survival of the Revolution in the Soviet Union depended on the success of revolution elsewhere. Stalin would have accepted that the ultimate logic of Marxism-Leninism lay in socialism spreading throughout the developed world but his name became associated with the idea of 'socialism in one country'. This meant that the USSR should create its own socialist base by means of industrialisation and building up military strength, thus acting as an impregnable bulwark of socialism against the outside world.

Although Stalin's ultimate goal was the same as Trotsky's, the tactics were different, and the tactics seemed to became an end in themselves. Stalin's arguments had much to commend them to the new generation of post-Revolutionary Communists. They were being offered an opportunity to forge their own future. This was appealing to a tough generation hardened by the brutalities and privations of civil war and economic dislocation. Action was preferable to waiting for world revolution to succeed. To nationalistically inclined Russians there was something uncomfortable in the idea of their country depending upon the 'advanced' working class of Western Europe to prod them into revolution, instead of depending upon the USSR's own fledgling proletariat. Trotsky's vision, dependent as it was upon the success of events outside Soviet borders, could easily be made to appear defeatist.

Comrade Stalin speaking to railway workers in Tiflis 1926.

Trotsky had other problems in his fight with Stalin. These were to do with his Menshevik background, his Jewishness, his flaunting of intellectual superiority, his failure to build a base of support in the Party, and the fear of 'Bonapartism' which his military successes engendered – but he also weakened his position first by disputes with Zinoviev and Kamenev; and then by forming with these two protagonists the Left or United Opposition to Stalin in 1926. This was factionalism rampant, and it was Stalin's rivals, not Stalin, who appeared responsible. Trotsky's defeat, his expulsion from the Party, his exile, and his eventual deportation from the USSR in 1929, may be ascribed partly to his own errors and failings, but Stalin still had to take advantage of the opportunities. The methods were varied: for example, Stalin secured the postponement of the Fourteenth Congress of December 1925 until he was sure of his majority. Stalin became adept in debate as he grew in confidence, and was particularly skilful in quoting Lenin, whose writings he had mastered, in order to support his own position. Another successful tactic was to quote back at rivals their earlier pronounce-ments. Exploiting such inconsistencies helped justify Stalin's accusations of factionalism and opportunism. Such tactics were necessary: until the end of 1927, political battles were still fought on the floor of the Central Committee or the Party Congress. Anybody, including Stalin, could be challenged. There would be votes taken, interruptions and heckling. Stalin eventually defeated the opposition in these forums, but could not suppress it entirely. Even during Stalin's dictatorship in the 1930s, opposition certainly existed underground, although it is difficult for us to quantify its strength.

It would be a mistake to portray Stalin as a one-man band imposing his will simply through ruthless determination. Alan Bullock, in his massive study of Hitler and Stalin, detected parallels between the two dictators: 'During the period 1924–29 Stalin was as intent as Hitler on securing power, and, like Hitler, saw the party as a means of achieving it.'

Whilst it is true, as Bullock claims, that Stalin never allowed himself to be diverted by ideological discussions from the real issues of power – which was true also of Lenin, an intellectual who had little time for other intellectuals – it is dangerous to portray Stalin as someone with a long-term plan. Often he reacted to events. He also probably had the support of many in the rank and file of the Party, particularly as NEP came increasingly under attack.

The economic debates of the 1920s were complex. However, the essentials were that the Left argued for a rapid and forcible drive to industrialisation, involving a squeeze on the peasants in order to provide the labour and resources for it. Trotsky and Preobrazhensky were the leading spokemen of this view. The Right, whose spokesman was Bukharin, stressed the close links between industry and agriculture: development of the former depended upon the development of the latter. Allowing the peasants to enrich themselves would increase the demand for consumer goods and lead to more factories. Industrialisation could occur without draconian measures against the peasants, which carried the danger of a violent reaction such as had occured in the days of War Communism.

Stalin followed the arguments rather than initiating them. He was evasive about the future, although in 1925 he stressed the importance of the peasantry in providing a market. But having supported the Bukharin line, the defeat of the Left in 1926 saw Stalin taking over its strategy and arguing for a drive towards industrialisation. Bukharin and the Right were isolated.

AGRICULTURE IN THE FRONT LINE

By 1927 agricultural output had become a serious issue. Peasants were increasingly reluctant to produce for the market, even with the incentives of the NEP. In 1927 the government procured half the quantity of grain of the previous year. The state purchasing price was simply too low for many peasants. They retained their grain and sold livestock instead. Although the government increased the supply of manufactured goods to the countryside for the benefit of the peasants, it also resorted to coercion. In January 1928 Stalin toured Siberia, speaking out against the hoarding of grain and speculation. Grain was confiscated. This so-called 'Urals-Siberian method' of requisitioning was in fact a reversion to the old policy of War Communism. The policy worked, at least in the short term. The Right probably saw the policy only as a short-term expedient. To what extent Stalin's response represented a real change of ideas or was a pragmatic response to a grain crisis is difficult to say; but certainly he seems to have decided at some point that the situation must be avoided whereby the peasants could once again control the distribution of grain and threaten the Soviet economy. By defeating Bukharin and his colleagues in 1929, Stalin was effectively in control, and by the time of his 50th birthday in December 1929, collectivisation was well under way. However, it is doubtful whether Stalin began to think about long-term economic strategy until he had consolidated his power base.

Bukharin was expelled from the Central Committee in November 1929. The defeat of the Right was to signal the end of the New Economic Policy.

THE QUALITIES OF A DICTATOR

Stalin's rivals had been unable to prevent his rise to power. Why did they not take Stalin seriously enough until it was too late? Was it intellectual arrogance, the belief in their innate intellectual superiority? Defeated politicians fostered the legend that, intellectually, Stalin was a mediocrity, albeit a cunning one. Certainly Stalin himself never claimed to be an eminent Marxist theorist. Perhaps that is why he was careful to master Lenin's works and cite them as his authority. But Stalin showed considerable skill in establishing the claim to be the interpreter of orthodox Marxist views. In so doing he undermined colleagues who were conducting their own political and ideological quarrels. Stalin acted gradually: Bukharin called him the 'master of dosage', because he was able to administer poison by degrees. A contemporary, Bazhanov, left a revealing account of Stalin's methods at the Politburo and Central Committee meetings over which he presided:

> He smoked his pipe and spoke very little. Every now and then he would start walking up and down the conference room regardless of the fact that we were in session. Sometimes he would stop right in front of a speaker, watching his expression and listening to his argument, while still puffing away at his pipe . . .
>
> He had the good sense never to say anything before everyone else had his argument fully developed. He would sit there, watching the way the discussion was going. When everyone had spoken, he would say: 'Well, comrades, I think the solution to this problem is such and such' – and he would then repeat the conclusions towards which the majority had been drifting.

Stalin did not posses the intellectualism of a Bukharin or the rhetoric of a Trotsky, but he could fight his corner very effectively. This is Stalin speaking to the Fifteenth Congress on 3 December, 1927, justifying the expulsion of the Left Opposition from positions of influence:

> How could it happen that the entire Party, as a whole, and following it the working class too, so thoroughly isolated the opposition? After all, the opposition are headed by well-known people with well-known names, people who know how to advertise themselves (*Voices:* 'Quite right!'), people who are not affected with modesty (*Applause*) and are able to blow their own trumpets.
>
> It happened because the leading groups of the opposition proved to be a group of petty-bourgeois intellectuals divorced from life, divorced from the revolution, divorced from the Party, from the working class. (*Voices:* 'Quite right!' *Applause*) . . .
>
> Have we the dictatorship of the proletariat or not? Rather a strange question. (*Laughter*) . . .
>
> If the opposition want to be in the Party, let them submit to the will of the Party, to its laws, to its instructions, without reservations, without equivocation. If they refuse to do that, let them go wherever

they please. (*Voices:* 'Quite right!' *Applause*). We do not want new laws providing privileges for the opposition, and we will not create them. (*Applause*).

This was calculated to win the support of rank and file Party members and is not the speech of a drab, unintelligent apparatchik. The audience may have been largely selected, but Stalin knew how to appeal to it, how to play on its fears and emotions.

Comrades greet Stalin on his 50th birthday.

Stalin's contribution to the canons of Marxism was not entirely unoriginal. As he grew more confident, and began to implement economic policies, Stalin propagated the notion that the State could produce changes in the economy and the consciousness of the people. Perhaps it was obvious that politics could change the economy, but it was Marxist heresy to suggest that politics rather than economics might be the prime force. Was politics more than the superstructure? Stalin claimed that in a backward country like the USSR, and in a revolutionary situation, relations between economics and politics were more fluid than orthodox Marxism allowed for, and therefore the policies of the State could have a decisive effect upon economic progress. Thus the theoretical justification for the Five Year Plans.

The theory might be crude, but the fact was that by 1929 Stalin was in a position to begin the second great revolution in twentieth-century Russia. The first had been the seizure of power in 1917, a political coup in which Stalin had not played a major role, but which brought him closer to the centre of events. The second revolution was to be presided over by Stalin, and it was this revolution which began the process by which the USSR was transformed into an industrial power. Stalin was very cynical about other peoples' motives, and it is not necessary to accept Bullock's claim that Stalin, like Hitler, believed that he himself had a historic mission. Nevertheless, Stalin was now to make tough decisions and create systems which were to last in essentials thirty years beyond his own death.

timeline	1924	January	Death of Lenin
		April	Publication of Stalin's *Foundations of Leninism*
		May	Central Committee agreed to support Stalin and suppress Lenin's *Testament*
		November	Publication of Stalin's *Trotskyism or Leninism?*
	1925	April	Stalin presented 'Socialism in One Country' to the Fourteenth Party Conference
	1926	January	Publication of Stalin's *Questions of Leninism*
	1927	January	Trotsky and Kamenev expelled from the Politburo
		October	Trotsky and Zinoviev expelled from the Central Committee and the Party
		December	Collectivisation agreed at the Fifteenth Party Congress
	1928	January	Stalin visited Siberia and ordered requisitioning of grain
	1929	January	Trotsky expelled from the USSR
		April	First Five-Year Plan presented to Sixteenth Party Conference
		November	Bukharin expelled from the Politburo Stalin announced mass collectivisation and liquidation of the *kulaks* (self employed, property owning peasants)

Points to consider

1) **Why were Stalin's rivals unable to prevent his rise to power in the 1920s?**
2) **How significant were the debates about economic policy within the Communist Party during the 1920s?**
3) **Were ideas or opportunism the main driving force behind Stalin's rise to power by 1929?**

4

THE SECOND REVOLUTION

THE CHANGE IN ECONOMIC POLICY

The New Economic Policy (NEP), the semi-private, semi-State economy of the 1920s, had always been a worrying phenomenon for those in the Party who saw it as a toleration of and even encouragement of capitalist tendencies. However, probably few of those anxious to replace the NEP with socialism envisaged the process quite as it was undertaken by Stalin.

Stalin's perception of the Soviet situation in 1928 was shared by many Russians. The USSR was perceived as potential prey for surrounding hostile capitalist states, seeking its destruction. They had failed in the aftermath of the Revolution, but they might succeed in the future. Only an industrially strong and militarily prepared Soviet State could resist the threat. Stalin was adamant on this point. In February 1931 he was to declare:

> It is sometimes asked whether it is not possible to slow down the tempo somewhat, to put a check on the movement. No, comrades, it is not possible! The tempo must not be reduced! On the contrary, we must increase it as much as is within our powers and possibilities. This is dictated to us by our obligations to the working class of the whole world. To slacken the tempo would mean falling behind. And those who fall behind get beaten. But we do not want to be beaten. No, we refuse to be beaten! . . . We are fifty or a hundred years behind the advanced countries. We must make good this distance in ten years. Either we do it, or we shall be crushed. This is what our obligations to the workers and peasants of the USSR dictate to us.

Thus Stalin transferred his personal sense of grievance against the powerful and the privileged, first expressed in his Georgian childhood, on to a wider stage.

There were practical as well as ideological reasons for a change of policy in 1928. The USSR had recovered economically to its 1914 position, but there was no private enterprise at the highest level to stimulate further investment. The State had to step in. Planning was deemed necessary because the market was too erratic to be relied upon. Hence the Five Year Plans and accompanying collectivisation.

Industrial and agricultural change had to go together. Large industrial cities could not be built unless there were workers to work the factories and produce to feed them. Regular and cheap food supplies necessitated an agricultural system that was more efficient and therefore by implication more productive, and also more closely controlled by the State. The millions of small farms in existence were difficult to influence, and the Party had never had a strong base in the countryside.

COLLECTIVISATION

For Stalin there was a significant element of class warfare in the decision to collectivise, once the immediate grain shortage of the late 1920s had been overcome. Small peasant farmers did not make good socialists, and better-off peasants or *kulaks* did so even less. The possibility of eliminating what was seen as a class enemy seems to have appealed to Stalin. Out of the window went Lenin's ideas of influencing peasants by moral persuasion and good example, ideas which Stalin himself had advocated as recently as 1927. Now, said Stalin, 'we have passed from the policy of *restricting* the exploiting tendencies of the kulaks to the policy of *eliminating* the kulaks as a class.'

The 1928 campaign to procure food seemed to suggest that the peasants could be made to yield to pressure, and agricultural output might be increased without massive injections of capital or machinery. Practical decisions had to be made. Collectives had to be established before the spring sowing, in order to minimise disruption. But 'eliminating' meant, in effect, murder. *Kulaks* – and the term was arbitrarily defined from area to area – were prevented from joining the new collective farms. Dispossessed of land and property, *kulaks* were exiled to different parts of the country or imprisoned. Probably over three million *kulaks* died during this collectivisation process.

The drive to collectivise was far from smooth. The key phase began with the decision on mass collectivisation in the autumn of 1929. Already in *Pravda* in November 1929 Stalin was writing about the successes which had occured: about one million households were collectivised by mid-1929. Now the pace was to be increased drastically. Alongside the establishment of collectives went the building of motor tractor stations, based upon earlier experiments. They became centres of Communist propaganda as well as sources of tractors.

Peasants were persuaded or forced to move on to collective farms, and meet quotas set by the government. Stalin displayed his cunning or his pragmatism when peasant resistance retarded the process and threatened serious disruption. In a speech of March 1930 Stalin called for a halt to the process, blaming over-exuberant local officials for being 'dizzy with success' and pushing too hard. But Stalin only intended the succeeding lull to be temporary. After bewildered Party officials adjusted their methods, the process of forcible collectivisation was resumed with vigour, until by the mid-1930s most of the USSR's agricultural land was collectivised. During the process there were many examples of personal distress, but particularly disastrous was the famine of 1932–3, when about seven million peasants died. This was at a time when the USSR was exporting grain and foreign aid was being refused.

Zealous Party officials were very active in implementing these policies at the local level. But there can be no doubt that Stalin approved of them. His aim seems to have been to crush all potential resistance and buttress his total authority. Stalin told Churchill during the Second World War that collectivisation had involved him in the most difficult struggle of his career, but he was not apologetic. And he achieved some of his aims. Collectivisation may not have been an economic success: the immediate impact was a catastrophic decline in numbers of livestock and output of grain, and pre-collectivisation levels of production were not equalled again until the late 1930s. Many of the economic problems caused by collectivisation were to plague Stalin's successors. The cost in human suffering was also incalculable. But politically Stalin achieved a remarkable success. For the first time since the Revolution the Party established a real hold over the countryside. Some twenty five million individual farms were replaced by a quarter of a million collective units.

Each had a chairman who was a Party member and appointed by the State. Party directives could be got to the peasants, and life on the farm (*kolkhoz*) closely supervised. Moreover, the Government did succeed in feeding the towns, since its call on the resources of the *kolkhoz* took absolute priority. The State's quota of grain was sold at a considerable profit in the towns. Urban workers were not well fed, but neither did they starve.

The term '*kulaks*' was an imprecise one, apparently embracing millions of peasants. We may find the notion of them as an antagonistic and threatening class a strange one, but Stalin appeared to perceive them in that way, and he did eliminate them. During the rest of his lifetime and beyond there was scarcely a whisper of organised peasant resistance to government measures. Some peasants were perhaps mollified by the concession of having private plots. Others showed their dissatisfaction by half-hearted efforts in the fields. Many hoped for an end to the system during the Second World War. But the spirit of overt resistance was broken by sheer brutal coercion, with more than a dash of propaganda. In these crude political terms Stalin fulfilled his aims, although the cost in human terms was unforgivable.

SOVIET INTERPRETATIONS OF COLLECTIVISATION

In the Gorbachev era of *glasnost*, Soviet writers began to speak out against Stalin's policies for the first time. V. Shubkin declared in August 1988:

> Stalin decided to eliminate NEP prematurely, using purely administrative measures and direct compulsion; this led, speaking mildly, to pitiable results. Agricultural production was disrupted, in a number of districts of the country famine began.

The historian Danilov had made a similar point in November 1987:

> The use of methods alien to socialism not only contradicted its objectives but also led to their distortion . . . The treatment of the cooperative of peasant households not as an independent objective of the socialist reconstruction of society, the achievement of which had its own internal logic and its own criteria of success and failure, but as a means for solving other problems, was a violation in

principle of Lenin's cooperative plan and involved other distortions.

Less than a year later Danilov declared, nevertheless, that 'Collective farms and collective farmers survived the severest test of war and made an immeasurable contribution to the great victory.' Clearly any assessment of Stalin's policies involved much soul-searching amongst Soviet historians.

THE FIVE-YEAR PLANS

Industrialisation proceeded apace with collectivisation. The new factories and steel works were to be paid for by the efforts of peasants and were in many instances to be manned by them also. Links between peasants and workers would be forged, and the way ahead to a classless Communist society opened up.

The Five-Year Plans revolved around the setting of gigantic industrial targets and the subordination of all economic and social life to the fulfilment of preordained goals. Communist commitment motivated some workers; even more were coerced by the threat of force or persuaded by Stalin's propaganda to give of their utmost. The gulag system of forced labour camps, swollen in the 1930s, also fuelled the drive for industrialisation. In the new Stalinist command economy, all supply and demand was determined by the State. The economic plan had the status of law: underfulfilment of the plan was therefore a criminal offence.

The First Five-Year Plan was approved at the Sixteenth Party Conference in 1929, although the Plan had already been agreed in 1927 and was begun in October 1928. The precise achievements of the plan can be debated at length. The human cost, as with collectivisation, is probably incalculable. The USSR was forced up the league of world industrial powers not by sophisticated economic mechanisms but by sweat and brute force. The population simply worked harder and the workforce was swollen by the addition of even more hands, especially female ones.

Western estimates usually put the increase in the output of civilian industries between 1928 and 1940 at 260 per cent. The output of munitions rose by 7,000 per cent, a clue to Stalin's other priority. Crude statistics mean little. Impressive superficially, they hide many of the problems which existed by 1937. Although many new resources had been created, many existing resources, including trained personnel who suffered during the purges (see Chapter 5), were destroyed. Great advances were made early on, but the pace was too quick to sustain. By the late 1930s many projects were incomplete, and the resources to finish them were not available. Pressures mounted, but the government explained away failures as sabotage.

The second revolution was well under way by the time of the Third Five-Year Plan, begun in 1938. At the head of the whole process stood Stalin, whose paranoia and appeals to Soviet nationalism increased in proportion to his power. He claimed later that his economic policies had laid the foundations of the Soviet success against Germany in the Second World War. It is difficult to assess the validity of this claim. Stagnation had set in in many sectors of the economy by the late 1930s, and then economic growth was resumed early in 1941. Could the Soviet economy have expanded by less draconian methods?

Stalin himself had no doubts about his success. In his report to the Seventeenth Congress of the Party, in January 1934, he was already exuding confidence:

> Marxism has achieved complete victory in one-sixth of the globe. And it cannot be an accident that the country in which Marxism has triumphed is now the only country in the world which knows no crises and no unemployment . . . comrades, this is not an accident.

It may have been no accident, but Stalin had probably, unconsciously combined the belief by the Right that the USSR could build socialism by its own efforts with the Left's insistence that the peasantry could be coerced into footing the bill. Stalin achieved on a massive scale what Peter the Great and Witte had begun in earlier centuries. Peter had begun the transformation of Russia into a superficially modern state two hundred years before Stalin, and had employed considerable brutality in the process. Stalin was to go to much greater lengths, both in the scale of his achievements and the degree of coercion applied, a coercion made all the more pervasive by the apparatus of the modern police state which Stalin inherited and then refined.

timeline	1928 October	First Five Year Plan
	1929 September	Collectivisation policy begins
	1930 March	Stalin's 'Dizzy with Success' article
	1933 September	Second Five Year Plan
	1938	Third Five Year Plan

Points to consider

1) Were Stalin's motives in the drive to collectivise primarily political or economic?
2) What was the rationale behind the Five-Year Plans?
3) 'Economically disastrous but politically successful'. Is this a valid assessment of Stalin's economic policies in the early 1930s?
4) Did Stalin create Socialism in the USSR?

TERROR AND TYRANNY

THE FUNCTION OF STATE TERROR

The use of terror as an instrument of political control is probably as old as history itself. Lenin had used terror against his rivals after the Revolution, just as the Whites had employed it against the Bolsheviks. But Stalin was to push terror to new heights in the 1930s. Authoritarian dictatorships often seek to induce popular compliance through, on the one hand, propaganda, and on the other, coercion, or the threat of coercion, against those suspected of less than wholehearted support for the regime. The ability of a dictator in the twentieth century to control and manipulate the media has increased the power of governments. Government controls were not implemented surreptitiously in the USSR. Propaganda in the Soviet system was seen as a legitimate means of projecting the particular world-view of the regime. Pluralism was never a possibility. The Party sought a monopoly of power in all spheres of life, social and cultural as well as political and economic.

For those not convinced by Stalin's propaganda, overt opposition was dangerous and certainly rare. If Stalin sought to keep his people in a state of fearful suspense, afraid of real or imagined enemies, and looking to himself and himself alone as their saviour, he probably succeeded. What we cannot know is how many citizens conformed out of genuine belief in the system, and how many simply lay low in order to save their own skins, although lying low was no guarantee against identification as an enemy of the people.

STALIN'S MOTIVES FOR THE TERROR

Terror in the sense of wholesale arrests, imprisonments and executions began in the 1930s. It would be absurdly simplistic to dismiss Stalin as mad, as some commentators have done. Although his rivals in the Party were in the shadows after 1929, Stalin could still not feel secure. Overt opposition there was not, but Stalin's old enemies and defeated rivals were still around, possibly plotting. It was the sort of situation Stalin reacted to – he rarely initiated policies himself without feeling provoked in some way – and now he felt compelled to preserve the Party's, and his own, power. Influential figures were alarmed at the dislocation and hardship caused by Stalin's economic policies. Groups of Party members were certainly discussing the possibility of Stalin's replacement as General Secretary in the early 1930s, to be followed by a relaxation of the draconian economic programme. Ryutin, a senior figure in the Party, circulated amongst colleagues a fierce written attack on the 'evil genius' Stalin. Ryutin and some others were expelled from the Party, but the fact that the Politburo was able to prevent Stalin from inflicting the more drastic punishment that he wanted showed that Stalin could still be restrained from complete arbitrary power at this stage. Also Kirov, head of the Party in Leningrad and a Stalin protegé, at one time very close to the dictator, spoke against Stalin in this affair. Therefore Stalin still felt vulnerable. Perhaps it was at this moment, when Stalin may also have been temporarily disturbed by the suicide of his second wife, that he decided to eradicate all real or potential opposition, particularly among the Bolshevik old guard who had been even closer to Lenin than he himself had, a fact that Stalin found difficult to come to terms with.

The intricacies of Stalin's psychological make-up have certainly exercised Soviet commentators in recent years. 'Evidence' has been unearthed, although unfortunately it has a fairly thin basis. There is, for example, the fact that, in 1916 Stalin quoted approvingly in his notes a sentence attributed to Ghengis Khan: 'The death of the vanquished is necessary for the calm of the victors'. In 1988 an old Bolshevik Petrovsky, was reported as saying:

> At one of the plenums of the Central Committee at the beginning of the 1930s, Kaminsky, a doctor, said: 'We must cure comrade Stalin, he is seriously ill.' He meant psychic illness. Stalin heard out

Kaminsky very respectfully. But after this meeting the doctor did not return to his home.

There is little firm evidence on which to speculate further. But if Stalin was thinking in terms of revenge by 1932, his determination can only have been strengthened by his experience at the Seventeenth Party Congress two years later. Here there was certainly a discussion of the desirability of sacking Stalin, and replacing him as General Secretary by the younger Kirov. Stalin is supposed to have manipulated the voting to prevent this situation occuring.

THE MAJOR PURGES BEGIN

Before 1934 was over Kirov had been assassinated. Circumstantial evidence points to Stalin's complicity in the crime. This is still a matter of debate, but the significance of the event lies in Stalin's use of it as an excuse to institute a drastic purge of the Party. Arrests and executions were arbitrary. Before 1934, many of the victims of the regime, im-

Kirov's funeral procession December 1934.

prisoned or exiled, had been professionals from various walks of life, but usually branded as 'bourgeois specialists'. Now the net was spread much more widely. As a percentage of the population, members of the bureaucracy, the Party, the armed forces and the intelligentsia now suffered most, although many workers and peasants also became uncomprehending victims.

A brief lull in the arrests was accompanied by the promulgation of a new Constitution in 1936. It was largely the work of Bukharin. It added to the fiction that the USSR was a democratic state with guarantees of citizens' rights. For Stalin, it was the opportunity to present his country to the world as a modern, progressive society. It was also the prelude to the next wave of terror. 1936 saw mass arrests and the show trials of old stalwarts like Kamenev and Zinoviev. Later trials, confessions and executions included Bukharin, Rykov and Yagoda, Head of the NKVD until 1936. Victims confessed to a range of charges, including membership of a Trotskyist conspiracy, spying and sabotage.

As the denunciations grew, and victims were swallowed up by day and night, the Purges appeared to take on a momentum of their own. However, Stalin personally signed thousands of death warrants and surely had a very precise purpose in stimulating an atmosphere of uncertainty and intimidation, making the very idea – let alone the act – of opposition dangerous.

Between 1935 and 1940 some twenty million people were arrested, of whom seven million were executed. Many others lingered or died in prison camps. Stalin was ultimately in control. The mass terror, which was also applied to the armed forces – thousands of officers were shot – was suddenly halted as Stalin established new priorities, not least of which was the problem of dealing with the threatening international situation.

Stalin was well on the way to creating a new class of functionaries and experts who had risen under him, filled the places vacated by the Purges, and owed everything to him. But he had also weakened his armed forces and demoralised many of his subjects.

AN EXPLANATION OF THE TERROR

There have been many attempts to explain the Terror. In Stalin's own lifetime, the Stalinist argument was that in the 1930s there was a plot to overthrow the regime and restore capitalism. The plot was supposedly organised from exile by Trotsky, who had been undermining the regime since 1917, and was now in league with the Gestapo. Later writers tended to interpret things differently. Some historians like Deutscher, seeking a rational explanation for the horrors, decided that Stalin foresaw the coming war and felt the need to eliminate a potential fifth column. Anti-Stalinists claimed that the Terror was simply a tactic used to create a totalitarian state and remove the hated old guard. Some Soviet and Western writers saw the origins of the Purges in the clash between the hard-line Stalin and supposed moderates like Kirov who favoured less dramatic action against 'oppositionists'.

There were certainly many Soviet citizens, including perhaps Stalin, who genuinely believed at the time that thousands, or indeed millions, of traitors were at large amongst the population. They had to be rooted out lest the USSR be fatally undermined during forthcoming struggles. That was certainly how Stalin's propaganda machine portrayed the situation.

Some Western historians have tended to play down Stalin's personal role in implementing the Terror. This trend has been bound up with the argument as to how far the USSR was a totalitarian state in the 1930s. It has been pointed out that local bureaucrats frequently initiated drastic security measures without direction from Moscow. Soviet historians have been less apologetic towards Stalin. Certainly there is now considerable documentary evidence of Stalin's personal involvement in the Purges, such as the many death lists bearing his signature. Stalin personally humiliated leading colleagues like Kalinin, the President, whose wife was imprisoned in a labour camp from 1938 to 1945.

STALIN AND STALINISTS

What about Stalin's relations with his entourage? Even powerful individuals like his fellow Georgian Beria, Head of the NKVD from 1938, had to bow to Stalin's will. The experienced Foreign Minister Molotov, according to Marshal Zhukov, was independently minded and was prepared to argue with Stalin, just as he did with Hitler, but even Molotov agreed with the Purges of 1937 and 1938. It is not easy to ascertain the precise relationship of Stalin to his leading henchmen. Beginning with Khrushchev's denunciation of the dead dictator in 1956, some old Stalinists were understandably eager to unload responsibility for acts of brutality and mistakes on to Stalin personally, thereby magnifying his power.

TOTALITARIANISM

Was Stalin's USSR a totalitarian state in the 1930s? Totalitarianism implies a state run by a dictator or a single political organisation that suppresses all political opposition, along with individual liberties, and seeks total allegiance from its citizens, both in thought and deed. By this definition the USSR was such a state, at least in intent. It is true that administration was sometimes chaotic and confused, and that local initiative was thereby not stifled – although local initiative was exercised by Party members. It is true that there were still factions within the Party, and personality clashes. Disagreements occurred between local and central committees. Molotov favoured a more rigorous campaign against 'oppositionists' than Ordzhonikidze, who paid the price for his moderation. Zhdanov welcomed criticism from rank and file Party members in the spirit of Lenin, whereas the Security Chief Yezhov favoured a strict adherence to the official line. It is also true that fewer individuals were expelled from the Party as the 1930s wore on, and the majority of expulsions from the Party were for non-ideological reasons such as theft and indiscipline. Readmissions to the Party began after 1936.

Russians refer to the years of the Purges as the 'Yezhovshchina', after Yezhov, Head of the NKVD between 1936 and 1938. According to one historian of the Purges, the Yezhovshchina

> was not the result of a petrified bureaucracy's stamping out dissent and annihilating old radical revolutionaries. In fact, it may have been just the opposite. It is not inconsistent with the evidence to argue that the Yezhovshchina was rather a radical, even hysterical, *reaction* to bureaucracy. The entrenched officeholders were destroyed from above and below in a chaotic wave of voluntarism and revolutionary puritanism.
>
> (J. Arch Getty, *Origins of the Great Purges*, 1985)

The same author concludes:

> The existence of high-level personal rivalries, disputes over development or modernisation plans, powerful and conflicting

centrifugal and centripetal forces, and local conflicts made large-scale political violence possible and even likely.

There is an element of special pleading here. Such conditions have existed in other societies without leading to the Terror of Stalin's USSR. The historian Fainsod described the USSR as an example of 'inefficient totalitarianism.' Stalin would doubtless have ironed out the inefficiencies had that been possible. Stalin was not an evil and one-dimensional spider at the centre of a gigantic web. Even at the height of the cult of personality, Stalin was capable of uttering soothing noises about relaxing the period of struggle whilst simultaneously calling for greater vigilance. He was a complex man. But powerful Stalin certainly was, and those afraid of him had good reason to be. Popular jokes are often a good indication of public sentiment. One Soviet joke used to go:

> Stalin went into a cinema to find out what people really thought of him. After the feature film there came a newsreel which naturally highlighted Stalin in every scene. The whole audience stood and applauded long and vigorouly. Stalin remained modestly seated.
>
> After a few moments the man next to Stalin nudged him and whispered: 'Most people feel the same as you do, Comrade. But it would be safer if you stood up.'

Stalin was at the height of his power inside the USSR on the eve of war with Germany in 1941. What were his personal characteristics and lifestyle at this time?

FAMILY LIFE

The only period when Stalin enjoyed a relaxed family life was during the 1920s, when he was only one member of a collective leadership. Power destroyed personal happiness. His second wife, Nadezhda Alliluyeva, became very depressed at developments in the country and shot herself in 1932. Stalin never recovered from this event, and, according to his daughter Svetlana, was both mortified and furious. Thereafter Stalin lived either in a simple Kremlin flat or a dacha on the outskirts of Moscow. Occasionally there was a holiday, but no personal happiness. One of his sons was captured during the war and died in German captivity, Stalin refusing to exchange him for a German prisoner. Stalin's other son died an alcoholic. His daughter Svetlana grew apart from him by the time of the War years. Much later she defected to the West. Stalin allowed some of his own relations to become victims of the Purges. The families of both of his wives were shot.

Stalin's personal life was frugal, without a breath of scandal, in contrast to effervescent contemporaries like Lenin and Trotsky. Stalin lived surrounded by bodyguards, he slept late and worked in the afternoons in the Kremlin. One of his few relaxations was to watch Soviet or foreign films. He rarely travelled, and seems to have studiously avoided meeting ordinary people.

CHARACTER
—

Stalin's character had been formed long before he came to power. The legendary 'rudeness' of which Lenin had complained never left him. He was always subject to fits of violent temper, and was vengeful. Although resentful of those he felt had been born with more talent or greater advantages in life, Stalin was confident in the rightness of his policies, that is, when he had finally made up his mind. Stalin had spent years in the underground and learnt to conceal his thoughts. He rarely acted impulsively, but, having decided upon a course of action, he could be unshakingly dogmatic in carrying it out. He resented criticism, and anyone with the temerity to challenge him was liable to a dressing down or worse, since Stalin regarded ruthlessness as a virtue, and anyway was inherently suspicious of the motives of anybody who did challenge him.

What was the driving force in Stalin's life? It is tempting to say simply, 'power'. But he could never have imagined the position to which he was to rise back in the pre-Revolutionary days of struggle. Perhaps he was surprised at his success, and that is why he never trusted anyone, even his closest colleagues. Stalin apparently had no religious beliefs. He did profess orthodox Marxism, in so far as it could be applied to Russia, and this partly explains his concern for economic advancement. He was content to acknowledge Lenin's contribution to Marxist theory, although he was not averse to exaggerated claims about his own achievements as presented by Soviet propaganda. However, Stalin would never permit use of the word 'Stalinism', in case it gave the impression that he had somehow initiated something un-Marxist in the USSR. Stalin always insisted that everything he had achieved inside his country was a true expression of Marxism-Leninism.

Stalin was involved in other things besides politics and economics. He was greatly interested in the arts, but was extremely traditionalist and hostile to the artistic experimentation which had flowered after the Revolution. He frequently interfered in the cultural sphere, either promoting Socialist Realism or denouncing that which he considered perverted. Famous composers like Shostakovich and Prokoviev were directly bullied by Stalin into producing works 'directly accessible to the masses.'

In the last resort perhaps it did all come down to power. But Stalin's regime did not depend solely on coercion. A whole class of bureaucrats, promoted under the regime, loyally supported every Party and government directive. So, no doubt, did many ordinary citizens, even if life was hard and often dangerous. It was to be the Nazi invasion of the USSR and not his own people that almost destroyed Stalin's regime. The people were prepared to fight for Mother Russia and even for Stalin, once he was astute enough to identify himslf with the country and tap the patriotism of the people rather than their love for himself or his Party.

timeline	1932 November	Suicide of Stalin's wife Nadezhda Alliluyeva
	1934 January–February	Seventeenth Party Congress
	July	GPU reorganised as the NKVD
	September	USSR joined League of Nations
	December	Assassination of Kirov and beginning of the Terror
	1935 January	Zinoviev, Kamenev and seventeen others arrested
	July–August	'Popular Front' policy announced at Seventh Comintern Congress
	1936 August	Decision to involve the USSR in the Spanish Civil War
		Show Trial of Zinoviev, Kamenev and fourteen others
	September	Yezhov became Head of the NKVD and launched Great Purge
	December	New Constitution adopted
	1937 May	Purge of Red Army began
	June	Tukhachevsky and leading Army officers executed

1938	March	Bukharin, Rykov, Yagoda and others tried and shot
	September	Munich Agreement over Czechoslovakia
		Short History of the CPSU published
	December	Beria became Head of the NKVD
1939	March	Stalin declared an end to the Great Terror

Points to consider

1) **What were Stalin's motives for the Great Terror?**
2) **Was the USSR a totalitarian state in the 1930s?**
3) **To what extent did Stalin carry out a social and cultural revolution in the USSR?**
4) **By 1941 Stalin had been a dictator for twelve years. Had he weakened or strengthened the USSR during that period?**

WAR AND THE TRIUMPH OF PATRIOTISM

The Second World War revealed both the weaknesses and strengths of the Stalinist system. The war was possibly Stalin's severest test and his greatest triumph, although the extent to which the Soviet victory was due to Stalin or came about in spite of him is still a matter of debate. The war devastated the USSR and many of the achievements of Stalin's economic revolutions were undone, but Stalin emerged from the war in 1945 even more powerful than before, and as a player on the international stage as well as domestic despot.

PRE-WAR FOREIGN POLICY

Most foreign policies are a compound of pragmatism and ideology. Stalin's foreign policy was no exception. He operated in the belief that his country was endangered by surrounding capitalist states, many of which had tried to overthrow the fledgling Bolshevik State after the Revolution of 1917. An important motive for the industrialisation programme had been to strengthen the USSR militarily in a hostile world. This had certainly been achieved, at least in terms of military hardware, although Stalin undid much of the good by his decimation of the officer corps in the Purges of the late 1930s.

Stalin identified the survival of Communism with the continued existence of his Soviet State. This was a convenient doctrine, for it legitimised for Stalin the subordination of all Communist activities abroad to the interests of the USSR. Foreign Communists were purged on Stalin's orders, just like Soviet ones. Stalin's agents spent much of their time during the Spanish Civil War rooting out and eliminating rival groups on the Spanish Left, particularly the hated Trotskyists, 'internationalists' who rejected Stalin's claims to be at the head of the world Communist movement.

Stalin and Fascism

When Stalin did allow ideological conviction its head, the results could be disastrous. This was notably the case in 1933, the year of the Nazis' accession to power in Germany. The Soviets held to the Marxist notion that the Great Depression heralded the coming collapse of capitalism. Fascism was simply the extreme form of capitalism, and signified the coming Armageddon. Therefore the advent of Fascism should actually be welcomed by Communists, including German ones. Stalin ordered the German Communist Party to focus its attacks on the German Social Democrats in the months before Hitler's take-over. Social Democrats, labelled 'Social Fascists' by the Communists, were seen as the true enemy, since their programme of moderate reform and compromise threatened to divert the German working class from the road of revolution. The stupidity of this policy was soon evident when, within months of taking power, the Nazis put thousands of German Communists into concentration camps. Some German Communists survived to wage a dangerous underground war against the Nazis in Germany, but most suffered badly from Stalin's mistake.

At least Stalin eventually acknowledged his error and in 1935 the Communist International, or Comintern, addressed the problem. The Comintern had been created as Lenin's vehicle for the encouragement and aid of Communist movements abroad. At its final Congress in 1935, the Comintern called for the formation of Popular Fronts, alliances of all left-wing movements, to resist Fascism. Unfortunately for Stalin, Western governments were as suspicious of him, sometimes more so, than they were of the Nazis. Stalin did not have a monopoly on mistrust.

Stalin reverted to his pragmatic mode. He allowed the USSR to join the once-reviled League of Nations, an organisation that had already displayed its ineffectiveness as a peacemaker in major crises. Stalin made alliances with France and Czechoslovakia, and worked to persuade the Western democracies to join him in a policy of collective security. Mutual suspicions hindered progress, and the Soviet position was weakened by German successes in the Rhineland and Austria, and the victory of Fascism in Spain. To make matters worse, the Czechoslovakian crisis, which had been simmering since May 1938 and which came to a head in September, was solved by a Four-Power Conference of Germany, Italy, France and Britain. Stalin was not invited, despite his ties with the Czechs. There seemed no reason why the West should trust Stalin, and it is not certain that Stalin would have come to the aid of the Czechs in the event of a German invasion, but his exclusion from the Munich Conference confirmed his suspicions that the West would never stand up to Hitler. He was also probably aware that a section of opinion on the Right in Britain and France looked much more favourably upon the Nazis than they did upon the Soviets.

The Nazi-Soviet Pact

Stalin became increasingly concerned about the international situation in the latter stages of 1938 and 1939. Even after the German break-up of Czechoslovakia in March 1939, the British and French governments were reluctant to abandon appeasement as a policy. Somewhat half-hearted feelers were extended to Stalin. But Stalin was in a dilemma. The British position seemed illogical. They had not fought for the Czechs in 1938; yet now they were guaranteeing Poland, a much more difficult country for the British to defend. In fact they would have to rely upon the Soviets in the event of a German attack on Poland. Stalin could see possibilities in an alliance with the West, but he was also aware that many in the West would be content to see him embroiled in a war against Germany, whilst the West sat on the sidelines. Another option was an agreement with Hitler, and that was the path which Stalin chose in August 1939.

It is strange that the Nazi-Soviet Non-Aggression Pact of August 1939 should have excited so much surprise and criticism at the time and ever since. True, the Nazis and Soviets had been at each others' throats for years, but politicians do not usually allow prejudices to interfere with prospects of advantage, whatever their political persuasion. Stalin had a grudging respect for his fellow-dictator, a feeling which was reciprocated, and the advantages of the Pact were obvious. It removed the threat of an immediate German attack upon the USSR, a threat which Stalin dare not contemplate, given the unready state of the Red Army in the aftermath of the Purges – the leadership of the Armed Forces and thousands of officers had been wiped out during the Great Terror.

Stalin also stood to gain part of Poland as a buffer territory, and Hitler's acquiescence in his annexation of the Baltic states, which Stalin carried out in 1940. Hitler avoided the prospect of a two-front war when he carried out his attack upon Poland. The possible alternative to the Pact for Stalin, an alliance with Britain and France, would probably have involved Stalin much sooner in a war with Hitler. Stalin was also fearful of danger from another quarter: there had already been serious clashes in the Far East between the USSR and Russia's old enemy Japan.

Therefore in the context of the international situation in 1939, Stalin's actions were logical and probably sensible. After all, he, like most people, even the experts, could not foresee Hitler's rapid triumph in western Europe in 1940, which upset calculations and the balance of power. Stalin might reasonably have hoped for a longer breathing space in which to get his military house in order. Stalin did in fact use the period after August 1939 to reform the Red Army. The latter's performance in the war against Finland of 1939–40 was to simply emphasise the need for such reform. Where Stalin can be blamed is if he persuaded himself that the Non-Aggression Pact was anything more than a temporary truce. Hitler had long made it clear that his ultimate ambition was a war of conquest against Russia. It is unlikely that Stalin trusted Hitler more than any other individual, and yet he seemed surprised when Hitler broke the Pact in 1941. This could have been due to the tendency which Stalin had, despite his pragmatism, to simply refuse to accept facts which stared him in the face if they were particularly unpalatable. This was a serious fault in the leader of a country ordained by Hitler to have a miserable existence as a province of the Third Reich.

The Russo-Finnish War

In the months after the Pact, Stalin certainly did make errors of judgement. In order to give more protection to the vulnerable city of Leningrad, he pressured the Finns to adjust their frontier with the USSR and to allow Soviet bases in Finland. Finnish refusal led to the Winter War of November 1939 to March 1940, a war which the Soviets won, but at a very heavy cost. There was logic in Stalin's demands on the Finns, as Finland was part of the Soviet sphere of influence following the Nazi-Soviet Pact, but the Soviet mistake was to underestimate the difficulty of subduing the Finns, a mistake which cost unnecessarily heavy Soviet casualties. Finland joined the Nazis in their invasion of the USSR in 1941.

Worsening Relations with Germany

Stalin also miscalculated in his relations with Hitler in the months following the Pact. A visit by Molotov to Berlin in 1940 was disastrous for Soviet-German relations. Hitler tried to tempt the USSR into his Tripartite Pact with Italy and Japan. Molotov's response was to propose an increase in Soviet power by mooting further large areas of Soviet influence in Eastern Europe and the Balkans. Perhaps Stalin thought that Hitler's involvements elsewhere would lead him to accede to these demands. If so it was a miscalculation, and Hitler was simply confirmed in his determination to attack the USSR. Stalin was bluffing and the enemy knew it. On the other hand, since Hitler fully intended to attack the USSR at some time, Stalin may be accused of provoking Hitler on this particular issue, but not of causing a fundamental change in his policy.

THE NAZI INVASION

Where Stalin's critics are unanimous in condemning Stalin's behaviour is over his actions immediately preceding the Nazi attack of 22 June 1941, and his strategy, or lack of it, immediately afterwards. There had been reports of German preparations for an invasion, and in a desperate bid not to provoke Hitler, Stalin left his frontier forces without clear orders other than the command that they must do nothing to incite the German troops massing on his frontiers. Some warnings came from the Western powers, and Stalin was too suspicious to believe them.

When the attack came, Soviet troops were caught largely helpless. The huge losses suffered by his troops and airmen in the early weeks of the German campaign were in large part Stalin's responsibility. Stalin's nerve broke, and he disappeared off the scene for several days.

One of Stalin's first actions was to look for scapegoats, by ordering the execution of those generals whose forces were overrun in the early days

Treachery Strikes. 'Forgive me Comrade'. Daily Mail *23 June 1941. Hitler tears up the Nazi-Soviet Pact.*

of the campaign. Some generals were still being accused of 'panic and cowardice' supposedly displayed at this time, as late as five years after the war. When Stalin recovered his nerve, he spoke with impressive gravity about the serious situation facing the country, setting the tone for the rest of the war. The speech was in a radio broadcast to the nation on 3 July 1941:

> The enemy continues to push forward . . . A grave danger hangs over our country . . . It is essential that our people . . . should appreciate the full immensity of the danger that threatens our country . . . The issue is one of life and death for the Soviet State, for the people of the USSR; the issue is whether the peoples of the Soviet Union shall remain free or fall into slavery . . . All our work must be immediately reconstructed on a war footing, everything must be subordinated to the interests of the front and the task of organising the demolition of the enemy.

The determined tone was typical of Stalin's style throughout the war. For example, on 21 September 1942 he ordered his Leningrad commanders to be ruthless in countering the tactics of the Germans, who sometimes sent ahead captured Russians to plead for peace. Stalin had no compunction in ordering his Army to fire on such civilians who were unwittingly aiding the enemy:

> It is said that the German scoundrels approaching Leningrad are sending ahead of their troops old men and old women, women and children, delegates from areas occupied by them to ask the Bolsheviks to surrender Leningrad and make peace. My advice is: don't be sentimental, but hit the enemy and his auxiliaries, willing or unwilling, in the teeth. War is merciless, and it will bring defeat in the first instance to him who shows weakness and vacillation.

Harsh orders indeed, but Stalin was only displaying his recognition that this was a war of survival. After all, Hitler's orders were that Leningrad should be destroyed, and eventually the whole Russian people was to be enslaved once Jews, Communists and other undesirables had been liquidated. The war was being waged ruthlessly on both sides.

The USSR survived the Nazi onslaught for several reasons: the vast distances which rendered the German blitzkrieg less effective than in Western Europe; German tactical mistakes such as switching the focus of their assault at critical moments; the Russian winter; and above all the heroism and sacrifices of the long-suffering Soviet people. But what was Stalin's contribution?

STALIN'S LEADERSHIP

It has become fashionable to find fault with Stalin's military input into the war. His culpability at the beginning of the war has already been discussed. Other pre-war chickens came home to roost, for example his refusal to allow partisan training before 1941 on the grounds that any war would be fought on the enemy's territory, not Soviet soil, and therefore in Stalin's view such training was unnecessary. Stalin's interventions in particular campaigns during the war were sometimes disastrous for his troops, as in the preliminaries to the Battle of Stalingrad in the summer of 1942.

In fact the evidence about Stalin's skills as a war leader is often contradictory. Zhukov, Stalin's greatest general, wrote different things about Stalin at different times. For example, in a letter he stated that

> a particularly negative side of Stalin throughout the war was that, because he had poor practical knowledge of the preparation of operations ... he proposed completely unrealistic dates for operations to start.

However, on another occasion Zhukov was more complimentary:

> At the beginning of the War he (Stalin) mastered strategic questions poorly, but his mind, the logic of his thought, his general knowledge and his grasp all served him well. In the second period of the War, after Stalingrad, he was entirely the right person as Supreme Commander ... he comprehensively studied in advance an issue to be discussed or the plan of a future operation. Having carefully examined the information, he summoned people, military specialists, and came to the meeting fully equipped. He did not tolerate superficiality and vagueness. Incidentally, he was able to listen to objections. It is not true that it was impossible to criticise Stalin. I objected and showed he was wrong – more than once!

Few people did disagree openly with Stalin, but Stalin had the sense to appreciate Zhukov's qualities.

There has been criticism of Stalin for not visiting the front during the war. As neither Churchill nor Hitler paid that many visits to the front themselves, such criticism is irrelevant. Successful leaders in modern wars need many qualities, but the fighting skills of an Alexander the Great are not among them. The test of a modern war leader comes in different areas: the ability to pick good generals and support their decisions; the ability to inspire his people; the ability to galvanise a nation in the context of total war. By these criteria Stalin's reputation should stand high.

THE CONDUCT OF WAR

Having recovered his nerve early in July 1941, Stalin displayed considerable resolve, even to the extent of remaining in Moscow when it was under direct German threat. More so than his antagonist Hitler, Stalin learnt from his mistakes. Staff appointments were based on military rather than political criteria.

The command structure created by Stalin was far more effective than the mish-mash of competing bureaucracies that characterised the Third Reich. Although Stalin always remained the dominant personality in the conduct of the war, he gave rein to able subordinates. Voznesenskii supervised economic planning; Molotov was responsible for diplomacy; Khrushchev, Kosygin, Mikoyan and Zhdanov all played key roles in the administration. Deficiencies in the Soviet system of command – there was initially no single organisation to determine strategy and to control operations – were rapidly corrected. Within two days of the German attack, STAVKA was created. STAVKA, the General Headquarters of the High Command, was initially under the leadership of Marshal Timoshenko, with Stalin as one of the members. In July 1941 STAVKA became 'STAVKA of the Supreme Command', under Stalin's chairmanship. In August Stalin became Supreme Commander. He had direct lines of communication to the people who mattered. Stalin was briefed by the General Staff, but kept firm political control over the military. Although political commissars, reintroduced into the armed forces in July 1941, were abolished again in October 1942, the influence of the military in planning, if anything, declined. Possibly Stalin was persuaded of his skills in generalship by his own propaganda. At the very end of the war it was Stalin's own strategy for the capture of Berlin that was implemented, rather than that of his generals.

The Stalinist command economy also proved far more adaptable to the needs of total war than the system of other countries, including Germany. The Soviets were able to physically shift factories to the security of the east and go over to total war production with relative ease. The planning mechanisms were already in place. Stalin was closely involved in this economic planning. Since he also played a key diplomatic and military role it is no exaggeration to say that Stalin exercised more control over his country's war effort than any other Allied or enemy leader.

Stalin had never been a demagogue, and was never renowned for the oratorical skills of a Trotsky, but he did discover during the war that he could inspire his people. He did this by appealing to their patriotism, not their belief in Marxism-Leninism. The people were exhorted to fight for Mother Russia. Stalin even reopened the churches to allow the people to invoke divine aid in their struggle. Stalin's own cult of personality was promoted, just as before the war, but now his image was identified not with the struggle for socialism, but the more tangible and immediate cause of defence of the motherland. This was a cause with which every citizen could identify. True, there were Soviet citizens who welcomed the Germans as liberators in the early stages of the war, but the brutal behaviour of the invaders relinquished most of this potential support. Stalin did strike a chord with most people. One soldier recalled his reaction to a Stalin order issued in July 1942, at one of the many critical moments of the war:

> All my life I will remember what Stalin's Order meant . . . Not the letter, but the spirit and the content of this document made possible the moral and psychological breakthrough in the hearts and minds of all to whom it was read . . . The chief thing was the courage to tell people the whole terrible and bitter truth about the abyss to whose edge we were then sliding.

Stalin also courted his Western Allies, at the same time as berating them for the delay in opening the Second Front, whilst the USSR bled. The Comintern was dissolved. Stalin lived up to the cosy image of 'Uncle Joe' which somewhat incongruously flourished in the West.

Stalin permitted little publicity about himself during the difficult months of 1941 and early 1942, but thereafter he was constantly portrayed as the heroic war leader and organiser of victory, rather than General Secretary of the Party. He took credit for a great deal, and we must disentangle his real achievements from the excesses of the Party's propaganda machine that accompanied and often exaggerated them. Dictators do seem to have a need to decorate themselves with the highest honours they can bestow, or even invent new ones – Stalin did both – but Stalin did perform consummately the role of war leader and personification of his country's resistance. This is somewhat ironic, since there is some evidence that in the dark days of October 1941 Stalin was considering whether to attempt a deal with Hitler, offering areas of Soviet territory to the Germans in return for a halt to their attack. However, the situation was desperate, and perhaps the incident simply confirms that Stalin was not infallible.

Stalin was responsible for brutal decisions during the war, and they cost many lives, as when he refused to allow units of the Red Army to retreat when they were in hopeless positions. Yet many elderly Russians can still look back nostalgically to the period when Stalin was 'the man who won the War'. The USSR suffered terribly in the war, and millions of its citizens, military and civilian, died. We may argue about Stalin's responsibility for many of these deaths. Modern warfare is a terrible experience and Stalin may be excused on some counts. Far less forgiveable was the lack of generosity and compassion shown by Stalin during the war and at its conclusion towards those whose only crime was to fight for their country. Stalin's concerns with threats to his regime, real or imaginary, did not relax with the onset of war. His security forces were more active than ever. Many thousands of Soviet citizens already accused of political opposition were shot by the NKVD in the first months of the war. Thereafter, any citizen suspected of disloyalty, either as an individual or as a member of a national group, was liable to arrest or deportation. Whole national groups were displaced and resettled. Failure in the performance of duties was treated with the utmost severity. Soldiers who had suffered the hardship of German captivity, and even civilians who were unfortunate enough to have lived in areas under German occupation, were automatically suspect, and liable to investigation and 'retribution'.

BUSINESS AS USUAL

At the end of the war Stalin was treated with reverence as the saviour of his country. Yet no respite was permitted. The iron discipline returned. It had never really been absent, but now it had to be directed towards new causes. Reconstruction was at the top of the list. But first there had to be retribution for the unworthy. During the war Stalin had spent as much time on security matters as military affairs. Little changed now: the leopard could not change its spots. Even the Party leadership of Leningrad, which had resisted the Germans heroically and undergone terrible privations during the nine-hundred-day Siege, was purged. Stalin had emerged from the war as the unchallengeable leader of a victorious superpower, but the steel was still in his soul and the 'sickly suspicion', as later characterised by Khrushchev, still gripped his mind.

timeline	1939	August	Nazi-Soviet Pact signed
		September	Germany attacked Poland
			Soviet occupation of eastern Poland
		November	Soviet invasion of Finland
	1940	March	Katyn massacre
		July	Baltic States incorporated into USSR
		August	Assassination of Trotsky
	1941	June	Germany invaded USSR
			Stalin appointed himself Chairman of the State Committeee of Defence
		July	Stalin became Commissar of Defence
		August	Stalin became Supreme Commander
	1942	August	Churchill and Stalin met in Moscow
	1943	January	German surrender at Stalingrad
		March	Stalin became Marshal of the Soviet Union
		April	USSR broke off diplomatic relations with the Polish government in Exile
		May	Comintern dissolved
		November–December	Teheran Conference
	1944	July	Soviet-controlled Polish government established in Lublin
		August	Warsaw Rising
		October	Churchill and Eden visited Moscow
	1945	February	Yalta Conference
		May	Germany surrendered

Points to consider

1) 'Inconsistent and short-sighted'. Is this a valid assessment of Stalin's foreign policy between 1929 and 1941?
2) What were Stalin's motives for signing the Nazi-Soviet Pact?
3) 'The USSR won the War in spite of Stalin, not because of him'. Do you agree?
4) To what extent did the war demonstrate the strengths and weaknesses of the Soviet system?

STALIN THE OMNISCIENT

In 1947 an official biography of Stalin was published in the Soviet Union. Stalin was at the height of his power, bathing in the glory of an all-pervasive personality cult, and admired and feared both as the victor of the war and the head of one of the world's two superpowers. The following extract reflects the tone of most Soviet propaganda of this period:

> Stalin is the brilliant leader and teacher of the Party, the great strategist of the Socialist Revolution, military commander, and guide of the Soviet state. An implacable attitude towards the enemies of Socialism, profound fidelity to principle, a combination of clear revolutionary perspective and clarity of purpose with extraordinary firmness and persistence in the pursuit of aims, wise and practical leadership, and intimate contact with the masses – such are the characteristic features of Stalin's style . . .
>
> Everybody is familiar with the cogent and invincible force of Stalin's logic, the crystal clarity of his mind, his iron will, his devotion to the party, his ardent faith in the people, and love for the people . . . Stalin is wise and deliberate in solving complex political questions where a thorough weighing of pros and cons is required. At the same time, he is a supreme master of bold revolutionary decisions and of swift adaptations to changed conditions.
>
> Stalin is the worthy continuer of the cause of Lenin, or, as it is said in the Party: 'Stalin is the Lenin of today'.
>
> (G. Alexandrov, *Joseph Stalin: A Short Biography*, 1947)

This is typical of the style of Stalinist propaganda both in the tone and the mixture of truth and untruth: few would argue for example with the epithets 'firmness' and 'persistence' as applied to Stalin, but there is no evidence that Stalin ever enjoyed or wished to enjoy 'intimate contact with the masses'.

STALIN'S FINAL YEARS

The reality of Stalin's final years in power from 1945 until his death in 1953 is well documented. Certainly supreme and unchallengeable, Stalin also lived in isolation, surrounded by sycophantic subordinates, all afraid of a resurrection of the Terror of the pre-war years, that might yet sweep them away. Stalin made only two speeches after 1946, and his interventions in the day-to-day business of governing became rarer. His poorer state of health after the war had a lot to do with this. His daughter Svetlana wrote of his 'loneliness, emptiness and lack of human companionship'. He was as suspicious as ever of those around him. Whilst doubting the sincerity of the enormous flattery he received, culminating in the extravagant tributes paid to him on the occasion of his 70th birthday in December 1949, he demanded such treatment anyway. Organised enthusiasm had long been an intregal part of the Stalinist system.

Stalin spent more time in his dacha and less in the Kremlin. Much of the autumn would be spent on the Black Sea coast, his favourite resort. He still confirmed decisions made by his ministers, but their Council sessions often took place in his absence. Stalin appeared in public even less than before. When Stalin travelled – and it was always by car or train – the isolation continued: roads and railway lines would be cleared, and his only companions would be the ever-growing corps of body-guards and security troops. In his dacha, Stalin would continue his practice of watching films and dining with a few prominent colleagues who had always to be on hand to indulge the old man's whims. Stalin's successor Khrushchev painted a portrait of an unhappy man who admitted that he could trust nobody.

Stalin did make one more notable appearance before his final decline. The Nineteenth Congress of the Communist Party was summoned for October 1952. It was the first Congress since 1939. It may have been called because there were new economic plans on the horizon, and amendments to Party rules on the agenda, but another purpose may have been to resolve the uncertainty about the leadership which was becoming evident. What is not certain is whether the decision to hold a Congress came initially from Stalin.

As a portent of the future, Stalin attended few of the sessions of the Congress, and unusually, he did not deliver the Report of the Central Committee himself. But he did make one last speech towards the end of the Congress, in which he proposed changes to the Presidium, which had replaced the Politburo, and offered his own resignation as General Secretary of the Party. This was less of a bombshell than it appeared at first sight, since most delegates regarded this simply as a ploy to bring Stalin's would-be successors out into the open. Not surprisingly, Stalin's resignation was not accepted, and Stalin went on to make considerable changes in the personnel of the Presidium and to openly criticise prominent colleagues like Mikoyan and Molotov. Nobody could feel safe. Stalin's speech lasted for one and a half hours, proof that his stamina had not entirely deserted him.

In fact Stalin's methods of government did not change much during the last years. His method was still essentially that of 'divide and rule'. Although the Party's influence in the Army was restored at the end of the war, it was a largely passive instrument as far as Stalin was concerned. The Party, the government, the police and the Army were all balanced against each other. Khrushchev was brought into the Politburo in 1949 as a counterweight to Malenkov and Beria. The latter was greatly distrusted by Stalin. The long-serving Foreign Minister Molotov was replaced by his deputy Vishinsky in 1949. Bulganin and Mikoyan were shifted to different departments. Zhdanov was thought by many experts to be Stalin's likely heir, but he was already falling from grace before his sudden death in August 1948. Zhdanov had been Secretary to the Central Committee and a hard-liner. Stalin was convinced that Zhdanov had been murdered, although he had been in bad health, and the repercussions were to be felt before Stalin's own death several years later. Malenkov and Beria gained from the demotion of experienced colleagues like Molotov, Mikoyan and Bulganin after Zhdanov's death, but nobody could feel secure. All the changes were decided by Stalin personally, or else he was persuaded to make them. The insecurity was best illustrated by the case of Voznesenskii. Voznesenskii had become Head of the State Planning Agency in 1938, played a crucial role in the direction of the wartime economy, joined the Politburo in 1947, and had been publicly praised by Stalin. Yet in 1948 he was suddenly arrested after accusations of having 'lost' important documents. Although acquitted, he immediately fell from Stalin's favour, was rearrested in 1949, tortured into confessing to treason, and shot in the following year.

Stalin had his own sisters-in-law arrested in 1949. He was almost certainly contemplating further bloodletting right up to the time of his own death. But meanwhile, there were other preoccupations at home, notably the economy.

POST-WAR RECONSTRUCTION
—

The task for Stalin of restoring the economic and social damage of the Second World War was a formidable one. The western areas of the Russian Republic, the Ukraine and Belorussia had all suffered enormous devastation. There was a shortage of machinery and labour, even after demobilisation. This was particularly true in the villages, since skilled workers tended to return to industry rather than to rural areas.

War factories were converted to civilian production and the Fourth Five-Year Plan was drafted, to operate from 1946 to 1950. The ambitious objective was to exceed pre-war levels of output by 1950. Almost 90 per cent of industrial investment went into heavy industry. 1946 was a poor year in terms of output: the dislocation caused by conversion to a peacetime economy, combined with a drought, led to actual falls in production levels. Stalin reimposed draconian controls, for example over collective farms, which had experienced some relaxation during the war. The obligation to supply food to the State as the first priority was reinforced, and procurement quotas could be arbitrarily varied from region to region as the government saw fit. This was depressing for villagers who had hoped for a further relaxation or even abolition of controls in the aftermath of victory. Instead additional burdens were imposed, such as higher taxes in 1948, and the duty to plant forests and build canals in steppe areas at the farmer's own expense.

Although Stalin himself was unsympathetic to the plight of the peasantry, his regime did attempt to increase agricultural efficiency. Brigades of agricultural workers were set up, to be paid by results; and smaller collective farms were merged into larger units – which also made them easier to control. The basic agricultural problems were not solved. Stalin's last years were certainly not beneficial to the peasantry. He remained distrustful of the peasants, and just before his death he was contemplating measures to transform more and more collective farms into state farms.

Industry fared better. After the difficulties of 1946, industrial recovery was rapid. In certain areas of the economy, pre-war production figures were equalled by 1950, a remarkable achievement. It was officially claimed that industrial production by 1950 was 73 per cent above the 1940 figure. Much of the recovery was due to the same combination of hard work, Stalinist propaganda and coercion as had prevailed before the war. But improvements were also partly the result of administrative reforms. During 1946 and 1947 several new ministries were created, or existing ones were subdivided. Ministries were run by professional administrators, supervised by the Party but less subject to arbitrary political intervention than in the past. The bureaucracy was anxious to protect itself from the arbitrary purges of the pre-war years, and although repression continued, it was possible to detect a gradual curb on the exercise of arbitrary power, at least below the higher echelons of the Party, where political infighting continued. Whereas between 1934 and 1936 up to one third of all managers in heavy industry were removed from their posts within one year, and the average length of tenure of directors of enterprises in the 1930s was three years, by 1950 directors were remaining in the same posts for an average of ten years. There was a dawning recognition that whatever the rationale for coercion in the early stages of industrialisation, it was not necessarily the most effective instrument for promoting efficiency in industry at a higher technological level. There was to be more experimentation with material incentives. How much Stalin approved of these measures is difficult to say. He still gave every appearance of ruling from the Kremlin with an iron fist.

Soviet propaganda in the post-war period depicted a people labouring intensively and with enthusiasm to restore the war-ravaged economy. A later General Secretary wrote:

> On literally all sections of the job, people were working with devotion, talent and initiative. It often happened that they did not go home for several days in a row, until the particular assignment had been completed. They would take cat naps in the shade for a couple of hours, and then go back to the job.
>
> (L. Brezhnev, *Rebirth*, 1978)

LIFE IN STALIN'S USSR

Life for Stalin's people was hard for the workers and peasants, although it was the latter who suffered most. Rationing of foodstuffs ceased in 1947, more consumer goods were produced, and real wages rose, although the figure at the time of Stalin's death was very close to the 1928 figure. Before the war Stalin had claimed that socialism had been achieved in the USSR, and the way was ready for the transition to Communism. But wage differentials were greater at the end of Stalin's life than at the beginning of his economic revolution. Workers in priority industries were relatively well-off, but the lowest-paid workers and peasants found life grim. A currency reform of 1947 effectively wiped out the value of savings. The shortage and low quality of housing was an even greater problem. During the war over 50 per cent of urban living space in the occupied territories had been damaged or destroyed; and elsewhere accommodation had deteriorated. By 1950 there were six million more urban dwellers than in 1940, but housing construction and repair did not keep pace.

The labour force increased by twelve million between 1945 and 1950. The increase came from demobilised veterans, peasants moving to towns from collective farms, pensioners who could not live on their pensions, and more women coming on to the labour market. There was also considerable reliance until Stalin's death on convict and prisoner-of-war labour.

The post-war Soviet Union was no workers' paradise. But Soviet citizens knew the sacrifices that had been necessary for survival and eventual victory in the war, and the Stalinist propaganda machine found it relatively easy to translate the slogans of sacrifice for war into those of sacrifice for peace. Stalin was still the leader at the helm, whose judgement must be infallible. Stalin himself had no doubts. In February 1946 Stalin made one of his rare speeches to claim that victory in the war had vindicated his policies of collectivisation, industrialisation and purging. After the usual claims of far-sightedness and the obligatory references to Lenin for authority for his policies, Stalin proceeded to summarise the experience of the Terror:

> It cannot be said that the Party's policy encountered no resistance.
> Not only backward people, such as decry everything new, but many

prominent members of the Party as well, systematically dragged the Party backward and tried by hook or by crook to divert it to the 'usual' capitalist path of development. All the anti-Party machinations of the Trotskyites and the Rightists, all their 'activities' in sabotaging the measures of our Government, pursued the single aim of frustrating the Party's policy and obstructing the work of industrialisation and collectivisation. But the Party did not yield either to the threats from one side or the wails from the other and advanced confidently regardless of everything.

The message was clear: the Party, and by implication Stalin, was always right, and any opposition would not be tolerated.

But Stalin's apparent paranoia now stretched in new directions. Anti-Semitism reared its head in 1948. It was not a new phenomenon, and indeed had been common in Tsarist days, but it had not been systematic in the USSR until now. The new mood had been fostered by Zhdanov, as part of his campaign against 'cosmopolitanism', that is, foreign influences in Soviet culture. Both Stalin and Zhdanov championed a Soviet nationalism which denigrated any outside influences on Soviet culture, and Jewish influences were particularly unwelcome at a time in the Cold War when the United States was sympathetic to Zionism and the new state of Israel was calling for support from Jews throughout the world. Jews were subject to a range of restrictions, and it was easy for someone with Stalin's suspicious mind to conclude that all Jews were latent Zionists, and all Zionists must be hostile to the USSR, and a potential fifth column if they lived within its borders. Stalin's prejudices were only confirmed by his son's marriage to a Jewess and Svetlana's involvement with a Jew. Molotov's Jewish wife was imprisoned until after Stalin's death, and many other Jews suffered discrimination or imprisonment.

THE FINAL TERROR

Following the changes in top personnel after the 1952 Congress, the increasingly ailing Stalin embarked upon yet another round of purges. They began in his own household. Stalin's long-serving bodyguard was suddenly sacked and disappeared. His personal secretary was also dismissed and arrested. Then an informer to the secret police denounced

Stalin's personal doctor, Vinogradov, who was arrested along with other specialists at the Kremlin clinic reserved for use by the Soviet élite. Seven of the nine arrested were Jewish. Charges levelled against them included murdering Zhdanov in 1948, being members of a Zionist organisation, and plotting to poison Stalin and other eminent figures. Two hundred people had been arrested after Zhdanov's death; now a further eight thousand were arrested in the two months following the arrest of the nine doctors in January 1953. Stalin took personal charge of the 'Doctors' case'. Khrushchev was convinced that a new round of bloodletting was about to begin, reminiscent of the 1930s, and that it would include the feared and mistrusted Beria and the Party élite who had been shuffled and demoted at the recent Congress. The usual apparatus was put in motion, including a propaganda campaign and organised attacks upon Jews in particular.

We cannot know the extent to which Stalin genuinely believed in the existence of these 'plots', and the extent to which they were part of his strategy of destroying anybody or anything which might threaten his position as he perceived it. But this final outburst of vindictiveness, only weeks before his fatal stroke, confirmed the impression of Stalin's ruthlessness noted years before by Lenin, and commented on by many others before and since.

timeline	1946 February	Fourth Five-Year Plan announced
	1947 June	Marshall Aid offered to Europe
	1953 January	Kremlin 'Doctors' Plot'
	March	Death of Stalin

Points to consider

1) **What were the similiarities and differences between Stalin's rule in the pre-war and post-war Soviet Union?**
2) **How successfully had the USSR recovered from the effects of war by the time of Stalin's death in 1953?**

INTERNATIONAL STATESMAN AND COLD WAR WARRIOR

STALIN AND HIS ALLIES
—

Following the Nazi attack upon the USSR in June 1941, Stalin became closely involved in international diplomacy as well as military affairs. As early as 18 July 1941 he was urging Churchill to consider opening a Second Front in France in order to relieve pressure on the hard-pressed Soviet armies. Stalin continued to badger the British and Americans on these lines right up to the Allied landings of June 1944. Interim landings in North Africa and Italy did not satisfy Stalin; rather they confirmed him in his suspicions that the Western Allies were content to allow the Soviets to do the bulk of the land fighting against Hitler. Stalin's suspicion was certainly not allayed by a personal visit to the Soviet leader by Churchill in August 1942. If the Prime Minister's intention was to convince Stalin of the rightness of the Allies' strategy, he failed signally, although at this meeting the two wartime leaders conceived a mutual respect for each other. Stalin declared that:

> He and Churchill had got to know and understand each other and if there were differences of opinion between them, that was in the nature of things . . . The fact that he and Churchill had met and got to know each other and had prepared the ground for future agreements had great significance.

The Second Front was one of Stalin's priorities. Another was to persuade his new Allies to acquiesce in Soviet territorial gains made under the Nazi-Soviet Pact. Stalin attempted this as early as the winter of 1941, but British reluctance to concede Stalin's ambitions led to Stalin putting them on ice. This merely delayed an intractable problem, which emerged again in the later stages of the war.

Stalin dissolved the Comintern in May 1943. This was more than simply a gesture designed to persuade public opinion in the West that the Soviet priority was to defeat the Nazis in alliance with the capitalist democracies, rather than undermine the latter by means of promoting Communist subversion. Stalin appears to have been genuinely in favour of Communists joining forces with parties of the Left in other countries, and dissolving the Comintern certainly made such alliances more palatable to the non-Communist Left.

Yet there were limits to Stalin's appeasement of Western opinion. When in April 1943 the Germans uncovered evidence of the Katyn Forest massacre, and the Polish government in Exile sought to investigate the circumstances of the deaths of fifteen thousand Polish officers, Stalin broke off relations with the Poles in London, accusing them of antipathy towards the USSR. The Soviets had massacred the Polish officers after their deportation to the USSR in 1939, but Stalin was hardly likely to admit it. He was already sponsoring his own Polish government in Exile, on his territory. The germs of the post-war disputes over Poland and Eastern Europe were already taking root.

Teheran

Stalin's appearance on to the world stage was marked by the first Conference of the Big Three Wartime leaders – Stalin, Roosevelt and Churchill – at Teheran, 28 November to 1 December 1943.

At the Teheran Conference Stalin did not get all he had wanted, since the Second Front was fixed only for 1944, but in many ways the conference was a great success for him. Stalin was recognised as the equal of the other two statesmen, he enjoyed the moral superiority of being the leader of the country which was doing the bulk of the ground fighting against Hitler, and Roosevelt demonstrated a keenness to be on as good terms with him as he already was with Churchill. It was important for Stalin not to have the British and Americans in a diplomatic alliance against himself, and this he avoided. Stalin's success was not just due to the desire of both Roosevelt and Churchill to curry favour with him, but also to his own adroitness as a negotiator. Stalin avoided a firm line being taken on Poland, and the Western Allies did not object to the idea of Stalin keeping the part of Poland which he had overrun in 1939.

Stalin displayed the same skills in international negotiations that he had shown during the political and economic debates inside his own country in the 1920s. That is, he listened more than he spoke, he weighed up the other personalities and the arguments carefully, he played on others' weaknesses when he had deduced them, and then he intervened with an effective mixture of firmness and reasonableness. For someone with a supposedly narrow perception of life outside his country's borders, Stalin was quick to appreciate the changing realities of the world situation. He paid special attention to Roosevelt, basically agreeing with him that the days of the British Empire were numbered. Stalin certainly appreciated this fact before Churchill did.

Stalin displayed at Teheran other qualities for which he was already well known. During discussions on the future of a post-war Germany, Stalin proposed the execution of fifty thousand German officers as part of the process of destroying Germany's military capacity. He responded to Churchill's shock and anger by assuring him that he had not been serious. However, it would not have been out of character for Stalin to have made such a proposal in all sincerity.

Poland

Stalin built upon his success at Teheran, demonstrating a combination of diplomatic skill and ruthlessness. The latter was particularly evident in his dealings with the Poles. The Soviets, advancing westwards, established their own Communist Polish Committee of National Liberation in Lublin. When the non-Communist Polish government in London, desperate to assert its own authority, ordered the Poles in Warsaw to rise against their German occupiers, the Red Army stood cynically by whilst the Germans crushed the rising and destroyed the city. Stalin preferred to see the non-Communist elements in Poland liquidated before his own troops took over, and the Germans obligingly did the job for him. Stalin knew that the West was too dependent on the Red Army to do more than protest. This episode is often quoted as an example of Stalin's inhumanity, but Stalin was not responsible for initiating the rising, which actually took him by surprise. Also, the Red Army was temporarily recouping for the next stage of its advance, and could not easily have made more than a gesture to save the Warsaw Poles even had Stalin wanted it to.

STALIN'S AMBITIONS

Some Western commentators later accused Stalin of deliberately attempting to create a Soviet-controlled satellite empire in Eastern Europe even before the war was over. However, this is Cold War politics projected backwards. The liberation of Eastern European countries from German occupation – and after all, it had been Hitler who had initiated war, not Stalin – was a complicated matter. It was far more than a simple military operation. There were different political groupings competing for power; there were also enormous economic and social problems confronting the victors. Stalin did not in fact insist upon Soviet-controlled Communist parties seizing power in Eastern Europe. He was aware of the disadvantages involved in alienating opinion in the West. Stalin was however determined to create a buffer against future German expansion. Such a buffer would include his territorial gains of 1939–40, but there is no evidence that at this time he thought specifically in terms of a Soviet Eastern Europe. As a practical measure, local Communists in Bulgaria, Romania and other liberated territories were encouraged to work with other left-wing and peoples' parties. In the north, Stalin granted very moderate terms to the Finns, despite their alliance with Hitler in 1941. He also stuck to his agreement with Churchill that Greece should be in the British sphere of influence, and would give no help to Greek Communists. The Yugoslavs, determined to retain their independence after driving the Germans out of their country, succeeded in doing so, despite the assistance they received in the process from the Red Army.

YALTA

The next meeting of the Big Three was at Yalta, 4–11 February, 1945. It was testimony to Soviet prestige that the Western leaders agreed to Stalin's insistence on a meeting on Soviet soil, despite Roosevelt's poor health. Stalin, at a preliminary meeting with Churchill, agreed to the Prime Minister's proposals for a division of the Balkans into Soviet and British spheres of influence. Stalin's aims had not changed since Teheran, and so he remained firm in his stance on Poland. Areas of Poland which had been under Soviet rule were to be retained by the USSR; and a sphere of influence created in Eastern Europe, principally the areas occupied at that time by the Red Army. These areas were to sustain governments friendly to Soviet interests. Stalin can scarcely be criticised for these objectives, given the Russian experience of invasion from the west over the previous forty years. Yet hostile commentators were to see this as evidence of a Communist plot for eventual world domination. They were less able than Stalin to discern the difference between the demands of ideology and perceived national interest.

THE ROCK

Allied solidarity at the conclusion of the Yalta Conference? Daily Herald, *13 February 1945.*

Stalin was in a strong position at Yalta. The ailing Roosevelt was anxious to secure a Soviet commitment to the war against Japan and to involvement in post-war international organisations. Nevertheless, Stalin played his own role skilfully again. He took the initiative over arrangements for the post-war Germany, although Churchill's opposition to his proposals for the dismemberment of Germany and tough reparations prevented Stalin from having his way completely.

Stalin once again showed himself to be at ease in the company of two other world leaders, and those at the conference were impressed by his memory for facts and his negotiating skill. Stalin's bearing at Yalta confirmed what had already been achieved by the Red Army in the field, namely the arrival of the USSR as a Great Power on the world stage.

Although relations between the wartime Allies were at their highest point, Stalin still acted circumspectly. It is true that he felt slighted at the abrupt way in which the USA suspended Lend-Lease deliveries to his country on 8 May 1945, and was offended by the American refusal to grant credit for reconstruction within the USSR, a refusal which partly

An American View: 'Officer Stalin's idea of policing the world.' Chicago Sunday Tribune *18 February 1945.*

accounts for the Soviet decision to strip materials from their zone of occupation in Germany and to transport them to the USSR. Nevertheless, as the war in Europe came to an end and governments were created in the liberated territories of Eastern Europe, Stalin ensured that other left-wing parties were represented alongside native Communists. However, in Poland, Stalin continued to stand firm: the USSR's security was the rationale of his policy there.

POTSDAM

The next great summit meeting at Potsdam, between 16 July and 2 August 1945, saw Stalin still in a very strong position. The other two participants, Truman and Attlee, had only recently assumed office. Stalin himself was not in good health, but Churchill's doctor wrote that

> Stalin's tenacity and obstinacy have no counterpart on our side. He knows exactly what he wants and he does not mind how he gets it. He is very patient too and never loses his temper.

Stalin achieved most of his objectives at the conference. The West was forced to accept his proposals on Poland's western frontier, mainly because the changes had already been made by the Soviets. He was less successful in his proposals on German reparations. The use of the atomic bomb by the Americans was a setback for the USSR, but nevertheless Stalin could feel satisfied that the military prowess of his forces had been translated into longer-term political advantages, a translation secured mostly by his own diplomatic efforts.

THE ROOTS OF THE COLD WAR

The wartime alliance soon disintegrated, now that the common enemy was no more. However, interpretations of the Cold War as having its origins in Communist expansionism are simplistic in assuming that poor relations between East and West were implicit from the very beginning of the alliance. As early as 1946 some Western commentators were tracing the roots of the Cold War back to the Marxist-Leninist doctrine of class-warfare and world revolution. It was assumed that Stalin was determined to undermine capitalism, whatever temporary concessions might be made to 'co-existence' for tactical reasons. According to this interpretation, the Americans were simply naive in their early hopes of the USSR being a genuine partner in a new world order. Eventually the mistake was learned, and it was the formation of NATO and measures to promote economic co-operation and post-war recovery in Western Europe which prevented Soviet expansionism.

This interpretation is simplistic, and ignores the fact that relations between the Powers deteriorated gradually, due to mistrust on both sides. Equally simplistic were some later interpretations, fostered by Soviet and revisionist historians, that Stalin's actions can be explained entirely as a defensive reaction to American economic imperialism, translated into political influence, particularly in Europe.

Relations between the USSR and the West did not seriously deteriorate until 1947. Up to that point Stalin had secured international recognition of the new governments in Eastern Europe. He was satisfied that victory in the war had vindicated his system. In a speech on 9 February 1946, he had declared:

> The war was something like an examination for our Soviet system, for our State, for our Government, for our Communist Party, and it summed up the results of their work, saying to us as it were: 'Here they are, your people and organisations, their deeds and their lives. Look at them well and reward them according to their deeds.'

Stalin did take exception to Churchill's 'Iron Curtain' speech with its accusation of the 'boundless expansionist tendencies of the Soviet Union'. In March 1946 he replied to Churchill in *Pravda*, reminding his former ally of the devastation that the War had inflicted upon the USSR and the reasons for the growth in Communist influence:

> The influence of the Communists grew because during the hard years of the mastery of fascism in Europe, Communists showed themselves to be reliable, daring and self-sacrificing fighters against fascist regimes for the liberty of peoples ... Of course, Mr. Churchill does not like such a development of events. And he raised the alarm, appealing to force. But he also did not like the appearance of the Soviet regime in Russia after the First World War.'

Churchill had attempted to overturn the Revolution by intervention and had failed:

I do not know whether Mr. Churchill and his friends will succeed in organising after the Second World War a new military expedition against eastern Europe. But if they succeed in this, which is not very probable, since millions of common people stand on guard over the peace, then one man confidently says that they will be beaten, just as they were beaten twenty six years ago.

This was the declaration of a leader confident in the strength of his position in Europe, suspicious of the West and on his guard, but not committed to conflict at all costs. There were other priorities. Stalin was heavily involved in domestic issues and economic recovery from the war. In fact after Potsdam, Stalin took little part in the conferences which were to show up increasing differences between East and West, for example the meeting of the Council of Foreign Ministers during March and April 1947, in the course of which the Truman Doctrine was announced. Even at this stage, Stalin was cautious and even moderate. He told the American Secretary of State, Marshall, in April 1947 that;

Differences had occured in the past on other questions, and as a rule, after people had exhausted themselves in dispute, they then recognised the necessity of compromise. These were only the first skirmishes and brushes of reconnaissance forces . . . he (Stalin) thought that compromises were possible on all the main questions, including demilitarisation, the political structure of Germany, reparations and economic unity. It was necessary to have patience and not become pessimistic.

Despite this apparent reasonableness, Stalin was clearly resolved to maintain Eastern Europe as a sphere of Soviet influence, and he tried to obstruct American plans to provide economic aid to Europe. There was some justification for Western fears of Soviet interference in its political affairs, since Stalin did issue instructions on political tactics to the powerful French and Italian Communist Parties, although he seems to have been aiming at Communist participation in the governments of those states, not armed revolution. In fact Stalin's tactics in France and Italy were unsuccessful. However, he did achieve his prime objective of hardening Soviet control of Eastern Europe, partly through the establishment of the Communist Information Bureau, or Cominform, in September 1947.

THE COLD WAR IN EARNEST

The battle lines for the Cold War were really drawn up in 1948 and the first half of 1949. A test of will developed between Stalin and his former allies. The Cominform was used by Stalin to mount a propaganda campaign against the Marshall Plan, since the prospect of massive American aid to Europe might threaten Soviet influence. The Czech coup of 1948, which brought the Czech Communists to power, may not have been planned by Stalin, but he benefited from the results and presumably approved of them. The coup was certainly viewed in the West as an example of Soviet expansionism.

To date Stalin had displayed a sure touch in his post-war diplomatic dealings, but his reactions were to grow more clumsy. His attempts to bring down Tito in Yugoslavia were misguided. Tito had taken his own path towards socialism. Stalin thought that the Yugoslav regime, proclaimed in November 1945, would collapse. But it did not, and it was helped by American aid. Stalin had Yugoslavia expelled from the Cominform in 1948, but the affair showed that Stalin was not master of the entire Communist world.

GERMANY

Stalin also underestimated the West's resolve in the Berlin Crisis. Stalin, like most Soviet citizens, was alarmed at the prospect of any revival in German power. In a speech to the Moscow Party in November 1944 he had declared:

> After her defeat Germany will, of course, be disarmed economically, as well as militarily and politically. It would be naive to think, however, that she will make no attempt to recuperate her strength and embark on new aggression. It is common knowledge that the German rulers are already making preparations for another war. History shows that quite a short period, a matter of twenty or thirty years, is sufficient to enable Germany to recover from defeat and recuperate her strength.

In many respects, fear of a resurgent and powerful Germany was still the dominant force in Soviet thinking on foreign affairs after the war. Stalin would probably have preferred Germany to be united but under

Soviet control rather than split into East and West. Short of that, a strong degree of Soviet influence in a divided and occupied Germany was the next best scenario. Thus far this goal had proved elusive. In fact a revival of German power did appear to be a possibility as the British and Americans co-operated in helping their zones of occupation to recover economically.

The USSR was in a good position to apply pressure on the Allies in Berlin. The city was well inside the Soviet zone. Stalin applied the Blockade in March 1948, with the intention of forcing the West to withdraw from its zones inside Berlin or to agree to Soviet ideas on the future of Germany. Stalin wanted war no more than the West. The Soviets denounced the formation of NATO, but the success of the Berlin Airlift persuaded Stalin to call off the Blockade. The Soviets went ahead with the creation of a separate East German State. It was proclaimed in October 1949. Thereafter Soviet tactics were confined to proposing a unified but neutralised and disarmed Germany.

Stalin had not got his way in the dispute over Germany. Yet he did have the great advantage over contemporary leaders in the West in that diplomatic or tactical setbacks had no significant effect upon his domestic position. Stalin's propaganda machine saw to that.

THE COLD WAR WORLDWIDE

Stalin had concerns elsewhere in the world. As usual, he was cautious in the policies he pursued. For example, Stalin interfered in the politics of Iran, and the Soviets would certainly have welcomed a say in the control of the Straits which linked the Black Sea and the Mediterranean, and the acquisition of a naval base in the Mediterranean. After all, these areas were close to the USSR and were important to its security. But there is no evidence that Stalin was preparing to invade Iran, Greece or Turkey. The Soviets flexed their muscles occasionally, as Great Powers are wont to do, but Stalin behaved little differently from pre-Revolutionary Tsarist governments in these areas.

The USSR certainly had a direct interest in the Middle East, which bordered upon its own Muslim regions. The Soviets supported Syria, the Lebanon and Egypt in those countries' attempts to force the British and French out of the region. The USSR was the first state to recognise the existence of Israel in May 1948, since it marked the departure of the

British from Palestine. Unfortunately for Stalin, in taking this step he offended the Arab world, whilst fears of Soviet influence in the Middle East prompted the USA, Britain, France and several smaller powers into closer co-operation and eventually led to the Baghdad Pact and CENTO (Central Treaty Organisation).

Stalin's touch certainly deserted him over China. He had long assumed that the Chinese Nationalists held the key to China's future, and had therefore given little help to Mao and the Chinese Communists. The Soviets were surprised at the speed of Mao's success and the formation of the People's Republic of China in 1949. Fortunately for Stalin, Mao was conciliatory, because he wanted aid from Stalin and an alliance with the USSR.

KOREA

Korea was a greater problem for Stalin. He had trained and armed the North Korean army which invaded South Korea in June 1950. The Soviets had pulled out of North Korea in 1949, leaving a Communist government behind. Stalin ordered caution on Kim Il-Sung, the North's leader, but then gave his approval for the attack, apparently on the assumption that there would be a simultaneous Communist uprising in the South, and that the USA would not react. In fact the speed of reaction to the attack surprised Stalin. He had miscalculated by boycotting the United Nations in protest at the American refusal to allow Mao to occupy the Chinese seat on the Security Council. Presumably Stalin did not anticipate a resort to the Security Council, because he was not in a position to veto the United Nation's decision to send aid to South Korea. However, when the tide of war turned in the UN's favour, it was Chinese and not Soviet troops which intervened. Stalin kept his distance: as with Berlin, he was not prepared to risk open war with the Americans. Ultimately, he probably gained from American involvement in a long, energy-sapping conflict.

STALIN AND SOVIET SECURITY

If the USSR wished to control areas outside its borders, it had to physically occupy those areas. Unlike the USA, the Soviets did not have the economic power to assert influence more indirectly, through 'economic imperialism'. Therefore there were severe limits to Stalin's freedom of action. After the Second World War he would have been content to reach an agreement with the Americans. However, the Americans would not recognise the depth of Stalin's concern for Soviet security, and so they refused to see Stalin's attempts to bolster Soviet security along his borders in anything but the most sinister light. Thus in one sense, Stalin, as the representative of the weaker of the two super powers, was forced into following the course he did.

Stalin did make miscalculations in foreign policy, and bears some, though not all, responsibility for the Cold War, with its state of armed confrontation between East and West. By turning the USSR into a superpower, and helping to initiate an expensive arms race with the USA, Stalin contributed to the Soviets' growing economic problems. Given the course of the Second World War, he may have had little alternative. Having borne the brunt of the land war against Germany, and in the process of defeating Hitler having occupied most of Eastern Europe, it was difficult to conceive of the USSR suddenly retreating back into a shell. Stalin had acquired superpower status for his country, with its attendant problems and responsibilities, whether he liked it or not. There is no evidence to suppose that Stalin regretted his new high international profile, and the Soviet people were proud of their achievements in war. However, this is not the same as saying that they or their leader were aiming for an expansionist world role from the pre-war days.

`timeline`	1945	July–August	Potsdam Conference
		August	Oder-Neisse Line agreed as frontier of Poland
			USSR declared war against Japan
	1947	March	Truman Doctrine announced
		October	Cominform established
	1948	June	Berlin Blockade begun
	1949	May	Berlin Blockade lifted
		September	First Soviet atomic bomb tested
	1950	June	Outbreak of Korean War
	1951		Fifth Five-Year Plan
	1956	January	Khrushchev denounced Stalin in speech at Twentieth Party Congress

Points to consider

1) To what extent did Stalin achieve his aims at the wartime conferences of the Big Three?
2) What were Stalin's ambitions for Poland and the other countries of Eastern and Western Europe?
3) Explain Stalin's policy towards Germany in the post-war years.
4) What responsibility does Stalin have for initiating the Cold War?
5) How extensive was Soviet influence in the world between the years 1945 and 1953?
6) 'Security was the driving force behind Stalin's foreign policy'. Do you agree?

THE KING IS DEAD:
LONG LIVE THE KING!
STALIN AND STALINISM

STALIN'S DEATH

One of the few detailed descriptions of the ageing Stalin was given by Milovan Djilas, a member of the Yugoslavian Mission sent to have talks with the Soviet leader in Moscow in March 1944. In his book *Conversations with Stalin*, Djilas described the old dictator vividly. Of all the participants at the meeting, he declared, Stalin

> was the plainest of all, in a Marshal's uniform and soft boots, without any medals except a golden star – the Order of Hero of the Soviet Union . . . This was not that majestic Stalin of the photographs or newsreels – with the stiff, deliberate gait and posture. He was not quiet for a moment. He toyed with his pipe, which bore the white dot of the English firm Dunhill, or drew circles with a blue pencil around words indicating the main subjects for discussion which he then crossed out, and he kept turning his head this way and that while he fidgeted in his seat.
>
> I was also surprised at something else: he was of very small stature and ungainly build. His torso was short and narrow, while his legs and arms were too long. His left arm and shoulder seemed rather stiff. He had quite a large paunch and his hair was sparse. His face was white, with ruddy cheeks, the coloration characteristic of those who sit long in offices, known as the 'Kremlin complexion'. His teeth were black and irregular, turned inwards.

Not even his moustache was thick or firm. Still the head was not a bad one; it had something of the common people about it – with those yellow eyes and a mixture of sternness and mischief.

I was also surprised at his accent. One could tell that he was not a Russian. But his Russian vocabulary was rich and his manner of expression vivid and flexible, full of Russian proverbs and sayings. As I realized later, Stalin was well acquainted with Russian literature – though only Russian.

One thing did not surprise me: Stalin had a sense of humour – a rough humour, self-assured, but not entirely without subtlety and depth. His reactions were quick and acute – and conclusive, which did not mean that he did not hear the speaker out, but it was evident that he was no friend of long explanations.

(Milovan Djilas, *Conversations With Stalin*, 1962)

Nine years later Stalin was dead. Some time on 1 March or 2 March 1953 he had a stroke. The exact time is imprecise because he had been alone and his entourage was afraid to disturb him. He was found

Stalin lying in state.

eventually, and took three and a half days to die. His last moments were recorded by his daughter Svetlana:

> The death agony was terrible. God grants an easy death only to the just. He literally choked to death as we watched. At what seemed like the very last moment he suddenly opened his eyes and cast a glance over everyone in the room. It was a terrible glance, insane or perhaps angry and full of fear of death . . . Then something incomprehensible and terrible happened that to this day I can't forget . . . He suddenly lifted his left hand as though he were pointing to something up above and bringing down a curse on us all. The gesture was incomprehensible and full of menace . . . The next moment, after a final effort, the spirit wrenched itself free of the flesh.
>
> (Svetlana Alliluyeva, *Twenty Letters To A Friend*, 1967)

It was difficult for people to comprehend Stalin's death, particularly within the USSR. Millions wept, including some of his victims in the labour camps. He had seemed a fixture, towering over a system apparently as inflexible as himself. In fact his system lived on, and it became popularly known as 'Stalinism', a word Stalin himself had not allowed to be used in his lifetime.

STALIN AND STALINISM

Stalin the person is difficult to divorce from his 'system', yet through the 'system' his influence lasted long after his death, both within and outside the USSR. The reasons for this raise awkward questions. They raise issues such as to what extent Stalinism was synonymous with Communism; and to what extent the persistence of Stalin's system arose from its inherent strength, its totalitarianism, or its apparent success. The Communist movement as a whole gained prestige from the Soviet success in the Second World War. The Stalinist economic system was taken as a model by several emerging Third World countries seeking to expand their economies rapidly from a primitive base. Politically, Communism, or the Stalinist version of it, appealed to many Third World politicians seeking to eradicate the vestiges of colonialism.

The hegemony of the Communist world was destroyed by the Sino-Soviet split in the 1950s and Mao's refusal to recognise Stalin's successors as leaders of the world Communist movement. For some leaders of underdeveloped countries, Maoism became a more attractive beacon than Stalinism. Cracks in the image also occurred with Khrushchev's revelations in 1956 about Stalin and his activities, and attempts in the Eastern European satellite states to break free of Soviet or Stalinist influence. A realisation that the Soviet economy was running into serious difficulties, and a growing awareness of the evils that had been an integral part of Stalin's USSR, further damaged the reputation of Communism. Yet it was difficult to shake off the past, even as Communist regimes in Eastern Europe collapsed in the late 1980s; and even within the USSR, the reforming Gorbachev ran into many problems in his attempts to exorcise Stalin's ghost.

There were some very prosaic reasons for the survival of Stalinism in the USSR for such a long time after Stalin's death. Stalin's successors in the leadership and the bureaucracy were all Stalinists, in the sense that they had all earned their spurs in his lifetime, and presumably believed in many of his policies. Khrushchev, who denounced Stalin in 1956, owed his rise to Stalin. In his famous speech of 1956 he was careful to blame Stalin himself and not the Party for Stalinist excesses. To have blamed the Party would by implication have been blaming himself and his colleagues. The successors to Khrushchev, Kosygin and Brezhnev, had also risen to prominence under Stalin, although Kosygin narrowly escaped arrest and death in Stalin's post-war Purges. It was not until Gorbachev in 1985 that a leader emerged who had not served his political apprenticeship under Stalin and was prepared to really challenge the Stalinist system. Khrushchev was a reformer, but he only tinkered with the system. Too many older Russians could not believe that the system which had overcome Hitler was other than fundamentally right. Too many people in positions of influence enjoyed privileges under the existing system to want to destroy it. The shadow of Stalin was therefore difficult to erase.

The word 'Stalinist' and the phrase 'Stalinist system' have been widely used, both in this book and elsewhere, so we should be precise in defining and using the terms. Stalinism has political, economic, social and cultural aspects, which developed at different times and at different paces. It did not suddenly appear from nowhere, but emerged from events. To what extent Stalinism was actually implicit in the processes of the Russian Revolution itself is an issue which has been debated at length.

Graeme Gill, in a short book called *Stalinism* published in 1990, attempted to define the principal components of the Stalinist system. He identified them as comprising a highly centralised economic system, which gives priority to heavy industry; a social structure which initially allows for considerable social mobility, but then hardens into a hierarchy of privilege; a cultural policy which makes cultural and intellectual life subordinate to and reflective of political aims; an emphasis on personal dictatorship reinforced by coercion; the total politicisation of life and, paradoxically, a weakening of central State control; and a prevailing orthodoxy, very conservative in nature, which replaces the initial revolutionary ethos.

Gill sees Stalinism as a phenomenon which emerged in the late 1920s and early 1930s; he maintains that a survey of the USSR in 1927 would have shown little evidence of what was to come later. Other historians have been far less sure of this. Both the argument and the evidence need examination. The question of Stalin's personal responsibility for the origins and development of the Stalinist system will be examined in the next chapter. Let us first look at the highly centralised economic system, or command economy.

THE STALINIST ECONOMY

The centralised, planned economy, with its twin bastions of the Five-Year Plans and collectivisation, was certainly an innovation. There was no inherent logic in the transition from the semi-private economy of the New Economic Policy to the highly centralised command economy of the 1930s. The transition did not occur gradually: it was a revolution from above, forced upon a relatively backward economy. While Marxists assumed that industrialisation was a pre-requisite for socialism, no real-life model for such a planned economy existed. It is a moot point as to how far Stalin was personally involved in the formulation and imple-mentation of the Five-Year Plans. Arguments about economic policy were bound up with political struggles. Initially Stalin had been a moderate, but after his defeat of the Left, he adopted the policy of all-out industrialisation and collectivisation. This won the support of many Party activists and therefore was far more than Stalin's personal policy. To many he probably seemed the leader who was essential in order to force through necessary measures. After 1934 Stalin took more arbitrary measures, on his own initiative sometimes, and in that sense was less of the mouthpiece of the Party than his own man, although there is no doubt that his policies were still welcomed by many activists. Stalin appears to have thought of industrialisation in terms of creating power and military defence as much as creating socialism with its economic and social potential for bettering the lot of ordinary people. But Stalin went along enthusiastically with the process of 'creating socialism', albeit relying upon a combination of draconian labour legislation, propaganda and appeal to idealism, in order to produce the necessay results.

The ability of this command economy to cope with the demands of war has already been described. Just as significant in the long term was the fact that this command economy became fossilised and the basis of the Soviet economic system long after Stalin's death. This was as true of the system of state and collective farms as for industry. An industrial system which depended on meeting quantitative targets, with little or no regard to quality, and which depended upon central planning agencies to establish priorities and to allocate resources without regard to consumer demand or changing needs, was adequate to give the infant Soviet economy a push early on. However, it was incapable of meeting the more sophisticated demands of the post-1945 world. In Stalin's day, and therefore for decades afterwards, meeting the quantitative targets was everything. Criticism of the system or suggested innovations were dangerous. Conservatism, or rather stagnation, set in. Tinkering with the system, like Khrushchev's limited decentralisation of economic controls and ministries, could not solve the problems. Growth rates suffered, and the USSR lurched into the years of economic stagnation under Brezhnev. Gorbachev, and after him Yeltsin, found it extremely difficult to change this economic system. Ideas of a market economy were anathema to old Stalinists, and in any case, workers and managers lacked the experience to change their ways easily. Restructuring meant uncertainty and possibly unemployment. People were not used to taking risks under the Stalinist system. An economy which had developed by increasing and intensifying the input of labour could not easily take on board technological advance and gear itself to demand. This may be regarded as Stalin's legacy in the economic field, although it should be remembered that this system had proved relatively effective in boosting heavy industry in the early stages of development, and it gave the USSR a sound economic basis on which to fight a major war.

STALINISM AND SOCIETY

What about the social structure under Stalinism? Within Russia and then the USSR, changes had been under way before the Revolution and during the 1920s. Before 1917 there had been the growth of a relatively small industrial proletariat. In a largely agricultural society, a small class of *kulaks* or better-off peasants was developing. After the Revolution, the economic power and social position of the middle and upper classes was smashed, and this was reflected in their immediate loss of political influence. Under NEP, there had been some recovery of 'bourgeois' wealth and values, albeit in new hands, but one of the most significant changes had been in the social basis of the Party and bureaucratic caste. More and more people from a working-class background, and a smaller percentage of peasants, progressed up the social scale, usually when they became Party members. Then, with Stalin's economic revolution, industrialisation increased the demand for factory labour. It was not just unskilled labour that was required, but also skilled workers, foremen and managers. Social mobility was aided by improvements in educational opportunities. In addition, the Purges created the need for ever more replacements. However, privilege came to feature prominently in the system also. Experts earned considerably more than ordinary workers, even though it was the latter who were feted in the art and propaganda of Stalin's USSR. Party members acquired special privileges. Aspirations rose. Thus, ironically, a new society of hierarchy and privilege was born, although it was based less upon money, as in capitalist states, then on the possession of influence, which, for example, gave exclusive access to certain goods and services. By the time of Stalin's death, privilege, or the lack of it, was increasingly important. The system became self-perpetuating: Party members were more liable to have access to the better schools for their children, who therefore got a better start in life; and they had access to goods and services denied to most of the population. Those with a stake in the existing state of things are often those most resistant to reform. After all, reform means change, and those who are already the 'haves' may lose out. Genuine reformers like Khrushchev and Gorbachev found their efforts at reform blocked mostly by middle-ranking Party careerists who had the most to lose by change. Conservatives like Brezhnev played safe and aimed for consensus. Social conservatism was reflected in the political structure: members of the ruling élite in the post-Stalin USSR were generally old. It was increasingly difficult for thrusting young intellectuals to come quickly to the fore, as they had in Lenin's day. In Stalin's USSR the population was divided into three classes, supposedly equal in status: workers, peasants and intellectuals, the latter group presumably being recruited from the ranks of the other two classes. This rigid classification was the basis of Soviet social classification long after Stalin's death.

Such social and political conservatism is not the exclusive province of Stalinism. It is a feature of many dictatorial or one-party states. It is not inevitable: Mao called for 'permanent revolution' in China as a means of periodically renewing and revitalising society. But such dangerous and unpredictable radicalism was not to the taste of Soviet bureaucrats and leaders learning to enjoy a security of tenure they had not experienced in Stalin's day. Lenin had been greatly concerned by the growth of 'bureaucracy' towards the end of his life, and did not approve of the developments described above, some of which were beginning to happen in his lifetime. Whether he could have prevented them is another matter. Stalin does not appear to have had qualms. Thus the irony: a man whose early career was one of struggle against authority, who resented those born into positions better than his own, came to preside over a society, which, after the shock waves of radical change in the 1930s, settled into a conservatism which permeated his country long after his death, and frustrated most genuine attempts at reform.

STALINISM AND CULTURE

The subordination of culture to political dictates was very much part of Stalinism and owed much to Stalin himself. It had long been Marxist orthodoxy that a society's culture reflected the interests of the ruling economic and political élite. Culture was simply part of the 'super-structure' which overlaid the economic 'base'. Radical Marxists in the USSR hoped for the rapid emergence of a genuine 'proletarian culture' after the Revolution. The Revolution certainly gave a great fillip to experimentation in the arts, although the experimentation had already been in the air, and the radical artists were not all Communists, although they welcomed the opportunity to appeal to a wider audience and therefore gave their approval to the regime. Lenin believed that a new 'proletarian consciousness' would develop naturally, in time. This was too slow for Stalin, and the climate of cultural change became very different towards the end of the 1920s and beyond. The State increasingly dictated what was ideologically correct in all artistic fields.

Stalin was a patron of the cinema, the theatre and the opera. He had been a poet, and he was knowledgeable in the Russian classics. However, respect for writers and artists did not prevent him from having very dogmatic views on what was 'correct'. Stalin did not just let his wishes be known. He frequently interfered more directly, in the writing of history for example. In 1931 he complained strongly about Soviet historians. He accused them in a written article of 'rotten liberalism' and encouraging a falsified version of history which played into the hands of the Trotskyists and other enemies of the regime. Those in positions of influence got the message, and changes were soon in evidence. One change was an increasing emphasis on Stalin's role in Soviet history.

Socialist Realism

Stalin was very hostile to Western influences or 'cosmopolitanism' in the arts. However, perhaps his most notorious example of direct interference was in the area of 'Socialist Realism'. All artists were required to display the regime and its achievements in a positive light. Heroic but basically ordinary individuals should be given prominence. The cause they fought for, the building of socialism, must always be seen to triumph, even if the hero did not survive to witness the triumph. In other words, art should reflect the reality which Stalin wanted. Culture must also be 'accessible'. Stalin condemned Shostakovich's opera 'Lady Macbeth of Minsk' for being unartistic, perverted and unsound in every way. Experimentation in the arts was dangerous and soon became a thing of the past. Artists like Shostakovich were driven into conformity, silence, exile or imprisonment by Stalin and his cultural watchdog Zhdanov, who continued to make the same threatening noises after the war.

The Stalinist notion that the main role of culture was to contribute to the task of building and defending socialism continued long after Stalin's death. Khrushchev shared Stalin's aversion to modern art. Nevertheless, he did permit a moderate relaxation of the intellectual climate in the 1950s, as part of de-Stalinisation, but the relaxation was within very strict limits. Under Brezhnev, there was to be a new clampdown on dissent, which reached into the arts also. It was not until the emergence of *glasnost* or 'openness' in the late 1980s that it finally became possible in the USSR to experiment freely in the cultural field. Even then it was a halting, uneven process, because cultural freedom was a difficult concept to grasp in a society which under Stalinism had never experienced genuine pluralism, in politics or thought.

RELIGION

As to be expected in a Marxist and a man without humanitarian instincts, Stalin had little time for religion. His early experiences in the seminary left him with no liking for priests. Persecution of the Church was part of the attack on the traditional life of the peasants which began with collectivisation. Only those priests of the Orthodox Church who compromised with the State could feel relatively safe from arrest or even death. Being a pragmatist, Stalin reversed his regime's anti-clerical policy during the Second World War, when it was expedient to allow ordinary citizens to seek inspiration from any source, including the Church. Stalin never changed his own contempt for religion. The uneasy relationship of Church and State in the USSR continued long after Stalin's death.

NATIONALISM

Stalin was equally opposed to expressions of national sentiment from minority groups within the USSR. Nationalist groups were regarded as dangerous and reactionary, even where nationalism was an expression of cultural feeling rather than a direct appeal for political autonomy or independence. Although Stalin was not a Russian, he promoted Russian nationalism. Russians dominated the leadership and the higher ranks of the Party. This was to continue until the 1980s, and Stalin's successors, notably Brezhnev, tried to disguise this by promoting the idea of the 'Soviet' citizen rather than highlighting the separateness of particular Republics.

STALINISM AND DICTATORSHIP

The emphasis upon personal dictatorship, reinforced by coercion, is usually regarded as very much an important aspect of Stalinism, and likewise of fascism. Lenin frequently acted dictatorially and was dismissive of colleagues' intellectual arguments. He was also prepared to employ coercion. However, he did at last allow colleagues to put forward their ideas, and accepted that there should be a place for genuine ideological argument *within* the Party. Lenin never employed coercion on the scale of Stalin. There was something unique in Stalin's paranoia and suspiciousness, translated into his political system, whether it arose from his personality, his background, or the circumstances in which he rose to power.

Personality Cults

Stalin's dictatorship was reinforced by a personality cult promoted vigorously by the Soviet media. There is no doubt that Stalin himself promoted the cult, despite his protestations that it did not interest him, and his own cynicism about human nature and the real feelings of people who indulged in praise or flattery. Stalin allowed Lenin's body to be embalmed and to lie in state in Red Square, and Lenin came to be regarded almost as a god or a god-substitute. Lenin had to wait until his death for deification. Stalin came to seem like a living god in his own lifetime. The cult was carried to extraordinary lengths. Stalin was glorified in prose, in art, in music, in film. The composer Prokoviev penned the following ode to Stalin in 1939, to celebrate the leader's 60th birthday:

> Never have our fertile fields such a harvest shown,
> Never have our villages such contentment known.
> Never life has been so fair, spirits been so high.
> Never to the present day grew so green the rye.
> O'er the earth the rising sun sheds a warmer light,
> Since it looked on Stalin's face it has grown more bright.
> I am singing to my baby sleeping in my arms,
> Grow like flowers in the meadow free from all alarm.
> On your lips the name of Stalin will protect from harm.
> You will learn the source of sunshine bathing all our land.
> You will copy Stalin's portrait with your tiny hand.

Stalin was credited with extraordinary genius and intellectual capabilities. It is true that his writings filled several volumes, and were set alongside Lenin's collected works, and Stalin did sometimes join in intellectual or philosophical debates, but the results could be unfortunate. This was the case in 1948 when the scientist Lysenko had his theories on crop and tree growth taken up and promoted by Stalin. Thousands of scientists who disagreed with Lysenko's eccentric theories were dismissed for their 'bourgeois' attitudes, and a massive programme of tree planting was undertaken. It failed, because the theories were faulty, but who could challenge Stalin?

The cult of personality remained part of the Stalinist political system long after Stalin's death. Khrushchev's personality was very different from that of Stalin's. He was an effervescent individual who enjoyed meeting people and travelling at home and abroad. Yet this would-be man of the people courted popularity himself, although never to the heights of Stalin. His colleagues would not have allowed it in any case. Brezhnev, during his long tenure of office, increasingly encouraged a cult of personality on Stalinist lines. During the 1970s Brezhnev's speeches and portrait were displayed everywhere, and his war record was grossly exaggerated. Lenin himself had been a formidable personality, and it is a moot point as to how far a totalitarian society needs a leader to whom a whole variety of attributes and qualities have to be attached. The emphasis upon the individual had no place in the Marxist analysis of society, which emphasised social and economic forces rather than individual determinism; in promoting his personality Stalin had more in common with Mussolini, Hitler, Mao and other twentieth-century dictators.

Coercion

As stated earlier, coercion was an integral part of Stalinism. Coercion was probably inevitable in a society in which a small, largely unrepresentative group seized power, able to do so only because there was a power vacuum and a chaotic situation in which a relatively organised and disciplined group like the Bolsheviks could flourish; and then that group had to hold on to power in a hostile environment, fighting internal and external enemies. One of Lenin's first acts after the Revolution had been the setting up of the Cheka. But under Stalin the security system became even more firmly institutionalised and extended. The USSR in the 1930s was teeming with security police and informers. A vast convict empire spread across the country. The successive heads of the security services were as feared as Stalin, although their own positions and lives were not secure.

The security apparatus was continued after Stalin's death, although the powers of the police were modified. Certainly the activities of the security forces became less arbitrary. Citizens who kept their heads down and conformed no longer lived in fear of sudden arrest. Dissent or opposition could lead to great discomfiture, but not necessarily death. However, the instruments of the State were quickly utilised against any suggestion of intellectual or political dissent, right down to the 1980s. In this sense the Stalinist system continued, albeit in a modified form. The Stalinist Constitution remained in force until 1977, when it was superseded by the Brezhnev version. In both documents the guarantees of civil liberties were largely a paper exercise.

The Politicisation of Society

The total politicisation of life was an integral part of Stalinism. Since all human activity had a political significance, according to Marxist orthodoxy, Stalin would have found no difficulty in persuading

A memorial to Stalin in his birthplace, Gori.

Communists that imposing his world view on his people was a legitimate course, given that his interpretation of what that world view consisted of was accepted as orthodox and in the true spirit of Lenin. The really notable feature of Stalinism was the extent to which everyday life *was* politicised. Everybody, and everything, in the USSR had to serve the interests of the State, and by implication, Stalin.

Paradoxically, the tightening of central controls which accompanied the economic liberalism introduced by Lenin in 1921 did not mean that Stalin's system of government always resulted in close control over its own servants. Partly due to the size and diverse nature of the USSR, partly due to administrative inefficiencies and shortages of the right personnel, central control of everything from Moscow did not always remain at the same level. Local Party bosses sometimes exercised a considerable degree of local autonomy, although they were subject to arbitrary recall or arrest. Stalin's dictatorship certainly did not operate as smoothly as its structure on paper might suggest.

Khrushchev deliberately promoted a policy of decentralisation as a means of stimulating economic efficiency, thought and initiative. His efforts were frustrated by bureaucrats, particularly those who wished to remain in Moscow. So the administrative structure remained in essentials until the 1980s: a theoretically tightly controlled, centralised, bureaucratic state, which in practice never attained the degree of total control or efficiency which its leaders craved.

Conservatism

Finally, what about Stalinism as a conservative ethos? There is a paradox which is quite explicable. Having survived a ruthless civil war, and then a world war, and having initiated a major economic revolution, the prevailing orthodoxy among Communists was that the system must be doing its job. Moreover, those Party officials and bureaucrats who had carved their niche in society and in many cases benefited materially from entrenched privilege had no motive for further change. A revolutionary ethos could easily become a conservative one.

Stalin's foreign policy was conservative in the best orthodox tsarist tradition. He was no Peter the Great seeking to expand his territories and open up Russia to progressive Western influences. Stalin's ideas on cultural and social organisation were equally conservative. Therefore in Stalin's USSR, once the economic revolution was well under way, there was little further impulse for revolutionary change. Mao's concept of 'permanent revolution', with its constant reappraisal of values, held no appeal for the lumbering Soviet bureaucracy. Khrushchev failed to appreciate this fact fully, and was removed from power. Brezhnev learned the lesson, and became the arch-conservative, so much so that his conservatism degenerated into stagnation. It made it all the more difficult for the generation of Gorbachev and Yeltsin to promote change, even when it was seen as essential to the future health of the nation.

The Role of Stalin

Analyses of systems such as Stalinism should not blind us to the fact that, during his lifetime, Stalin was at the centre of the web. His ideas and thoughts were important. Events and structures were either initiated by him or he approved of them. An analysis of Stalinism which suggests that a large bureaucratic state operates simply by its own internal dynamics is in danger of underplaying the crucial role of Stalin himself. Other societies have moulded themselves on some elements of Stalin's USSR, but without a Stalin they did not necessarily succeed or even survive. Stalin was clearly far more than a figurehead. For this reason the role of Stalin and an analysis of Stalinism must go hand in hand. Much of the Stalinist structure, particularly in the economic sphere, survived his death, well into the 1980s. But with Stalin's death, there were also important changes of emphasis. This fact alone confirms the importance of Stalin both as a personality and a political figure, and makes the phrase 'Stalinist' one to be used with care, either as a term of political abuse by opponents of Communism or totalitarianism or as an analytical tool in the hands of political and social commentators.

Points to consider

1) What were the chief features of 'Stalinism' in the USSR?
2) Which features of the Stalinist system outlived Stalin?
3) To what extent had Stalin succeeded in having 'achieved socialism' in the USSR by the time of his death?
4) Why did Stalin's influence remain so strong after his death?

THE HISTORIOGRAPHY OF A MAN AND HIS GHOST

Each age reinterprets history anew. Good historians seek objectivity, but they bring their own prejudices to bear upon their studies, and we are all subject to many influences which determine our interpretation of the evidence before our eyes. When much of the evidence is hidden or missing, speculation is encouraged, and the historian should be appropriately humble in pronouncing judgement. However, humility has not been prominent amongst the qualities displayed by historians of Stalin and Stalinism. Many of the histories to date were written in an era when ideologies were at war with each other. In such a climate, in addition to the problems of perspective, or lack of it, historical interpretations are liable to become part of the battleground. This should not be surprising in the case of Stalin since he provoked strong reactions both during his lifetime and after his death.

STALINIST HISTORIOGRAPHY
—

Interpretations of Stalin within the USSR during his lifetime did not suffer from the complications suggested above. There could be only one 'official' interpretation of Stalin after 1929. Certainly once Stalin was firmly in power, Soviet historians were bound to consider his past, and to eulogise him for the benefits of the contemporary propaganda machine. The image created of Stalin was one of a wise, far-seeing comrade who had been Lenin's right-hand man before, during and after the Revolution. Details inconvenient to the regime, such as the role and very existence of Trotsky, were simply given a perverted interpretation or ignored. History became hagiography. Although Lenin had the position of honour on the pedestal, the deification of Stalin reached extraordinary heights. He was credited with every virtue and achievement imaginable. Not just pre-eminent in politics, Stalin was presented as a genius of philosophy, science, the arts and economics. Not just historians, but poets, painters, film-makers, journalists and novelists all added their grist to the propaganda mill.

Official Soviet histories of Stalin first appeared in the USSR in the late 1930s. In 1935 Stalin himself ordered work begun on the *History of the All-Union Communist Party*, usually known by the shorter title of the *Short Course*, because its purpose was didactic. Two years later Stalin had it redrafted, setting out new guidelines for the book. Although it was claimed later that Stalin wrote the finished product, he probably completed just the chapter on 'Dialectical and Historical Materialism'. The *Short Course* magnified the role of Stalin from 1912 onwards. Stalin was credited with being co-leader of the Party with Lenin. The impression was given that Stalin and Lenin had agreed on everything, and together they had foiled the attempts of traitors like Trotsky and Zinoviev to destroy the gains of the Revolution. The *Short Course* was published in 1938, and it included very unflattering references to the prominent victims of the recent Show Trials.

Although much of the *Short Course* is fiction, its importance should not be underestimated. The Central Committee decreed in November 1938 that it should be required reading for anybody seeking promotion within the Party or government. It became the Bible for Communists in the USSR and in other countries, being translated into sixty seven languages and being reprinted three hundred times down to Stalin's death in 1953. Thus it was taken to heart by millions of Soviet and foreign comrades.

For years, all Soviet history books were required to base their contents on the *Short Course*. Therefore not just Stalin's generation but the next also was educated in the belief that Stalin was the dominant force in Soviet history from even before the Revolution. The *Short Course* even overshadowed the eighty page official biography of Stalin published in Moscow in 1940. This book gave the same prominence and praise to Stalin, and was also read by millions at home and abroad.

POST-STALIN SOVIET HISTORIOGRAPHY

The disquiet created by Khrushchev's denunciation of Stalin in 1956 put a temporary stop to histories of Stalin and his regime. In 1959 a new Party history was produced to replace the 1938 edition. Although the new volume was printed in millions, it was given less official publicity than its parent. The 1959 *History* criticised Stalin for the first time. Whilst admitting that Stalin had acted correctly in destroying the Party's enemies in the 1930s, it stated that there had been too many innocent victims alongside the guilty. In other words, Stalin had gone too far, although it was implied that this has been due partly to the Heads of the Security Services having influenced Stalin in this direction. Stalin was still praised for his achievements, particularly in the economic field. He was criticised for the excesses of his personality cult – it was the Party itself rather than Stalin which should have had the limelight – and aspects of his leadership during the war were called into question, but the *History* concluded that Stalin's career had been beneficial to his country and to the world Communist movement overall. It must be said that the 1959 *History* was reasonably balanced, certainly compared to anything that had appeared in the USSR during Stalin's lifetime.

Khrushchev and Stalin

Interestingly, the 1959 *History* was more moderate in its criticism of Stalin than Khrushchev had been in his celebrated 'secret speech' to the Twentieth Congress of the Party in 1956. That indictment was indeed damning:

> The negative characteristics of Stalin, which, in Lenin's time, were only incipient, transformed themselves during the last years into a grave abuse of power by Stalin, which caused untold harm to our Party . . .
>
> Stalin acted not through persuasion, explanation and patient cooperation with people, but by imposing his concepts and demanding absolute submission to his opinion. Whoever opposed this concept or tried to prove his viewpoint, and the correctness of his position, was doomed to removal from the leading collective and to subsequent moral and physical annihilation.

Khrushchev claimed that Stalin played 'a positive role' in opposing the enemies of Leninism and socialism, but this legitimate action had degenerated into mass repression, and Stalin's concept of the 'enemy of the people' had precluded any constructive ideological argument:

> Instead of proving his political correctness and mobilising the masses, he (Stalin) often chose the path of repression and physical annihilation, not only against actual enemies, but also against individuals who had not committed any crimes against the party and the Soviet government.

Stalin's principal crime, Khrushchev continued, had been to deviate from the 'clear and plain precepts of Lenin'. This was a significant charge given Stalin's frequent claim that he had been the true heir of Lenin. Why had Stalin been so ruthless? Khrushchev gave a short character sketch of the dead dictator:

> Stalin was a very distrustful man, sickly suspicious; we knew this from our work with him. He could look at a man and say: 'Why are your eyes so shifty today?' or 'Why are you turning so much today and avoiding looking at me directly in the eyes?' The sickly suspicion created in him a general distrust even towards eminent party workers whom he had known for years. Everywhere and in everything he saw 'enemies', 'two-facers' and 'spies'.

Khrushchev concluded by calling for the abolition of the cult of the individual and a resurrection of the authority of the Party on the 'Leninist path'.

The context in which Khrushchev delivered this speech was a difficult one for the Party leadership. Two years before, a Party Commission into Stalin's Purges had begun to reveal the full horror of those years. Khrushchev and other leading Party figures were engaged in a struggle for power, but since evidence of the horrors of the Stalinist years was being made public, some official statement of responsibility had to be made. Khrushchev was attempting to absolve himself and others from responsibility for the crimes he revealed, and to set the limits for future discussion. Not all the truth was told, but even so Khrushchev aroused great hostility from some of his colleagues for the revelations he did make. Some colleagues accused him of power-seeking, and he had to tread carefully for several months after the speech. News of the details of the speech also helped to spark revolt against Stalinist regimes in Eastern Europe. Perhaps this accounts for the more moderate 'official' assessment of Stalin in 1959.

Nevertheless the attack upon Stalin's reputation was resurrected by Khrushchev at the Twenty-second Party Congress in 1961. After his speech, Stalin's body was removed from the Lenin mausoleum and interred by the side of the Kremlin wall. Stalin's name disappeared from books, street names and city names. Stalin's memory was kept alive in his native Georgia, but officially he became a 'non-person', like so many of his own perceived enemies before him.

Official Histories

The official histories of the Congresses, printed in 1975 and revised four times down to 1985, chart the changes in attitude towards Stalin. The Report on the Sixteenth Congress of 1930 and the Seventeenth Congress of 1934 outlined the achievements of the Five-Year Plans, but attributed them to the Party. Stalin was not mentioned. Nor was he mentioned in the Report on the Nineteenth Congress of 1952, celebrating recovery from the war. In the Report on the Twentieth Congress of 1956 there was simply the statement that:

> The Congress discussed the question of the Stalin personality cult that had arisen and drafted a series of measures to ensure that the cult was fully overcome and its consequences remedied in all spheres of Party, state and ideological work, and that the norms of Party life and the principle of collective leadership elaborated by Lenin were strictly observed.

BUKHARIN AND STALIN

Of course there had been criticism of Stalin and his methods by some Communists long before 1956, although such criticism had been extremely dangerous. Bukharin, one of the most notable victims of the Purges, gave his account of the background to the Show Trials in an interview in Paris with a Menshevik historian Boris Nicolaevsky, two years before Bukharin's trial and execution. Bukharin revealed something of the political intrigue which had taken place at the time of Kirov's assassination and later. He talked of Kirov's attempts to bring an end to the Purges, which had already begun, and how Kirov's death had simply led to an intensification of the Terror. According to Bukharin, Stalin had decided upon personal dictatorship because of his realisation that 'the mood of the majority of the old party workers was really one of bitterness and hostility towards him'. Stalin's response involved the creation of 'a new ruling caste.' Bukharin had been a loyal Party man, but his sense of betrayal was obvious and he was to pay the ultimate price for his earlier disagreements with Stalin.

TROTSKY AND STALIN

However, the most vehement Russian critic of Stalin during his lifetime was his great rival Trotsky. Trotsky's output of books and journalistic articles was prodigious until his assassination in Mexico in 1940. He was working on a biography of Stalin at the time of his death, although he was a subject about whom Trotsky had already written and spoken at considerable length. Although unfinished, the drafts of Trotsky's biography were published in 1946. Trotsky could not refrain from emphasising his own intellectual superiority: according to Trotsky, one of Stalin's principal faults was his 'contemptuous attitude towards ideas'. Trotsky had to concede that Stalin did possess certain qualities – determination above all others – but he was concerned to show that Stalin had employed his talents to pervert the course of the Revolution, creating a bureaucratic, anti-workers' state. Already in 1937 Trotsky had written of 'Soviet Bonapartism' in *The Revolution Betrayed*. He described Stalin's cult of personality as an essential element in his regime: 'Stalin is the personification of the bureaucracy. That is the substance of his political personality'. Stalinism represented 'the crushing of Soviet democracy by an all-powerful bureaucracy'. Stalinism and Fascism were 'symmetrical phenomena', both caused by the 'dilatoriness of the world proletariat in solving the problems set for it by history'.

These were strong criticisms on the scale of Marxist abuse, but their effectiveness was negated by the fact that Trotsky was as concerned to vindicate his own actions as to attempt an objective portrait of Stalin and an analysis of his system. The effects of his criticisms were also diluted by the onset of war and the boost which Stalin's international reputation received from the titanic efforts of the Soviets in their struggle against Hitler.

MODERN SOVIET HISTORIOGRAPHY

In the decades after Stalin's death, the history of the Stalin period was often retold in the USSR. In the 1970s and early 1980s Stalin's role was usually played down or even omitted altogether. Stalin might be a convenient scapegoat for past errors and crimes, but to criticise his memory continually might lead to embarrassing questions about his heirs also.

School textbooks idolised Lenin. Stalin's role in the Revolution, the Civil War, the economic revolution within the USSR, the Second World War, went unrecorded. On the few occasions when Stalin was mentioned by name, it was only as part of a collective leadership. Accounts of Soviet history were heavily sanitised: for example, the Purges were not mentioned.

Histories for adult readers were little different. An official *History of the USSR*, by Yuri Kukushkin, published in 1981, named Stalin as one member of a Central Committee which waged a 'determined, uncompromising struggle against the anti-Leninist elements who were trying to force the Party to abandon its struggle for socialism.' After several chapters containing detailed descriptions of the agricultural and industrial transformation of the USSR in the 1930s, without one mention of Stalin, Kukushkin finally devoted a few lines to the presiding dictator:

> The impressive progress made in socialist construction was, unfortunately, marred by both the objective difficulties and the subjective mistakes that were committed. Such mistakes were made by J. V. Stalin who for many years had held top Party post of General Secretary. Stalin had contributed much to the struggle against the enemies of Leninism and for the construction of socialism. However, as time went by, all the achievements in socialist construction were erroneously credited to him and his personal leadership. This was a mistake as the crucial part played by the Soviet people and the Communist Party, the two decisive forces in the building of the new society, was thus relegated to the background. Stalin began to abuse his power in flagrant violation of the Leninist principles of Party leadership. As a result, a Stalin personality cult developed. This was exploited by some political adventurists who, having infiltrated the higher echelons of the state security bodies, framed many honest Party and government leaders

and subjected them to totally undeserved repression. The Stalin personality cult did great damage. But even so, it could not stop the country's onward development. Later Stalin's personality cult was strongly condemned and its consequences were eliminated.

There is unconscious irony here in the fact that this passage was written at the time of Brezhnev, who had himself promoted a pervasive personality cult.

According to Kukushkin, it is the Communist Party which deserves the credit for mobilising the struggle against Hitler, along with the 'Soviet command' – but there is no mention of Stalin.

Finally, Stalin's name appears almost as a postscript:

In March 1953, J. V. Stalin, who had for years held the top posts in the Party's Central Committee and in the Soviet government, died. The enemies of socialism had hoped that his death would cause disarray in the communist ranks. But their hopes were dashed. The Party gave an all-round assessment to Stalin's life and work pointing out his merits and services to the nation and criticising the mistakes he had made. The Communist Party submitted to an in-depth analysis the reasons that underlay Stalin's personality cult and its consequences.

This was a very bland assessment which raises more questions that it answers. It has been quoted at length because it is typical of the attention given to Stalin in post-Stalin but pre-*glasnost* literature; and it is a remarkable example of an historian's ingenuity that a 270 page history of the USSR could confine mention of Stalin's name to the few lines above.

Medvedev and Stalin

There were a few honourable exceptions to the propagandist version of history. One of the most remarkable post-Stalin analyses of Stalinism was given by the philosopher Roy Medvedev in *Let History Judge*, published in 1971. Medvedev was a dissident who could not accept that Stalin alone was responsible for all the crimes committed in his name. Medvedev denied that Stalinism had been an inevitable development within the USSR. He argued that Stalin was bent on 'unlimited personal dictatorship', and it was a 'sad fact' that there had been no significant resistance to him. It was also 'an unavoidable fact that Stalin never relied on force alone.' In other words, there many Soviet citizens equally responsible for the crimes of the Stalinist era. Medvedev examined the paradox that Stalin reversed some of the gains of the Revolution, whilst at the same time relying upon the masses for support. Stalin was also successful, he concluded, because he was able 'to make extreme simplifications of complex ideas' which had the effect of 'vulgarising Marxism-Leninism.' Other dedicated Communists had not been able to adapt to changing circumstances, and so the way had been opened for Stalin.

POST-*GLASNOST* HISTORIOGRAPHY
—

Medvedev's views were not novel by Western standards, but it was courageous for a Soviet citizen to publish them in 1971. By the mid-1980s and the emergence of *glasnost*, it was considerably easier for Soviet citizens to be more open about their past. Soviet historians and commentators began to grapple with questions such as how Stalin had managed to come to power, whether indeed this had been inevitable in the conditions of the 1920s. The first major post-*glasnost* biography of Stalin was Dimitri Volkogonov's *Stalin*. The author had been in the Red Army at the time of Stalin's death, and although his family had suffered in the Terror, he had been an enthusiastic believer in Stalin. His biography was very critical of Stalin for his role in the Terror and his wartime leadership. Like Trotsky, Volkogonov was still convinced that Stalin had always been a mediocre figure.

Some historians writing in the 1980s were concerned with Stalin's apparent paranoia and his intolerance of criticism. In so doing, they were only repeating the main thrust of Khrushchev's 1956 speech, although they were able to flesh out their accounts with more detail than had hitherto been available to the Soviet public. Novelists also vented their opinions. In the *Literaturnaya Gazeta* of 22 June 1988, Yuri Bondarev wrote of Stalin as a 'despotic figure with the uncontrolled mercilessness of an avenging will'. Some commentators found it difficult to condemn the entire Soviet system and contended that although Stalin, like Bonaparte, had seized power and had established a personal dictatorship, the essence of Soviet society had remained socialist, that is, the system still represented the interests of the working class, whatever its faults. It was difficult, however, to accept that socialism had been developing at the same time as Stalin's dictatorship – after all, even Lenin had argued that democracy was necessary for socialism to survive in the long term. Gorbachev emphasised the point in his speech on the anniversary of the Revolution, in November 1987:

> Stalin's personality cult was certainly not inevitable. It was alien to the nature of socialism, represented a departure from its fundamental principles and, therefore, has no justification . . . (After the war) a contradiction between what our society had become and the old methods of leadership was making itself felt ever more appreciably. Abuses of power and violations of socialist legality continued. The 'Leningrad Case' and the 'Doctors' Case' were fabricated . . . In short, there was a deficit of genuine respect for the people.

Yet within months of this speech the Soviet magazine *October* published sixteen pages of readers' letters praising Stalin. One reader from Belogorsk regretted the removal of Stalin's body from the mausoleum in Red Square:

> Stalin and Lenin are the two bulwarks, the twin legs of our Socialist ideology. To remove either one means to cause irreparable damage to the cause of Communism . . . You may claim that the 20th Party Congress laid down the foundation of democratisation in Soviet society. But I think it was the reverse. The activities of Khrushchev and the writers who supported him like Solzhenitsyn and Tvardovsky, meant counter-revolution. And if it was not clear enough in 1956, it is today.

A 23 year old from Kishinev, criticising the posthumous publication of Tvardovsky's anti-Stalinist poem *By Right of Memory*, wrote:

> Ask the workers and peasants what they think about Stalin . . . If you try to convince them that it was under Stalin that the system of privilege for the top Party echelons began, they will tell you that it's rubbish, and every sane person knows these privileges grew up under your beloved Khrushchev.

However, the general trend in the USSR in the early years of *glasnost* was towards a hostile view of Stalin. A survey in April 1988 of 1200 students from eleven higher education establishments showed that 69 per cent 'approve the criticism in the press of the cult of Stalin's personality', whilst only 18 per cent 'consider that such publications can shake the faith of young people in the ideals of socialist society.' A survey of Muscovites in June 1988 revealed that 55 per cent felt that Stalin 'played a negative role in the life of our country'; 31 per cent found 'both positive and negative features in his activity'; and less than 1 per cent held 'a high opinion of Stalin's role in the history of our country'.

Some of the biggest problems were faced by schoolteachers, who found that their history exams were cancelled and their textbooks withdrawn at the end of the 1980s whilst new versions of Stalin and his contribution to Soviet history were written. The existing history textbooks had last been revised in 1981. The new ones, written by more than a dozen leading historians, and quoting from Western as well as Soviet sources, meant it was possible to have a genuine and open debate about Stalin almost forty years after his death, just when the USSR was breaking up. The new textbooks, for example, admitted that in Stalin's day 'The constitution and daily life were in sharp divergence'; Stalin's policy towards Hitler and the Finns was condemned; and only a few sensitive issues such as the precise role of Trotsky and the annexation of the Baltic states were skated over.

STALIN IN FICTION

Some of the most popular analyses of Stalin in the USSR were those which appeared in the format of popular fiction. Perhaps the most notable was Anatoli Rybakov's *Children of the Arbat*, published in the 1980s after years of suppression within the USSR. The novel, set in 1934, intertwines the lives of ordinary Russians living through the onset of the Terror with that of Stalin, plotting to assassinate Kirov and unleash the Purges. Rybakov portrays Stalin as suspiciously noting the shortcomings of all his subordinates, and coldly outlining his philosophy:

> Magnanimity toward a conquered enemy was dangerous: an enemy will never believe in your magnanimity; he will always regard it as a political manoeuvre and will attack at the first opportunity . . . The people's greatest enemy could be evoked only through suffering. Suffering could be used for destruction or for creation. Human suffering leads to God: the people had been nourished by that basic postulate of Christianity for centuries, and it had become part of

their flesh and blood, and we must use it. The earthly paradise of socialism was more appealing than a mythical heaven in the sky, even though to achieve it one also had to suffer. Of course the people must be convinced that their hardships were only temporary, that they served the attainment of the great goal, that the supreme authority understood the people's needs and cared for them and protected them from the bureaucrats, however high up. The supreme power was ALL-KNOWING, ALL-WISE, ALL-POWERFUL.

Rybakov was criticised by several historians for a one-sided portrait of Stalin and his times, although his portrayal of Stalin's scheming and suspicion is not very different from the descriptions of contemporaries like Khrushchev. Soviet writers still struggled to explain the roots of Stalinism, to differentiate the man from the system, and achieve anything like an objective analysis. The arguments continued to have contemporary relevance. The Soviet jurist Boris Kurashivli wrote in 1990 that Stalinism was a weapon used in the battles between political factions:

> The millions of still living modest men and women who in their simplicity continue to believe in Stalin, the millions of their spiritual heirs, convinced patriots and followers of socialism, are being insulted and rejected. Progressive forces have split over the attitude to Stalin, who, as a person, is worlds removed from the actual objectives of perestroika (Reconstruction). Criticism of deceased leaders of the day before yesterday is distracting attention from those who are still alive, those who are leaders of yesterday clinging to their offices and resisting perestroika.
>
> (*The Heartbeat of Reform*, 1990)

WESTERN HISTORIOGRAPHY

It might be expected that non-Soviet historians would find it easier to be dispassionate about Stalin. This has not always proved to be so, although Western historiography of Stalin has not had to undergo the same degree of soul-searching as its Soviet and Russian counterparts. In the West, opinion of the man and his system has been far from unanimous.

Levine

Writers in the West, often journalists, began to take a serious interest in Stalin in the 1930s. The first serious biography was *Stalin* by the Russian-born Isaac Levine, published in 1931. Levine's picture of Stalin was that of a man who was authoritarian but basically well-intentioned. This was to be the line followed by several other writers in the 1930s who were impressed by the apparent economic and social achievements occuring in the USSR, and often taken in by Soviet propaganda, although few accounts attained the level of the embarrassing panegyric of Stalin's Russia which was the Webbs' *Soviet Communism: A New Civilisation*, published in 1935.

Souvarine

In contrast, Boris Souvarine, a French citizen, but like Levine, Russian-born, wrote a detailed and damning indictment of Stalin in a biography published in London in 1939. Souvarine's views were coloured by his own Trotskyist inclinations. Nevertheless, his book was enlivened by portraits of Soviet leaders he had known personally, and it was based upon the available sources. Souvarine's conclusions were unambiguous: Stalin was not responsible for all of the ills in his country, but nevertheless he had set himself up as a dictator and had destroyed any good brought about by the Revolution.

Deutscher

One of the more interesting post-war biographies of Stalin was that of the Marxist historian Isaac Deutscher. His *Stalin* was published in 1949. Deutscher wanted to avoid the taint of Cold War polemics in vogue at the time, but this did not prevent considerable criticism of his book both by contemporaries and later historians. Deutscher portrayed Stalin as a hard man, but one who represented the views of many other people, and who forced through progressive economic and social changes at the same time as introducing mass terror to the USSR. Deutscher's explanation of the latter was that Stalin foresaw the war and needed to purge the country of potential fifth columnists. Deutscher lavished considerable praise on Stalin for his wartime leadership. A despot yes, but also a man of genuine popularity. Deutscher's attempt to write a balanced account of Stalin was praiseworthy, coming from an admirer of Trotsky, but many of his judgements were questioned. Interestingly, he tried to interpret what was going on inside Stalin's mind in a way similar to Rybakov a generation later.

Carr

A different tack was pursued by historians who concentrated less upon Stalin's personality, the defects of which were virtually taken for granted, and concentrated instead on the institutions of the USSR and the significance of the policies which were followed. The ultimate example of this approach was probably E. H. Carr's massive *History of Soviet Russia*, published in the early 1950s. The institutions of the USSR certainly received far more detailed treatment than the individuals, whether prominent personalities or ordinary citizens. Carr did make an assessment of Stalin, taking the not particularly original line that he was full of contradictions, although at heart he was a strong-minded dictator. Carr was not interested in making moral judgements about Stalin, which might be a virtue in a historian but perhaps makes for a duller as well as a bigger book that Deutscher's.

Liebmann

Certain themes have been prominent in the writings of other eminent historians of recent years, such as the extent to which Stalinism was a continuation or perversion of Leninism, and the extent to which Stalin's means were justified by the ends of his policies. The former issue has been debated at length in the old USSR also, but it was an issue among Western historians for many years before that. The view that Stalinism was essentially different from Leninism was argued by the French historian Marcel Liebmann in his *Leninism Under Lenin*, published in 1973. Whilst accepting that 'the bureaucratic and totalitarian degeneration of the Soviet regime does not begin with the death of Lenin', the author went on to discuss the essential differences between the two systems:

> Is not the latter (Stalinism) identified with the omnipotence of bureaucratic tyranny, with the domination of a pragmatism that is often incoherent, bold strokes punctuating a highly conservative policy – and, above all, with the exercise of unlimited personal dictatorship?

These, argued Liebmann, were not features of Leninism. As for the philosophical basis of Stalin's Marxism, unlike Lenin's,

> Stalinist dialectics was merely the ideological cover for the ramblings of a short-sighted pragmatism. If Stalinism is Leninism *plus* administrative tyranny and *plus* bureaucratic terror, it is Leninism *minus* dialectics. It is thus Leninism *impoverished* by being deprived of that leaven which has made of it, even in its mistakes, and in spite of its failures, one of the richest sources of inspiration in the fight for socialism, one of the most fruitful contributions to men's struggle for their emancipation.

Schapiro

In contrast to Liebmann's thesis, the historian Leonard Schapiro in his *History of the Communist Party of the Soviet Union*, published in 1963, argued that 'the foundations of the machine erected by Stalin for his tyranny were already laid down by Lenin'. Schapiro was interested in the concept of totalitarianism and he argued that 'It is in the nature of the rule of the totalitarian despot that he cannot tolerate any rival institution'. Thus Stalin attacked even the institution of the Party and destroyed its monopoly position, using the secret police and the State bureaucracy. Stalin's Party was 'essentially a body of retainers' who could be removed or promoted on a whim. Khruschchev was to restore the institutional framework. In this respect Stalin was unique compared to Soviet leaders who preceded and succeeded him.

Conquest

In 1968 Robert Conquest published his detailed study of *The Great Terror*. In a balanced assessment of Stalin's character, he admitted Stalin's political skills:

> Stalin's achievement is in general so extraordinary that we can hardly dismiss him as simply a colourless, mediocre type with a certain talent for terror and intrigue . . . because he did not elucidate and elaborate his views and plans, it was thought that he did not have any – a typical mistake of the garrulous intellectual.

Nevertheless, in the last resort

the drive for power was Stalin's strongest and most obvious motivation ... The one fundamental drive that can be found throughout is the strengthening of his own position.

Nove

As for the argument about the necessity or otherwise of Stalin's methods, opinions have also been varied. Alec Nove is the historian of the economic development of the USSR. He argued that, given the Communists' decision to collectivise and industrialise, it had to be done rapidly and could not have been voluntary:

> The strains and priorities involved in a rapid move forward required a high degree of economic centralisation, to prevent resources from being diverted to satisfy needs which were urgent but of a nonpriority character. In this situation, the party was the one body capable of carrying out enormous changes and resisting social and economic pressures in a hostile environment; this was bound to affect its structure. For a number of years it had already been in process of transformation from a political into a power machine. The problems involved in the 'revolution from above' intensified the process of turning it into an obedient instrument for changing, suppressing, controlling.
>
> This, in turn, required hierarchical subordination, in suppression of discussion; therefore there had to be an unquestioned commander-in-chief.
>
> (Alec Nove, 'Was Stalin Really Necessary?', *Encounter*, April 1962)

Nove believed that there were evil actions directly attributable to Stalin, the obvious example being the Purges, and those evils which flowed inevitably from the situation, and which arose from policy choices which were the responsibility of many other people besides Stalin. The latter included the 'stresses and strains' which flowed from rapid industrialisation.

Lewin

This attempt to distinguish between 'necessary' and 'unnecessary' evils was strongly criticised by Moshe Lewin, who argued that there were alternative economic policies that could have been pursued in the 1930s, and therefore it was difficult to excuse Stalin. Rather an essential precondition for analysis is the ability on the one hand to identify urgent social needs dictated by circumstances, and on the other to judge the practical solutions to these problems which were the result of subjective choice on the part of the leaders. By making this distinction, we are able to appraise the actions of historical personages, and to pass judgement on the quality of the leaders.

(Moshe Lewin, 'The Immediate Background of Soviet Collectivisation', *Soviet Studies*, October 1965)

Lewin perceived a struggle taking place in the USSR in the 1930s between two 'political models'. Between 1935 and 1938 'the theme of reinforcing legality, rehabilitating the concept of law, was being voiced and preached.' At the same time the arbitrary nature of coercion represented by the Secret Police and the camp system grew. The bureaucracy supported the first model, because 'legality allows the masses to identify with the system – otherwise the lawless system is felt as tyrannical and cannot be stable'; and 'the ruler, in order to control the state machinery directly and efficiently, requires a clear legal framework for the smooth working of state institutions and bureaucracies'. Stalin himself was aware of both developments, but even Lewin accepted that to some extent the dangers inherent in the process were beyond his control.

McCauley

The debate about Stalin and Stalinism continued into the 1980s. Martin McCauley wrote in 1983 that there were basically two ways of observing Stalin:

If one downgrades the Georgian and sees him as an intellectually limited, uncreative, ideologically bread-and-butter person, then the Soviet Union under his leadership must have derived its dynamism from some other source. This source is the revolution itself, something which is impersonal but with an inner dynamic . . . The other way of assessing Stalin is to see him as a great man . . . the moulder of events.

(M. McCauley, *Stalin and Stalinism*, 1983)

McCauley's own assessment was that Stalin was not a good man, but that he was a very skilful and gifted politician who did not get to the top by accident.

THE STALIN PHENOMENON

New biographies of Stalin and analyses of Stalinism appear regularly. For years after Stalin's death, the Stalin phenomenon merely interested the West, but thoroughly permeated the USSR itself. The failure of right-wing Russian plotters to bring down Boris Yeltsin in 1991 may have gone a long way towards finally exorcising Stalin's ghost. The plotters represented the hopes of an older generation which still believed in the ordered, regulated society which emerged under Stalin, once the arbitrariness of the Terror had subsided. It was a society which bore his particularly brutal stamp. Who is to say that dictatorship might not return to the Republics of the old USSR? Dictatorships of the Right or the Left might emerge, but is is difficult to believe that another Stalin could emerge from the shadows to emulate the 'crafty Georgian', who saved Europe from one tyranny, the Nazi one, but whose own version of despotic rule invoked feelings of fear and respect long after his statues were knocked down and his corpse was removed from its place of honour next to Lenin in the marble mausoleum. Or would that be to make the same mistake as the comrades who underestimated Stalin and smoothed his path to power all those years ago?

Points to consider

1) What changes have taken place in Soviet and Russian interpretations of Stalin since his death? How do you account for any changes?
2) What have been the principal themes of Western historiography of Stalin since his death?
3) What difficulties are there for a historian in writing an objective account of Stalin?
4) Is it possible to separate Stalin from Stalinism?

PERSONALITIES

Vladimir Ilych Lenin 1870–1924

He was born V.I. Ulyanov in Simbirsk. In 1887 he entered Kazan University as a law student. He then became a revolutionary and was expelled. In 1890 he was allowed to take his degree in St. Petersburg. In 1895 he was arrested, imprisoned and exiled. In 1898 he joined the SDP (Social Democratic Party). In 1902 he published the influential *What is to be Done?* and in 1903 he was leader of the Bolshevik group which emerged from the SDP Congress. He was back in Russia towards the end of the 1905 Revolution, but spent much of the next ten years in foreign exile. In April 1917 he returned to Russia, published the *April Theses* and called for the overthrow of the Provisional Government. Forced into hiding after the July Days, he returned to Petrograd for the October Revolution. Lenin was elected Chairman of the Council of People's Commissars and was head of government until his death. He survived an assassination attempt in 1918, but suffered a stroke in 1922. He finally died in January 1924.

Leon Trotsky 1879–1940

Born Lev Bronstein to a prosperous Jewish family, he became a revolutionary in 1897. He was arrested and exiled, but escaped abroad, where he met Lenin. He was prominent in St. Petersburg during the 1905 Revolution, and was Chairman of the Soviet. After prison, he spent several years abroad until returning to Petrograd in May 1917. After a brief imprisonment he was elected Chairman of the Petrograd Soviet. He abandoned his Menshevik past, became Lenin's ally, and played a prominent role in the October Revolution. In 1918, as Commissar of Foreign Affairs, he negotiated the Treaty of Brest-Litovsk. During the Civil War he created and led the Red Army. He was a member of the

Politburo from 1919. He advocated the New Economic Policy, implemented by Lenin, and suppressed the Kronstadt Rising in 1921. After Lenin fell ill, Trotsky was opposed by Stalin, Zinoviev and Kamenev. He failed to act decisively against Stalin, and was attacked for his ideas on 'Permanent Revolution' and his past record. He was sacked as Commissar for War in 1925. In 1926 Trotsky formed the United Left Opposition with Zinoviev and Kamenev, but was expelled from the Party in 1927. In 1928 he was exiled to Turkestan, and in 1929 deported from the USSR. After years of wandering around Europe, denouncing Stalin, Trotsky settled in Mexico in 1937. In 1940 he was assassinated by a Stalinist agent.

Lev Kamenev 1883–1936

In 1908 he joined Lenin in Geneva and became a propagandist for the Bolsheviks. In 1914 he took charge of *Pravda* in St. Petersburg but was arrested and deported to Siberia, to the same location as Stalin. He took charge of *Pravda* again in April 1917. Along with Zinoviev, he opposed Lenin's call for a Bolshevik coup in October 1917. Although elected president of the Central Executive Committee, and Head of the Moscow Party organisation, he lost support after Stalin became General Secretary. During Lenin's illness in 1922 he joined with Stalin and Zinoviev to oppose Trotsky. In 1926 he allied with Zinoviev and Trotsky against Stalin in the United Left Opposition. In 1928 he was persuaded to denounce Trotsky, but was himself expelled from the Party in 1932. Readmitted to the Party in 1933, he offered his support to Stalin. After Kirov's assassination he was arrested, given a Show Trial and executed in August 1936. The sentence was annulled by the Soviet Supreme Court in 1988.

Grigori Zinoviev 1883–1936

In 1901 he joined the SDP and became a member of the Bolshevik Central Committee in 1907. He joined Lenin in exile in 1907, and returned with him to Russia in April 1917, but along with Kamenev, opposed the decision for a Bolshevik coup. Between 1918 and 1926 he was in charge of the Petrograd Party organisation, and between 1919 and 1926 headed the Comintern or Third International. He was a member of the Triumvirate with Stalin and Kamenev against Trotsky, then a member of the United Left Opposition with Kamenev and Trotsky, against Stalin, 1926–7. He was expelled from the Party, readmitted in 1928, expelled again in 1932. Arrested in 1934, he was tried in 1935 and again in 1936. He was executed in 1936. His sentence was annulled by the Soviet Supreme Court in 1988.

Nicholas Bukharin 1888–1938

He became a Bolshevik in 1906, and later met Lenin and Stalin in exile abroad. After travelling widely he returned to Russia and took part in the October Revolution. He became editor of *Pravda*, and together with Preobrazhensky wrote the influential *ABC of Communism* in 1918. He changed from support for War Communism to support for NEP. During the mid-1920s he supported Stalin and the doctrine of 'Socialism in One Country', opposing the Left Opposition. In 1928, along with his 'Rightist Opposition' colleagues Rykov and Tomsky, he was attacked by Stalin. He was expelled from the Politburo, but came to prominence again in 1934, when he became editor of *Isvestia*. In 1937 he was arrested. In 1938 he was given a Show Trial and was shot for treason and other supposed crimes. In 1988 Bukharin was officially rehabilitated.

Sergei Kirov 1886–1934

He joined the SDP in 1905 and was later exiled to Siberia. Active during the Civil War, he then became the Soviet ambassador to Georgia in May 1920. In 1923 he joined the Central Committee, and in 1925 he replaced Zinoviev as Party boss in Leningrad. He joined the Politburo in 1930, and was prominent and popular at the Party Congress of 1934. In December 1934 he was assassinated.

Grigori Ordzhonikidze 1886–1937

A Georgian and a Bolshevik before the Revolution, he was a political commissar during the Civil War. He commanded the Red Army's invasion of Georgia in 1921, after working closely with Stalin. He helped to 'Russify' Georgia. In 1930 Stalin appointed him to the Politburo, and in 1932 he became Commissar for Heavy Industries. Ordzhonikidze argued for more moderate policies during the Terror. In 1937 he died. He may have been murdered, but the more likely explanation is suicide, after he had been denounced by more ruthless colleagues.

Nikolai Yezhov 1895–1939?

A St. Petersburg worker who joined the Bolsheviks in 1917. He became a member of the Central Committee in 1927, and was involved in actions against the *kulaks*. He became Chairman of the Central Control Commission of the Party in 1935, and replaced Yagoda as Head of the NKVD in 1936. He launched the Terror, known by Russians as the 'Yezhovshchina'. He was removed in 1938, arrested, and probably shot.

Andrei Zhdanov 1896–1948

He became Head of the Leningrad Party organisation after Kirov's assassination in 1934. He was also Secretary to the Central Committee. Renowned as the guardian of the Party's ideological and a strong opponent of foreign influences, he nevertheless favoured a decentralisation of authority.

Lavrenti Beria 1899–1953

A Georgian who joined the Bolsheviks in 1917, he worked in Intelligence from 1921. In 1934 he became a member of the Central Committee, with responsibilites in the Caucasus. In 1938 he replaced Yezhov as Head of the NKVD, and organised the later Purges. He was in charge of Security between 1941 and 1953. After Stalin's death he was made Minister of Internal Affairs but was arrested, tried and shot in December 1953.

BIBLIOGRAPHY

There are many relevant books on the History of the Soviet Union, but the following are just a few which are useful for a study of Stalin. Place of publication is London unless otherwise stated.

Bullock, A., *Hitler and Stalin. Parallel Lives*, Harper Collins, 1991.
˙Conquest, R., *The Great Terror*, Macmillan, 1968.
De Jonge, A., *Stalin and the Shaping of the Soviet Union*, Fontana, 1986.
Deutscher, I., *Stalin*, Oxford University Press, Oxford, 1967.
Gill, G., *Stalinism*, Macmillan, 1990.
Hingley, R., *Joseph Stalin, Man and Legend*, Hutchinson, 1974.
Lewis, J. and Whitehead, P., *Stalin, A Time for Judgement*, Methuen, 1990.
Lynch, M., *Stalin and Khrushchev, The USSR 1924–1964*, Hodder & Stoughton, 1990.
McCauley, M., *Stalin and Stalinism*, Longman, 1983.
McNeal, R., *Stalin, Man and Ruler*, Macmillan, 1988.
Medvedev, R., *On Stalin and Stalinism*, Macmillan, 1979.
Tucker, R., *Stalin as Revolutionary 1879–1929*, Chatto and Windus, New York, 1974.
Tucker, R., *Stalin in Power, The Revolution From Above 1928–41*, Chatto and Windus, New York, 1990.
Tucker, R., (ed.) *Stalinism, Essays in Historical Interpretation*, W. W. Norton, New York, 1977.
Volkogonov, D., *Stalin, Triumph and Tragedy*, Wiedenfeld and Nicolson, 1991.

The FA

LEARNING

The Official FA Guide to
Fitness for
Football

Dr Richard Hawkins

Hodder Arnold

A MEMBER OF THE HODDER HEADLINE GROUP

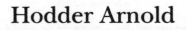

NORWICH CITY COLLEGE		
Stock No.	233 599	
Class	796 · 334 HAW	
Cat.	SSA	Proc	3wL

Orders: Please contact Bookpoint Ltd, 130 Milton Park, Abingdon, Oxon, OX14 4SB.
Telephone: (44) 01235 827720, Fax: (44) 01235 400454. Lines are open from
9.00–17.00, Monday to Saturday, with a 24-hour message answering service. You can
also order through our website www.hoddereducation.com

British Library Cataloguing in Publication Data
A catalogue record for this title is available from the British Library.

ISBN: 9780340816035

First Published 2004
Impression number   10 9 8 7
Year   2008

Copyright © 2004 FA Learning Ltd

All rights reserved. Apart from any permitted use under UK copyright law, no part of this
publication may be reproduced or transmitted in any form or by any means, electronic or
mechanical, including photocopy, recording, or any information, storage and retrieval
system, without permission in writing from the publisher or under licence from the
Copyright Licensing Agency Limited. Further details of such licences (for reprographic
reproduction) may be obtained from the Copyright Licensing Agency Ltd,
Saffron House, 6–10 Kirby Street, London EC1N 8TS.

Managing Editor: Jonathan Wilson, FA Learning

Typeset by Servis Filmsetting Ltd, Stockport, Cheshire.
Printed in Great Britain for Hodder Education,
338 Euston Road, London, NW1 3BH, by CPI Cox & Wyman, Reading, RG1 8EX.

Hachette Livre UK's policy is to use papers that are natural, renewable and recyclable
products and made from wood grown in sustainable forests. The logging and
manufacturing processes are expected to conform to the environmental regulations of the
country of origin.

Contents

LEARNING

The FA

LEARNING

Philosophy of the guides

The aim of these **Official FA Guides** is to reach the millions of people who participate in football or who are involved in the game in other ways – at any level.

Each book aims to increase your awareness and understanding of association football and in this understanding to enhance, increase, improve and extend your involvement in the world's greatest game.

These books are designed to be interactive and encourage you to apply what you read and to help you to translate this knowledge into practical skills and ability. Specific features occur throughout this book to assist this process:

■ Tasks will appear in this form and will make you think about what you have just learned and how you will apply it in a practical way.

Best Practice The Best Practice feature will give you an example of a good or ideal way of doing things – this could be on or off the pitch.

Quote │ 'Quotes throughout will pass on useful knowledge or insight or encourage you to consider a certain aspect of your skills or responsibilities.'

Statistic

The statistics included will often surprise and will certainly increase your knowledge of the game.

Summary

- **The summaries at the end of each chapter will recap on its contents and help you to consolidate your knowledge and understanding.**

You can read this guide in any way you choose and prefer to do so – at home, on the pitch, in its entirety, or to dip in for particular advice. Whatever way you use it, we hope it increases your ability, your knowledge, your involvement, and most importantly your enjoyment and passion to **be a part of the game**.

Introduction

When listening to the reports of commentators and the diagnosis of managers on a Saturday afternoon it is difficult to escape the fact that fitness played a deciding role in the outcome of the game being reported. Whether they realize it or not, it is not unusual to hear some reference to the physical qualities of an individual or the team as a whole during the post-match reports. For example, the centre forward climbed high at the far post to score with a downward header; the winger flew past the fullback to pull back a pin-point cross; the goalkeeper reacted sharply to a snap-shot which was goal bound. All things being equal, the fitness of a team will decide the outcome of a game.

We all relate to fitness in different ways, depending upon whether we are dealing with a Sunday league team or Premiership players. However, regardless of the level of importance that is placed on this part of the game, it is apparent that the benefits are the same at all levels. Benefits include enhanced performance, injury prevention and health promotion. Fitness is an integral part of football and as such it should be integrated into the system at various levels, albeit to varying degrees and seriousness. The fun component however should never be lost.

In the current era it is evident that the fitness qualities of World Cup winning teams have not developed by chance; fitness at the top level needs to be developed through appropriate methods of conditioning, in conjunction with, and in addition to, the game of football itself. At the top level the game of football is simply not enough.

Although many people have the dream of playing at the highest level, not everyone can play to this standard. However, it is still possible for people to contribute to and help others achieve success. Based on this reality, it is the aim of this guide to provide an overview of the components of fitness that are important for football and the methods of conditioning available to develop them. At all levels it is important that players, coaches, and parents alike have some level of understanding of the body to fully appreciate the impact that appropriate fitness training can have on a player and ultimately on the team's performance.

This introductory guide to fitness has been put together with the above in mind; at grassroots level players will be able to help themselves and be assisted by others. The guide covers a range of topics from the physiology of the player and how the body responds to exercise, to components of fitness and the different training needs of children compared to adults. This book will give you an insight into fitness as a whole, giving you new ideas of how to train, some fundamental principles of training that need to be followed if success is desired, and practical strategies for monitoring your own, or your team's, progress, in addition to provoking thought about your current beliefs on fitness.

Whether or not this guide is your first insight into fitness for football, I hope it will stimulate you to learn more and investigate this fascinating area of football further.

We must point out that it is always the responsibility of the individual to assess his or her own fitness capabilities before participating in any training activity.

The FA and publisher take no responsibility for accident, injury or any other consequence of following the exercises and advice herein.

Chapter 1

Basic physiology

THIS CHAPTER WILL:

- Give you an understanding of the basic structure and function of the key organ systems related to general fitness.
- Look at the respiratory system (lungs); cardiovascular system (heart); muscular systems; energy systems.

The workings of the human body are determined by the various organ systems. The majority of these play a role in influencing the human body and consequently have an impact on performance, however some are more relevant than others.

The systems that are more immediately related to fitness are the respiratory, cardiovascular, muscular and energy systems.

Crucial to understanding how individuals can improve their overall fitness is to first understand the workings of the major organ systems that have the biggest impact on fitness.

The respiratory system

At its most fundamental, the respiratory system brings oxygen into our bodies and rids us of excess carbon dioxide. It is the process used by all living things for gaining the energy that is essential for keeping the body's vital organs alive and working.

In humans this energy is gained from the breakdown of food materials (oxidation) by transporting the oxygen from the lungs into the bloodstream. Once in the bloodstream the oxygen can then be distributed to the body's cells, where it is used to unlock the energy from food.

Quote | 'The process of respiration is one of several characteristics shared by all living organisms.'

The process of breathing in and out

The process of 'breathing in' is called inspiration and involves the diaphragm lowering and the ribs rising to increase the volume of the chest cavity (thorax). Air is drawn into the lungs as the pressure decreases.

The process of 'breathing out' is known as expiration and involves the opposite movement of the ribs and diaphragm (ribs lower and diaphragm rises). This decreases the volume of the thorax, increasing the pressure and results in air being forced out of the lungs.

Once the individual has breathed in, the combination of gases (mostly oxygen and carbon dioxide) that makes up the air we breathe is transported into the lungs. The point at which these gases are exchanged from the lungs to the blood and vice versa (when breathing out) is at the wall of the alveoli, these are tiny sacs which fill with air during breathing.

Figure 1 **The diaphragm during breathing**

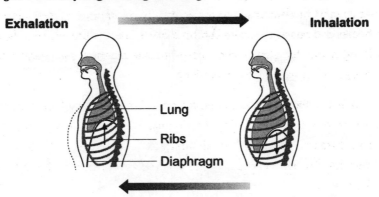

Exhalation   **Inhalation**

— Lung

— Ribs

— Diaphragm

The surface of the alveoli is thin and moist, allowing gases to pass through and be exchanged with tiny blood vessels called capillaries, which cover the surface of the alveoli. These narrow blood vessels have the job of transporting the oxygen via the bloodstream to the cells where it is used to unlock the energy from food.

It is this energy that is essential for keeping all the body's vital organs alive and fully functional.

Statistic

Alveoli are smaller than grains of salt and there are over **300 million** of them in the lungs. Collectively, their surface area is as big as half a tennis court.

While the process of 'breathing in' occurs to provide the body with oxygen to break down food and release energy, 'breathing out' occurs to rid the body of carbon dioxide.

Figures 2 and 3 **Anatomy of the lungs and gaseous exchange at the aveoli**

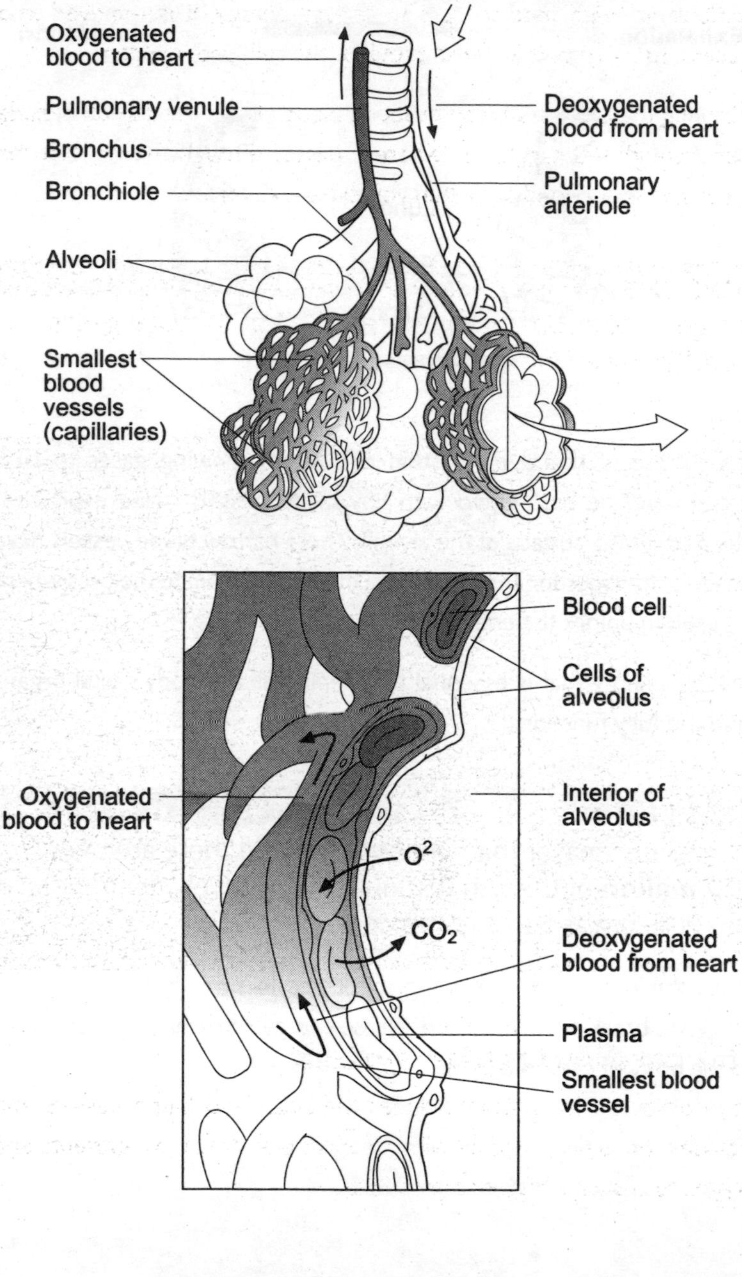

Oxygenated blood to heart

Pulmonary venule

Bronchus

Bronchiole

Alveoli

Smallest blood vessels (capillaries)

Deoxygenated blood from heart

Pulmonary arteriole

Blood cell

Cells of alveolus

Oxygenated blood to heart

Interior of alveolus

O_2

CO_2

Deoxygenated blood from heart

Plasma

Smallest blood vessel

Carbon dioxide is the waste product from the process of oxygen 'combusting' with food in cells to release energy. It is removed in a process that mirrors that which provides the cells with oxygen.

Following the process of 'combustion', blood carries the carbon dioxide back through the capillaries, where it passes through the walls of the alveoli and is breathed out when you exhale, as waste.

Statistic

Oxygen makes up approximately **21%** of the total gases found in the air we breathe.

The cardiovascular system

The cardiovascular system includes the heart and blood vessels and provides the active muscles with a continuous stream of nutrients and oxygen to sustain a high-energy output.

As with the respiratory system, the cardiovascular system is basic to life and like breathing, the beat of your own heart is an automatic function controlled by the brain.

Statistic

In a 70-year lifetime, an average human heart works for about **30 years** and rests for a total of **40 years**.

The heart is a tough, hollow muscle about the size of a fist that pumps blood around the human body. On average the human heart will beat 70 times per minute and with each beat pumps 140 ml of blood.

The heart is pear shaped, lies in the centre of the chest and has four chambers. The four chambers are made up of two atriums whose primary function is to receive blood, and two ventricles whose primary function is to pump blood.

A heart of two halves!

The right half of the heart receives oxygen-depleted blood from the veins of the body. Its function is to pump blood to the lungs where it picks up a new supply of oxygen.

The left side of the heart then receives this oxygenated blood and pumps it to the body through the arteries.

The right atrium receives blood from two large veins, the superior vena cava, which brings oxygen-poor blood from the upper part of the body, and the inferior vena cava, which brings oxygen-poor blood from the lower part of the body.

The right ventricle then pumps this oxygen-poor blood to the right and left pulmonary arteries which take it to the lungs. After the blood is oxygenated in the lungs it flows back to the left side of the heart by way of the pulmonary veins. The left atrium then receives this oxygenated

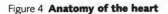

Figure 4 **Anatomy of the heart**

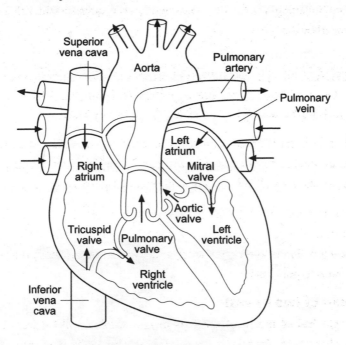

blood and the left ventricle pumps this blood out of the heart into the artery called the aorta.

The heart cycle

1   The right atrium is filled with blood from the vena cavas.

2   The blood is passed from the right atrium to the right ventricle.

3   At the same time oxygenated blood from the lungs comes from the pulmonary veins to the left side of the heart, filling the left atrium.

4   This blood is passed from the left atrium to the left ventricle.

5   To pass blood from the atriums to the ventricles the atriums contract to force the blood to pass into the ventricles.

6   The ventricles contract.

Statistic

The heart pumps approximately **4,000** gallons of blood each day.

Understanding blood

So far we have discussed the basics of the respiratory and cardiovascular systems but we have not yet looked at the crucial substance that is responsible for the delivery of oxygen and the removal of the body's waste – namely blood.

Blood is made up of a number of components all of which have important roles to play in ensuring that your blood can both deliver and remove the oxygen and waste from your body.

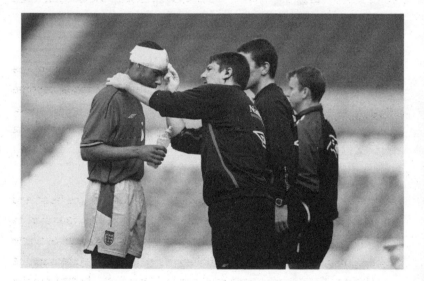

Red blood cells

These are responsible for transporting the oxygen to cells around the body and have a large surface to maximize how much oxygen they can carry.

White blood cells

These cells fight infection and make antibodies to surround and overcome bacteria.

Platelets

Platelets are in the blood so when blood is escaping through a cut, they are able to block it through the clotting process.

Plasma

This is the yellow part of the blood. It contains many substances dissolved in it such as the products of digestion.

Transporting blood

Once blood leaves the heart, it is transported around the body in three main types of blood vessels:

Arteries

Arteries transport the oxygenated blood away from the left side of the heart around the body. Like the branches of a tree, arteries become thinner as they spread out from the main arteries. These smaller branches are called arterioles, while the largest artery in the body, the aorta, is connected directly to the heart.

Veins

Veins transport used blood from all over the body back to the heart and lungs for re-oxygenation. Veins are often visible through your skin as blue lines. They are blue because they carry blood that is full of waste products and low in oxygen. The 'motorways' of the venal system are the vena cavae. The superior vena cava carries blood to the heart from the upper body, while the inferior vena cava carries blood from the lower body.

Unlike arteries veins have no pulse; there is no pump to push the blood through the venal system. Veins have thinner walls than arteries and they have lower pressure and a larger space inside. Therefore veins have to fight gravity to get the blood from the feet to the heart by using muscular contractions, which massage the veins and push the blood along. Veins also contain valves that help stop the blood falling due to gravity.

Capillaries

Capillaries are minute blood vessels that join onto the arterioles. They are one cell thick and are exchange points where the nutrients (oxygen and glucose) cross into the tissue cells (muscles) from the arterioles. Waste products from the tissues cross back into the bloodstream in the capillaries then into the venules (small veins).

Table 1 shows some of the key differences between the two main types of blood vessels:

Table 1 **Arteries vs. veins**

Arteries	Veins
Take blood away from the heart.	Take blood to the heart.
Walls are thick and elastic.	Walls are thin.
Transports oxygenated blood.	Transports de-oxygenated blood.
Has small lumen (tubular cavities inside).	Has large lumen.
Has a pulse and blood travels in spurts.	Has no pulse and blood travels smoothly.
Has no valves.	Has valves.

The muscular system

Muscles move and make us capable of a variety of actions by simply contracting and becoming shorter. Muscles are attached to bone by tendons and exert force by converting chemical energy into tension and contraction.

Muscles pull but they cannot push. They are made up of millions of tiny protein filaments that work together to produce motion in the body. In total more than 600 muscles are served by nerves which link the muscles to the brain and spinal cord.

Our bodily needs demand that muscles accomplish different chores, so we are equipped with three types of muscles:

1 Cardiac muscles – found only in the heart, power the action that pumps blood throughout the body.

2 Smooth muscles – surround or are part of the internal organs.

   (Both cardiac and smooth muscles are called involuntary muscles, because they are not consciously controlled.)

3 Skeletal muscles – the body's most abundant tissue; skeletal muscles are composed of highly specialized cells known as muscle fibre and are the only muscles to carry out voluntary movements.

Statistic

Skeletal muscles comprise approximately **23%** of a woman's body weight and about **40%** of a man's body weight.

Figure 5 **Anatomy of the skeletal muscle**

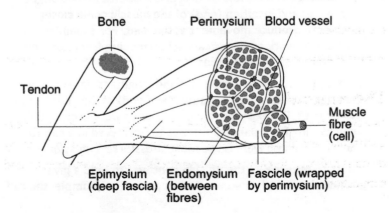

The muscular system is concerned with movement, the muscle tissue being made up of cells that have contractile properties. Skeletal muscles work in conjunction with the skeleton, whilst smooth and cardiac muscles produce movement of the internal organs.

Irrespective of whether muscle is skeletal, smooth or cardiac, the function of muscle is to generate tension and so exert force. The effectiveness of this force production has a fundamental impact on performance during sport and exercise.

There are four physical properties of a skeletal muscle:

1 Excitability – the ability to respond to certain stimuli i.e. from the nervous system.

2 Contractibility – the ability to shorten and generate tension in response to stimuli from the nervous system.

3 Extensibility – the ability to stretch and increase in length without damaging muscle tissue.

4 Elasticity – the ability to return to resting length and shape after stretching.

Types of muscle action

Skeletal muscle can produce three types of contraction:

1 **Concentric** – the muscle contracts and shortens. The origin (beginning) and insertion (end) of the muscle come closer together to produce movement at the joint. For example, the calf muscles work concentrically when moving from standing flat-footed to standing on toes.

2 **Eccentric** – the muscle contracts and lengthens under tension. The origin and insertion (beginning and end) of the muscle move further apart. For example, the calf muscles work eccentrically when moving from standing on toes to flat-footed in a controlled manner. Eccentric work is the most stressful to a muscle.

3 **Static (isometric)** – the muscle contracts to hold a given position. No actual movement takes place. For example, the calf

muscles work statically when holding the position of standing on toes.

Major muscle actions

The following is a brief overview of the principal skeletal muscles involved with body movement.

■ Use Figures 6 and 7 on page 15 to locate some of the muscles discussed below on your own body.

Back muscles

This muscle group surrounds the spine, acting to extend, flex laterally and rotate the trunk and neck.

Abdominals

The abdominals include rectus abdominis, the transverse abdominis (deepest abdominal muscle) and the internal and external obliques, running from the ribs to the pelvis. These muscles combine to stabilize, flex, laterally flex and rotate the trunk.

Gluteal muscles

The gluteal muscles include gluetus maximus, gluteus minimus and gluteus medius, which combine to abduct and adduct (move the leg out to the side and back), and rotate the hip. Gluteus maximus also acts to extend the hip, swinging the leg powerfully backwards during running.

Hip muscles (flexors)

These run from the pelvis down onto the thighbone. They act to flex the hip, bringing the thigh upwards, for example during the high-knee drive whilst sprinting.

Front thigh muscles

The quadriceps are made up of four muscles (rectus femoris, vastus medialis, vastus lateralis and vastus intermedius) acting as powerful knee extensors. Rectus femoris also acts to flex the hip joint as it passes from above the hip to below the knee, thus referred to as a two-joint muscle.

Rear thigh muslces

The hamstring muscles, biceps femoris, semimembranosus and semitendinosus are all powerful knee flexors, also acting to extend the hip joint.

Inner thigh muscles

The muscles around the groin (adductors) of which there are five, act to adduct the thigh, for example, bringing the leg back in when running sideways, some also acting as rotators and flexors of the thigh.

Lower leg muscles

Muscles at the front of the lower leg and around the shin act to dorsiflex the ankle (bring the toes towards the shin). Muscles at the back of the lower leg, namely gastrocnemius, soleus and tibialis posterior all plantarflex the ankle (this is to extend or straighten the ankle, point the toes down). The gastrocnemius muscle also assists in knee flexion (two-joint muscle).

Figures 6 and 7 **Major muscle groups**

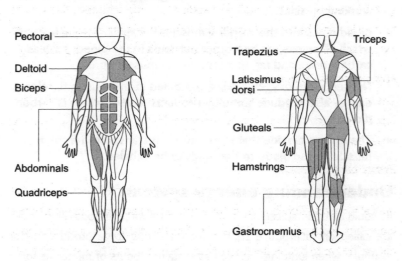

Quote	'Some muscles such as hamstrings and gastrocnemius cross two joints and are commonly torn or strained during football activities, such as sprinting and kicking a ball, particularly if the muscles are cold and tight or if they are fatigued – a common factor associated with muscular strains.'

Teamwork of the major systems

Now that you have read and begun to understand how the major systems of the body that are most directly connected to fitness work, here is a summary of their major functions and their relationship with each other.

- Exercising muscles gain a significant amount of energy through the combination of food stuffs (nutrients) and oxygen.

- Oxygen contained in the air is inhaled and passes into the lungs from where it diffuses into the blood.

- The heart acts as the pump supplying oxygenated blood to the working muscles.

- Blood flows into the working muscles in capillaries, the walls of which allow oxygen and other nutrients in the blood, such as carbohydrate and fat, to pass into the muscle fibres.

- Nutrients and oxygen having combined in the muscle to release energy also produce some by-products, one of which is carbon dioxide.

- The carbon dioxide that is produced, is transported from the muscle by the blood to the lungs to be exhaled.

Understanding energy systems

It should be understood that muscles produce force. In football, muscles are called on to produce short bouts of strong force production (for example, when jumping), as well as sustained bouts of moderate force production (for example, when jogging). In each case, if performance is to be effective, energy has to be provided to meet these demands.

Muscles need energy to function. This energy is derived from the breakdown of various substrates (fat, carbohydrate and protein).

There are two key methods of energy production and both are used in very different ways when performing different tasks.

Aerobic

Aerobic energy production refers to the process of energy production using oxygen. The aerobic energy system is used to fuel low intensity endurance activities, such as walking, jogging and running at low to moderate speeds.

It is this type of energy production that is improved as a result of 'endurance training' and is critical to provide any footballer with a strong fitness base from which he/she can improve other aspects of their overall fitness.

Improvements in the body's ability to produce energy aerobically increases the body's ability to recover from physical activity. In a footballing sense this means that if you're a speedy winger, you will be more able to recover quickly from sprints up and down the touchline, enabling you to make more forward runs and track back more often to help your defence.

When coaches talk about players with 'good engines' that can constantly run from 'box to box', this refers to the fact that they have high aerobic capabilities.

Anaerobic

Oxygen transported to the exercising muscles is not always sufficient for aerobic energy production alone to meet these energy demands. This is particularly true at the start of exercise when rapid changes in energy demand take place and also during periods of intense exercise.

In these instances energy is also produced in the absence of oxygen, namely through anaerobic energy production.

Good anaerobic power is needed for the performance of activities such as jumping, turning and accelerating since high levels of force are required to be produced quickly.

A high anaerobic capacity is important for sustaining periods of high intensity exercise such as repeatedly performing sprints with limited recovery periods.

Statistic

88% of all activities involve aerobic energy production.

▓ Next time you take part in any physical exercise think about which sources of energy you are using.

Summary

- The systems of the body that are more immediately related to fitness are the respiratory, cardiovascular, muscular and energy systems.

- Blood is responsible for the delivery of oxygen and removal of the body's waste.

- Oxygen is used to unlock the energy from food stored in the body's cells.

- Aerobic and anaerobic are the two key energy systems used by the body.

Self testers

- Name the process used to describe 'breathing in'.
- Why are cardiac muscles and smooth muscles described as involuntary?
- What is the difference between aerobic and anaerobic energy systems?

Action plan

Be more aware   The next time you're training or exercising be aware of which muscles and which energy system you are using, and think about how your heart and lungs are reacting to the increased workload.

Chapter 2

The body's response to exercise

THIS CHAPTER WILL:
- Give you an understanding of how the cardiovascular and respiratory systems respond to exercise.
- Look at the relationship between heart rate and exercise intensity.
- Consider the importance of the process of sweating and changes in body temperature.

During exercise, physiological mechanisms (respiratory, cardiovascular and muscular systems) operate to enable the individual to meet new energy demands. Providing that exercise (training) is of the appropriate frequency, intensity and duration, improvements in performance should take place and these improvements reflect physiological adaptations that have occurred.

The advantage of strong genes

Research has proven that there is a genetic component to success. However, performance is not only attributable to genetic factors and

training will determine to what extent an individual's genetic potential is realized. Furthermore, while some people are born with a head start, it does not mean that other less naturally gifted people cannot see massive improvements providing they train and work hard.

To make it to the top, most players will benefit from a combination of both natural ability (genetics) and a determination to succeed. This means plenty of sacrifice to improve all aspects of their natural game, including fitness levels.

As with all sports and at all levels, some people have to work harder than others to succeed and football is full of professionals whose determination to succeed has more than made up for their lack of natural ability. On the other hand, there are also many examples of very talented footballers who have relied too much on natural talent and never fulfilled their potential.

Quite simply, providing your training programme is well planned and designed for your appropriate level of fitness your body should respond positively to the exercise, which means that over a period of time you should begin to see an improvement in your overall fitness levels.

Quote	'Genetics play a major role in determining individual's physical characteristics so choose your parents wisely.'

Respiratory system

The body's respiratory system responds in quite obvious ways whenever we exercise, the most noticeable being a shortness of breath.

The reason for shortness of breath is because as we begin to exercise, the body uses more energy. When exercising, the muscles' demand for oxygen dramatically increases and in order to maintain the energy level

required the lungs will increase the rate at which they inhale and exhale in an attempt to increase the amount of oxygen being provided.

The reason for a reduction in the shortness of breath once we begin to take part in regular exercise is that our lungs begin to improve their 'capacity' and efficiency, also known as the 'rate of ventilation'.

The rate of ventilation refers to the amount of air inhaled or exhaled in one minute. When resting, a typical rate would be 5 l per minute, however during a match, the demands of a professional footballer can be as high as 200 l per minute.

By exercising regularly, our lungs begin to increase their ventilation rates and so with each breath they can inhale more oxygen and exhale more carbon dioxide. As the lungs become stronger and more efficient, fewer breaths are needed to maintain the oxygen levels required by the muscles and so shortness in breath is reduced, allowing players to maintain higher energy levels for longer.

A number of factors can affect ventilation, such as altitude. When playing at altitude the body compensates for the fact that there is less oxygen in the air by increasing the rate of ventilation. Clearly, this would have been a factor during the 1970 and 1986 World Cup finals held in Mexico. The reduction of oxygen in the air is the reason why many professional sportspeople and professional football teams use altitude training to improve fitness.

Quote | 'During their preparations for what was a successful 1986 World Cup in Mexico, the Danish players trained using equipment which lowered the oxygen content of the air breathed.'

Different types of exercise will impact differently on our lungs, depending on the activity and the energy requirements. Therefore it is important to design training programmes that incorporate the types of physical demands that will be placed on an individual during a match.

■ Next time you're playing in a match be aware of your body's response from a bout of high intensity work and judge how long it takes to recover and regain your breath.

Cardiovascular system

Several things happen to your heart while you exercise. Your heart rate (the number of times your heart beats per minute) increases to pump more blood to the muscles all over the body, which are working harder. Therefore, your cardiac output increases, which is the amount of blood that the heart pumps out to the body per minute.

As the heart rate increases so does cardiac output. The other important component to consider is stroke volume. This is the amount of blood pumped out of the heart with each contraction of the ventricle. An average adult's stroke volume is about 70 ml. When resting, the heart has a cardiac output of about 5 l.

The heart rate and stroke volume combined are therefore the two contributory factors to determining cardiac output.

Cardiac output

Cardiac output refers to the amount of blood that is pumped per minute by the heart. This gives an indication of the rate of oxygen delivery to the exercising skeletal muscles.

cardiac output = stroke volume × heart rate

At rest, cardiac output is roughly 5 l per minute rising up to 25 l per minute during intensive exercise. This increased cardiac output coincides with a redistribution of blood flow, with most of the blood directed toward active muscles.

Appropriate training will improve the heart's capacity to pump blood, which will increase cardiac output. A cardiac output of up to 40 l per minute has been recorded in highly trained professional footballers.

Enhancing cardiac output through training leads to increased blood supply and therefore oxygen delivery to the exercising muscles during intense exercise.

Heart rate
The heart reacts in a number of ways to exercise, the most obvious of which that can be felt by the individual is an increased heart rate, i.e. the speed at which your heart pumps blood around the body.

Heart rate, one of the two primary determinants of cardiac output also rises in line with work rate. At rest, heart rate can be as low as 30 beats per minute in well-trained athletes, with most people having a resting heart rate of approximately 60 beats per minute.

■   Measure your resting heart rate, and see how you compare to a well-trained athlete. Take your heart rate by measuring your pulse by placing two fingers over your wrist or the side of your neck.

Statistic
On average a heart beats approximately **86,400** times a day.

The environment will influence heart rate. Exercise at altitude and in the heat will lead to an increased heart rate response for a given bout of physical work. However, after a period of appropriate endurance training the heart rate will be lower at a given exercise intensity (see Figure 8). This is because as the cardiac muscles (found around the heart) become stronger they are able to pump more blood around the body in a single beat, increasing stroke volume, which means that fewer beats are required to meet the body's demands.

Figure 8 **Change in heart rate response following training**

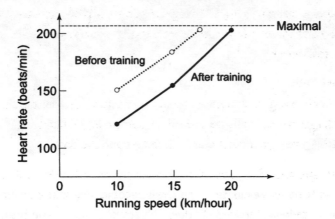

Stroke volume

Stroke volume is the other primary determinant of cardiac output, representing the amount of blood pumped from the heart during each beat.

Appropriate endurance training increases the strength of the musculature around the heart and allows the heart to hold more blood. As a result the heart is able to pump out more blood per heartbeat.

Heart rate varies according to the amount of exercise you are doing. When you are sleeping deeply, your heart rate drops to a very slow rate to give the heart time to rest. When you are exercising hard, your heart rate can go up as much as almost three times its resting rate.

When the heart is exercised regularly it becomes larger and the volume of the chambers increases, as does the stroke volume. The heart of a trained athlete can pump more blood, and therefore more oxygen and nutrients, to the working muscles in the body each time the ventricles contract. So each beat of the heart pumps more blood than the average person, because the heart is larger. Therefore it will require less effort by the heart to do ordinary things like walking up a flight of stairs or running for the bus.

Quote | 'The benefits accrued after a period of well-structured endurance training will include a significant increase in the amount of oxygen delivered to the exercising muscle.'

Blood

The average adult has 5 l of blood. Approximately one third of the blood consists of red blood cells and the other two thirds consist of a fluid called plasma.

Red blood cells contain the protein haemoglobin, which gives blood its red colour and transports oxygen around the body. The blood plasma transports essential nutrients to the working muscles, including carbohydrate, protein and fat. It also acts to remove waste products such as lactate. Lactate is a substance produced during anaerobic exercise which is associated with the sensation of fatigue.

Appropriate endurance training does not increase the concentration of haemoglobin but will lead to an increase in blood volume. Top endurance athletes have been reported to have up to 7 l of blood after many years of training. It follows that one's capacity to supply oxygen to the muscles is enhanced by an increase in blood volume.

How the body reacts to exercise

Body temperature

The internal temperature of the body is often referred to as the core temperature. This is normally kept within a narrow range of 36.5–37.5 °C, as it is at this temperature that many of the bodily functions work most efficiently.

A large portion of the energy generated during aerobic and anaerobic metabolism is lost as heat. This is partly beneficial as when we exercise the heat generated helps warm up the muscles which function best at a temperature of 38.5 °C. However, more than this can lead to poor functioning of body systems and it is therefore important for the body to distribute and release the heat from the body. One way of releasing heat is by sweating.

Sweating

Sweating plays an important role in regulating temperature during exercise. Sweat provides effective cooling as it evaporates, helping to maintain or reduce the internal temperature of the body. We rely on sweating to varying degrees, hence some people are seen to sweat a lot and others not so much. Sweating is not a sign of being unfit, but rather a sign of the body performing a role it is designed to do.

Heavy legs

Players often have the sensation of heavy legs during the early periods of the season. This is generally due to unaccustomed exercise and insufficient energy stores in the working muscles. Players can also get this type of sensation from brief bouts of high intensity exercise when there is an increase in the acidity of the muscle due to the production of lactic acid.

Aching muscles

Muscles are known to be sore or ache after periods of unaccustomed exercise or eccentric muscle work. This type of exercise can lead to a delayed onset of muscle soreness (DOMS), which may be experienced two days after a bout of exercise.

Good preparation and appropriate training will help reduce the severity of aching muscles.

Summary

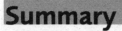

- **Genes play an important role in fitness levels but dedication to training is critical in developing fitness.**

- **By exercising regularly, our lungs begin to increase their ventilation rate and become stronger and more efficient.**

- **When you exercise your heart rate (the number of times your heart beats per minute) and cardiac output (the amount of blood that the heart pumps out to the body) increases.**

Self testers

- What is the average resting heart rate?
- Why do we get a shortness of breath when exercising?
- How do you calculate cardiac output?

Action plan

Be more aware The next time you're training or exercising be aware of your body's reaction to exercise in terms of cardiovascular system and measure your resting heart rate and then your heart rate at the end of your training.

Chapter 3

The game's physical and physiological demands

THIS CHAPTER WILL:

- Give you an understanding of the key elements that make up physical fitness.
- Introduce you to the four S's.
- Consider the different positions and roles within a team and their physiological demands on the player.

Quote | 'The demands imposed on footballers are numerous and require players to develop every aspect of their physiological capabilities.'

The physiological demands of football are more complex than in many individual sports since players require some of the physiological attributes of both marathon runners and sprinters. The demands on players vary depending on the level of performance, positional role and style of play incorporated by a team.

The various demands placed on players at all levels during a match include:

- Short sprints,
- Slow jogging,
- Walking,
- Running backwards, sideways, and diagonally,
- Accelerating and decelerating,
- Jumping,
- Tackling,
- Kicking,
- Changing direction,
- Contesting for possession,
- The ability to recover rapidly.

As a result, the various components that make up the overall fitness of a player as well as their energy systems within the body (the systems that produce energy either with or without oxygen) are put under various degrees of stress, so there is a need for them to be adequately developed.

Several researchers have studied the work-rate and activity profiles of elite professional footballers through match analysis techniques. The following player demands have been commonly identified during a game:

- Runs between 5–8 miles (8–13 km).
- Exercises at a pace that represents 70–80% of their endurance capacity.
- Walks, sprints, jogs, cruises, stretches, jumps, passes, heads, tackles and shoots.
- Contact with the ball for two to three minutes.
- Turns some 400–50 times through 90° or more during the game.

Football is commonly classified as a multiple-sprint sport characterized by short periods of high-intensity exercise randomly interspersed with periods of active or passive recovery. In addition to the physical activity, the player must be mentally prepared to make split-second decisions in an ever-changing environment. Although factors such as skill, technique and motivation will be crucial in the preparation of the player and team, fitness has an influence on them all.

The four S's

In general terms fitness is often referred to as being made up of four S's, namely:

- **Speed,**
- **Strength,**
- **Stamina (or cardiovascular endurance),**
- **Suppleness (or flexibility).**

Figure 9 **The four S's**

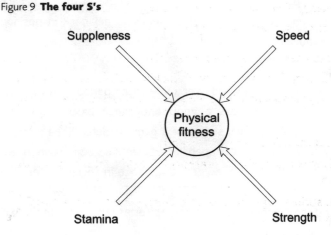

Quote | 'Through planning, natural attributes can be nurtured and improved.'

Strength

Strength enhances the performance and execution of many football skills. Every skill that a player must perform against resistance will benefit from the improvement of strength. Strength training is not just about improving a player in terms of his/her ability to be 'strong' on the ball, it is a fundamental component of training that will affect every movement that a player performs whilst on the field of play.

Speed

Speed is an essential component of the game today and it is therefore important that this area is thoroughly developed. It is also important to remember that not all speed work is about quick sprints but often about concentrated intensive spells lasting much longer than a few seconds.

Many activities in football involve intense periods of activity, which require a player to have a good level of what is termed speed endurance. For example, intense periods occur when a midfield player successively closes down opponents over a period of 30 seconds, or when a fullback goes on an overlapping run and then needs to get back in position because the move has broken down.

Stamina

The fact that the game is played over a 90-minute period highlights the need for players to possess a good endurance base. A player's performance during the final stages of a game is determined in many respects by his/her endurance capabilities. Scientific studies have shown that enhancing aerobic (with oxygen) endurance in soccer players can improve their performance by increasing the distance covered, the work intensity and the number of sprints and episodes involved with the ball during a game.

Be aware that muscles that are cold and tight or fatigued are more likely to suffer from strains and tears.

Sweating is not a sign of being unfit but rather a sign of the body performing a role that it is designed to do.

In general terms, fitness is often referred to as being made up of the four Ss, namely: speed

strength

stamina

suppleness

Football is a late specialization sport. With improved knowledge of training methods and nutrition players can maintain their career at the highest level for longer.

Quote	'The French team proved in the final of Euro 2000 that the ability to perform at the best of your abilities for the full 90 minutes and into extra time is vital at the highest level.'

Statistic

In a successful season a player can play over **6,000 minutes (100 hours)** of competitive football.

Suppleness

The flexibility requirements of footballers varies depending on the position and role of the player in the same way as it varies between sports. For example, footballers do not have to have the same levels of flexibility as Olympic gymnasts but they should be supple enough to complete the range of movements required during a match, e.g. stretching for the ball.

Different positions and their different requirements

Speed, stamina, suppleness and strength combine to produce the overall fitness level of the individual. However, it is important to realize that football is made up of a team of 11 individuals with different positions and roles to play and so the requirements for each player will be different.

In basic terms football teams are made up of four key positions (goalkeeper, defender, midfielder and strikers) but we are going to look at all the likely positions players may be asked to play within their teams, as highlighted in the following line up.

Figure 10 **4-4-2 formation using a 'diamond' shaped midfield**

Goalkeeper

The crucial physical attributes required by a goalkeeper are speed, strength and suppleness. For example, speed will need to be harnessed when the goalkeeper has to rush out of the 18-yard box to intercept a pass or rushes out to close down the angle of a striker's shot.

Suppleness is obviously a critical factor for goalkeepers so that they are flexible enough to stretch for the ball in an attempt to save a shot, while strength will be needed when a goalkeeper comes to claim a corner kick through a crowd of players.

■ The next time you watch a goalkeeper attempt to save a penalty think of the different physical attributes required at that moment.

Centre back

Centre backs need to be strong and quick as well as having the stamina to last for 90 minutes. Typically, centre backs will need to be able to jump and challenge for the ball as well as having the speed to cut out passes and then the strength to hold off attackers.

The position of centre back is one that requires a lot of power (strength and speed) that is released in quick short bursts of energy, while under sustained spells of pressure. The centre backs will also require stamina and a quick recovery time so that they can make numerous challenges, turn and sprint etc.

Fullback

The position of fullback requires a lot of stamina and speed as in a typical game a fullback will be expected to cover a lot of ground up and down the touchline.

Making attacking overlapping runs and then having to get back if the ball is lost to cover their defensive duties means that fullbacks require a great deal of stamina, while having to get back into position as quickly as possible means that speed is also an essential requirement.

Wingback

The position of wingback is the most physically demanding position and although it requires very similar attributes to a fullback, arguably the player's stamina levels need to be even greater. The role of wingback will mean the individuals are responsible for covering both roles as an attacking winger and defensive fullback. Eventually the position of wingback is a progression on from fullback.

■ The next time you watch a match, watch the fullbacks and count how many times they make forward runs and then have to track back to help with the defence.

Holding midfielder

In this position the player will be required to constantly put pressure on the opponent's midfielders and therefore cover a lot of ground, often with little time to rest and recover. This means that excellent stamina is critical for a holding midfielder.

If asked to play this sort of role, the player will also require excellent strength as he/she will be attempting to put in a lot of tackles and make many challenges in an attempt to win back the ball.

Winger

The attributes required for a winger are very similar to those required for a fullback – namely speed and stamina – as wingers will also usually be expected to assist their fullbacks defensively.

When playing on the wing the player will be expected to track back and assist the fullback as often as he/she is expected to push forward and create chances for the strikers. In order to do this the player has to have excellent stamina as well as speed.

Attacking midfielder

Speed, strength and stamina are all critical elements for anyone playing this role. In the same way as their more defensive-minded teammates, attacking midfielders will still be expected to make many tackles and challenges in the centre of the pitch. As a result strength is critical to ensure that tackles are won for the team.

When 'going forward' it is often the role of the attacking midfielder to arrive late in the box at the crucial time to get the vital goal – this is where speed is essential.

However, any attacking midfielder will still be expected to assist the team with their defensive duties. This means that they will also cover a lot of ground, which makes stamina an essential attribute.

Statistic

When tested some professional footballers have been known to run up to **15 km** in a single game.

Attacker (Target man)

The key attribute for this role is strength. The ability to perform this often thankless task for 90 minutes means that stamina is also an essential requirement of any striker.

If you think of successful strikers such as Emile Heskey, James Beattie or John Hartson, although they all have slightly different skills and attributes, they all possess excellent strength.

Attacker (Speedy striker)

The most obvious attribute required of a striker is speed, so that he/she can make runs on to through balls played from the midfield and get

ahead of opponent defenders. Strength and stamina are also crucial attributes when playing this role.

Strength is required to hold off defenders when running on to passes or when jumping to challenge for a header, while stamina is needed so that even in the 90th minute strikers can still look to make runs behind the defence and get that all-important goal.

Statistic

In the previous two World Cup finals more than **20%** of all the goals scored were in the final **15 minutes**.

In every match strikers make many forward runs that do not lead to a goal and in order to continue to do this throughout the game they require excellent stamina.

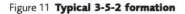   The next time you watch a match spend a few minutes following the strikers and observe how many forward runs they make.

How tactics define the attributes required

The role of a manager is to pick the team and the tactics, and often the tactics played will have a bearing on the physical attributes required of the players.

For example, if a coach is looking to play the 3-5-2 formation, as shown in Figure 11, there are a number of roles that will require certain key physical attributes from his/her players. In particular, both wingbacks will need to have very high stamina levels as well as being quick and strong if they are to perform the role effectively. While in this situation the

Figure 11 **Typical 3-5-2 formation**

manager will also need to have a strong and powerful player to play the role of target man alongside a player who has a lot of stamina and speed to play up front alongside him/her.

It will often be the case that a manager's tactics will be influenced not just by the skills of the players but also by their physical attributes and fitness levels. This is particularly the case in grassroots football where players will have less time to train and so should not be expected to be as physically fit as their professional counterparts.

Therefore, the manager will always need to be aware of his/her players' fitness levels as well as their technical strengths and weaknesses as this could affect their ability to play in certain positions for the team.

The other critical reason that a manager must be aware of the physical attributes of his/her players is so that he/she can provide training to match their needs in order to help the players improve their game. For example, if you have a player who is a great finisher but only ever lasts 45 minutes before becoming fatigued it should be the role of the manager to assist the player and improve his/her stamina, enabling performance of the highest possible level for the duration of the match.

Summary

- **The four S's are fundamental components of fitness.**

- **Different positions require different attributes.**

- **Different tactics will impact on the physical attributes required of the players.**

Self testers

- Name the four S's.
- What are the critical physical requirements of centre backs?
- What are the critical physical requirements of goalkeepers?

Action plan

The next time you watch a game take a look at the formation and tactics played by the coach and decide if you think it matches the physical attributes of the players.

Chapter 4

The differences between adults and young players

> THIS CHAPTER WILL:
> - Give you an understanding of the concept of trainability.
> - Provide information on the appropriate age to train youngsters and in what aspects of the game.
> - Help you to remember that the game is fun!

It must be clearly understood by coaches training young players that they are not 'mini-adults'. This can easily be forgotten.

As children grow and mature, their physical needs and capabilities change. Boys and girls differ in their responses to exercise which are more apparent following puberty. Strength levels are generally greater in males due to the smaller percentage of body fat while a smaller heart and blood volume contributes to a higher heart rate response to exercise in females. From as young as five or six years of age there are gender-related differences in children's responses to exercise.

These differences are magnified as boys and girls grow and it is vital that coaches involved in their development and training understand how to nurture talent whilst protecting the young players' welfare as they continue to develop physically.

Growth and maturation are closely related, although the two are totally different processes. Growth refers to an increase in the size of the body or its parts; maturation is progress toward the mature or adult biological state. Growth does not stop when maturity is reached but continues throughout life as in nearly every tissue and organ there is a cycle of growth, death and regeneration.

The principles according to which adults train and play cannot be directly applied to young players because of the differences in the maturity of the skeletal, muscular and cardiovascular systems. Training must be adapted to their development, being progressed slowly while laying down suitable foundations. This fact may easily be ignored by parents or well-meaning coaches who coax and cajole their pre-adolescent protégés to swifter, higher and stronger competitive levels.

Figure 12 **Growth dynamics to show average annual growth rates in boys**

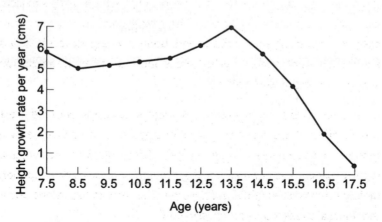

Figure 12 highlights that 'growth spurts' occur from ten years through to 15 years of age. However, it should be noted that significant growth occurs from 8.5 years through to 15.5 years of age and continues past 18 years of age for some.

Increased potential for injury

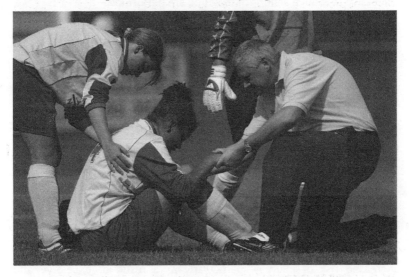

It is during the early and adolescent years of life that the body's muscles and bones develop and grow. The young player may be more susceptible to injury during this period. Bone in young players is still not mature; it has not yet fully ossified and is under considerable stress from strong maturing muscle action.

Injuries resulting from 'overplay' (playing too regularly with little rest) usually affect the parts of the skeleton that constitute attachments of tendons and ligaments. In children and adolescents who participate in regular training and competition, the strength of muscles develop more rapidly than the strength of the skeleton. This may be hazardous due to the unusual stress it puts on the skeleton.

It is proposed that bone grows faster than soft tissues such as muscles and tendons, which become tighter with growth, particularly during 'growth spurts'. This loss of flexibility can be a factor in increasing the risk of injury.

Football involves the forceful actions of running, jumping, landing, kicking and fast direction changes. The chance of injury can increase if excessive repetitive actions of this type are performed.

Because of the stages of development that the body is going through and particularly up until the age of 14/15 years of age, coaches need to be aware of the demands they place on their young players and adapt their training methods to the development of their players.

Statistic
Football is now the most popular sport played by girls as well as boys.

Different training needs for young players – keep it varied

As highlighted above, as young players' bodies develop there is an increased risk of injury – particularly as a result of excessive and repetitive movements that focus on a particular part of the body.

For example, if during a 90-minute training session, the coach runs three ten-minute sessions of jumping and heading practice there would be an increased chance of injury to the knees or ankle joints. This is because this would be the area of the body taking the impact of this particular training drill.

If the same coach had devised a 90-minute training session that only had one jumping and heading practice, one turning with the ball practice and one shooting practice, the chances of injury would be reduced. This is because different areas of the body would be taking the impact of these training drills.

Keeping training sessions varied and interesting will not only help young players to improve their chance of avoiding injury but should also assist the young players' interest and motivation levels.

The Official FA Guide to Basic Team Coaching title in this series looks at a variety of training sessions suitable for young players and will assist any coach looking to increase the variety in their training sessions.

■ If you're a coach of a team involving young players think about how varied you make your training sessions.

Coaches need to understand their younger players

The young player is physiologically unique from the adult and must be considered differently. Generally, the youngster will adapt well to the same type of training routine used by the mature athlete, but training programmes for children and adolescents should be designed specifically for each age group, bearing in mind the developmental factors associated with their age.

As we saw, Figure 12 on page 52 shows growth velocity for stature for boys. Statural growth occurs at a constantly decelerating rate – the child is getting bigger, but at a slower rate. The rate reaches its lowest point since birth just before initiation of the adolescent spurt.

Young players' growth patterns result in variations in anatomical factors such as limb length, the stability of muscle-tendon-bone attachments, relative muscle/bone length and vulnerability to bone at growth plates or muscle attachments. There are also physiological factors such as decreased cardiovascular endurance, muscle strength and flexibility.

Decreased flexibility is common in young players. It is generally caused by the different rates of growth in bones and muscles, so that the muscles are relatively shorter than the bones. The areas subject to the greatest growth are the back and the legs, therefore muscles acting on these areas i.e. the quadriceps, hamstrings, iliotibial band, and back extensor muscles are most likely to show this tightness.

Long-term development of young players

The section below summarizes the three phases of development and the types of training and areas of development that the coach should be focusing his/her attentions on in each phase.

Fundamental phase (6–11 years)

The fundamental phase of development is a multilateral phase that lays a foundation on which future development is built. This is the time when the young player will begin to learn the basic skills that will continue to be used throughout his/her playing career.

This is also the stage at which the young player is least developed physically and therefore has limited endurance (stamina) and strength levels, therefore training should be focused on technique and playing rather than fitness and strength training.

Football should be all about having fun, doing something you enjoy and being part of a team and so the coach needs to ensure that his/her players enjoy their first experiences of the game.

The key implications for coaches working with this age group are summarized below.

- **Basic skills should be developed, such as passing, shooting, heading, controlling the ball, turning with the ball, etc.**
- **Activities should be of a short duration with endurance being developed through play and games and not endurance training.**
- **Use slow progression in hopping and jumping activities and strength training should be limited to technique development.**
- **Specific activities and games should emphasize co-ordination.**

Training to train phase (11–14 years)

During this phase of development, athletic formation begins to take place with the body and its capacities develop rapidly.

This is also the time when the percentage of players that begin to drop out increases as players begin to find other activities; computer games, socializing with friends, other sports and discovery of the opposite sex demand more of their time, therefore coaches need to ensure that they maintain their players' interest in the game.

Ensuring training sessions are still fun, varied and involve competitive elements such as five-a-side matches will help maintain interest and hopefully begin to keep more teenagers in the game.

The key implications for coaches working with this age group are summarized below.

- **Remember that chronological age may not be the most appropriate way to group players as young people develop at different rates so compare height, body mass, strength, etc. instead.**

- Players should learn how to train during this phase, including physical, technical, tactical and ancillary capacities (e.g. warm-up, cool-down, nutrition, rest, recovery, etc.).

- Some previously learned skills might need refinement, as limb growth will impact on technique, balance and co-ordination.

- Focus on speed work either during or immediately after the warm-up and not when players are tired at the end of a training session.

Training to compete phase (14–20 years)

The biggest changes in training occur during this phase. The exercises undertaken are aimed at development, but with the intensity and volume of work gradually increasing.

The key implications for coaches working with this age group are summarized below.

- **Aerobic and anaerobic systems become fully developed and can be trained for maximum output.**

- **Strength training can be maximized to improve overall strength development and training of the nervous system should be optimized.**
- **Learning how to compete is important, incorporating all technical, tactical and ancillary components into performance.**

As highlighted in the 'Training to train' phase, as the young players' age increases more players drop out of the game and the role of the coach is critical to maintaining the interest and motivation of the young player.

Football as a sport has many positive outcomes for those that regularly participate, including:

- **Fitness,**
- **Teamwork,**
- **Competitiveness,**
- **Responsibility to others (i.e. teammates),**
- **Social skills.**

This is why we need to maintain the interests of young players in this age group at such a crucial time in their development and the coach is central to this along with teachers and parents.

Long-term development – summary

In the long-term development programme it should be apparent that there is a gradual change from general to specific conditioning of players as they pass through the various stages of athletic development.

The coach needs to be aware that at the younger age groups the players' training should concentrate on the technical aspects of the game as this is when basics skills are learned, while ensuring training is varied and the emphasis is on playing and having fun.

Best Practice Don't expect too much too soon and plan with the long-term development of the player as the overall objective.

As the players develop physiologically, training can begin to develop the physical aspects required, such as strength and stamina throughout specific and targeted training. However, coaches must remember that varied and competitive elements of training will be necessary to maintain the interest and motivation of players.

Early vs. late specialization

Figure 13 shows the difference between early and late specialization sports. In this example we have used gymnastics to compare with football.

Figure 13 **Early specialization explained**

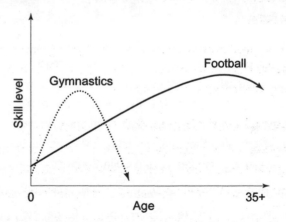

In gymnastics the training of young athletes is more intensive than in football and begins at a much earlier age as most gymnasts will only participate in competitions until their late teens, although many male competitors will continue to their early and mid 20's. When compared to football gymnastics is an early specialization sport.

The potential playing career of a footballer is much longer than a gymnast's, especially at grassroots level with players regularly participating well in to their 40's. Even within the professional game there are many examples of footballers continuing to participate at the highest level long after their 35th birthday. For example, Paulo Maldini, Rob Lee, Paul Ince, Stuart Pearce and Colin Cooper.

In football players improve and mature at different rates and in many cases the player's position (e.g. goalkeeper, defender etc.) has a major impact on the time taken to specialize. For example, many experts would argue that central defenders peak in their late 20's as key attributes other than the purely physical, such as decision-making and composure take time to develop.

If a player does not develop until his/her mid to late 20's, coaches need to realize that young players, and especially those just starting to play competitive football, should be able to have fun whilst learning the technical aspects of the game through playing matches and specific technical practices. They should not have to spend large portions of their training time working at the physical aspects until their bodies reach sufficient maturity.

It should also be remembered that playing regularly will help younger players to develop the physical aspects of their game naturally. Through training matches and competitive play young players will begin to develop stamina, strength and speed while also learning the skills that will improve their enjoyment of the game.

How much sport does the child play?

For many children football may be only one of a number of sports that the child plays on a regular basis. The sports available to children to play in an organized capacity are greater than at any time in the past and this can mean that although a child only plays football a couple of times a week his/her overall sporting schedule may be increasing their chances of overloading type injuries.

Although keeping track of a player's other sporting commitments is difficult for a football coach to be aware of (unless they coach them at other sports), it is important that the coach tries to keep in contact with the player and parents as excessive playing and training without suitable progression has the potential to be detrimental to the player's fitness and health.

Although we always promote a fit and active, healthy lifestyle involving plenty of exercise, it is important that young players allow their bodies time to recover from exercise.

Maintaining a sensible balance of rest and play should ensure that the chances of injury are reduced and that the playing careers of young players are extending into their 20's, 30's and 40's with a reduced number of injuries that are typically associated with over training.

■ If you're a parent think about how much sport your children play and look at whether they allow time in their schedules to rest and recover.

■ If you're a coach of a team, ask the players how many sports they play and how often, in order to gain an insight in to the stresses they place on their bodies.

Summary

- **Young players are not 'mini-adults'.**

- **As children grow and mature, their physical needs and capabilities change.**

- **Training must be tailored and aligned to the development of the young players' physical needs and capabilities.**

Self testers

- Why is there an increased risk of injury for younger players?
- What are the differences between early and late specialization sports?
- Why do football coaches need to be aware of other sports children play?

Action plan

Review your training programme for your team of young players and ensure that it meets their developmental needs, their physical capabilities and that it is FUN!

Chapter 5

Basic training principles – planning a programme

THIS CHAPTER WILL:
- Explain how to structure a training session.
- Provide pre-pre-season training advice.
- Show the importance of stretching and warming up.

Training programmes

All good training sessions will have specific aims and objectives, and must all begin with a sound warm-up. For players embarking on training programmes there are four basic questions to be asked. The answers to these questions vary according to the end results sought and are specific to the various components of fitness.

There is a certain amount of overlap between the identified fitness components. Without the necessary attributes individuals playing the game at any level will not be able to cope with the demands placed upon them.

Table 2 **Fitness components as identified by FITT**

F   **Frequency:** How often should the type of exercise be performed?
Frequency incorporates the principles of regularity and recovery.

I   **Intensity:** How hard should the exercise be?
Intensity incorporates the principles of overload and progression.

T   **Time:** How long should the exercise session be?
Time incorporates the principles of overload and progression.

T   **Type:** What types of activities train each component?
Type incorporates the principles of specificity and variety.

It is the combination of training volume (frequency and time) and training intensity that predominantly determines the long-term effect of training. Volume and intensity can be manipulated and are dominant at different stages of the season as shown below.

Volume

Volume refers to the quantity of training i.e. the sum of work conducted in a training session. Generally, volume of training dominates during the off-season and the early preparation period. It can be expressed by the following depending on the type of session, for example a running session or a weights session.

- **Time or duration of the training session,**
- **The distance covered in the training session,**
- **The total amount of weight lifted in a session,**
- **The total number of repetitions conducted in a session.**

Intensity

Intensity refers to the quality of training. In contrast to volume, intensity of training dominates prior to competitive periods and during the competition period. It is a crucial component of strength, speed and power development. It can be expressed by the following depending on the type of session, for example a weights session or an aerobic session.

- **Velocity of movement,**
- **Percentage of maximum heart rate,**
- **Percentage of one repetition maximum (see page 81).**

It is the appropriate manipulation of both volume and intensity that is important when devising a training programme to ensure that the desired improvements take place.

Best Practice Understand your fitness objectives and design your training routine accordingly.

To achieve a high level of fitness, training sessions need to be undertaken regularly by players, as it will be difficult for any individual who only occasionally turns up for training to see any real improvement.

Basic training principles

As discussed in Chapter 3, in general terms fitness is often referred to as 'the four S's', namely:

- Stamina or cardiovascular endurance,
- Strength/muscular endurance,
- Suppleness or flexibility,
- Speed.

More specifically, Figure 14 takes this theory one step further and identifies several fitness parameters and the links between them, all of which contribute to the player's performance.

Figure 14 **Fitness components contributing to the performance of players**

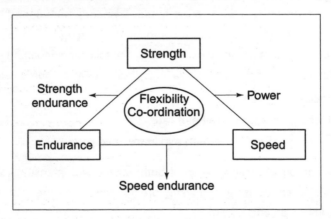

In order to improve any or all of these components certain principles will always apply. Adherence to these principles will ensure that the physical and physiological development of players will be optimal, whereas neglect can often result in unnecessary injury.

Table 3 describes five key training principles.

Table 3 **Basic principles of training**

Individuality	The time it takes for someone to adapt and the amount of change depends somewhat upon heredity. Not everyone possesses the same capacity to adapt to training. Because of individual differences, training programmes must take into account specific needs and abilities and therefore must be flexible and adaptable.
	It is therefore important to identify an individual's strengths and weaknesses so that players can be reviewed individually when setting training goals.
	As discussed previously it is important to take into account both the individual and their role/position within the team when devising individual training programmes, especially when dealing with senior players.
Specificity	The effect of training is specific to the type of training undertaken and its volume and intensity. Training, therefore, must be geared to the relevant energy systems, muscle groups and range of movements. Training programmes must stress the physiological systems that are critical for optimal performance in football in order to achieve the desired training adaptations.
Reversibility or Use it or lose it!	The effects of training are reversible; if training is infrequent or not sufficiently intensive, the training effects will diminish – so in other words, 'use it or lose it!'
Progressive overload or Gradual progression	Overload and progression form the foundation of all training. Without overload no improvements will take place and without appropriate progression individuals will not be given sufficient time to adapt to the training, with the likely result being injury.

Table 3 **continued**

To achieve this the intensity and duration of training sessions should be increased in a logical and reasonably progressive fashion.

The greater fitness a player displays, the higher the level of exercise stress needs to be in order to create an overload.

It is the manipulation of training volume and intensity that will determine whether the session will have a progressive training effect or simply help to maintain a player's fitness levels.

Recovery

The importance of recovery is often forgotten in the training process despite the fact that it is critical to ensure the optimal development of players at all levels.

Through the application of training principles an appropriate amount of activity will stress the system and result in a certain level of fatigue.

The adaptations that result from the training can take place more quickly if the fatigue that the training produced is reduced quickly, which is possible through the application of appropriate recovery strategies.

Recovery allows the body to replenish energy stores and assist in the repair of damaged tissues allowing subsequent training sessions to take place in a state of minimal fatigue. This provides a better opportunity for further physical improvements to take place.

Too much, too quick, too soon

An FA study into the injury patterns of professional players (1997/8 and 1998/9) highlighted, the principle of progressive overload is commonly neglected at all levels of the game.

Figure 15 shows the percentage of injuries sustained per month during training and competition in English professional football over the course of two seasons.

Figure 15 **Distribution of training and match injuries throughout the season**
Source: FA Injury Audit (2001), Hawkins (2001).

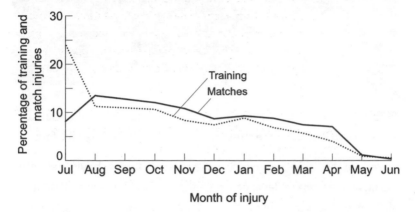

As you can see from the graph the greatest percentage of injuries happen in July. This is when players return to training from the 'close season' and in most cases these injuries will happen because training programmes are designed to expect too much, too soon.

Clearly, at the beginning of the season the players have not been progressively overloaded. Therefore most players tend to go from doing little or no exercise to physically demanding training sessions that can actually do more harm than good and cause injuries.

Figure 15 demonstrates that training injuries peak during July, and match injuries peak during the first month of the playing season after the pre-season training period, both show decreases during the remainder of the season. It seems possible that during the first month of the competitive playing season, the players have not yet reached appropriate levels of

fitness and are therefore not in optimal physical and physiological states to be able to withstand the stresses associated with competitive football.

To reduce the risk of injury early in the season, players should attempt to maintain a reasonable level of fitness throughout the year so that at the start of pre-season training the sudden increase in training intensity comes as less of a shock. Players should therefore view the 'close season' as pre-pre-season and seek to continue with regular exercise.

Pre-pre-season

This is the period from the end of the competitive season to the start of the traditional pre-season and is usually the time when players relax, put their feet up and forget about training, as the new season seems so far away. However, this is the time when players should be preparing for the new season and making sure that their fitness levels are able to cope with pre-season training.

Best Practice Maintain your fitness throughout the summer and make sure you build a pre-pre-season programme in to your training routine.

In order to maintain the required level of fitness we would recommend individuals take part in relatively short but intensive training programmes, ideally two to three times a week. To provide some guidance The FA has devised a series of training drills (page 76) that focus on short periods of intensive work.

The high intensity of training sessions limits the length of the training periods and the number of repetitions. For professional footballers we would recommend that four intervals of four minutes are very effective, however, this can obviously be reduced for those starting at a lower fitness level.

Less trained players would require shorter work periods or a lower number of intervals. It is worth noting that this high-intensity training has been shown to be effective when performing many forms of training, including incline running on a treadmill, completing a football-specific skills course, and small-sided games, providing the key requirement of intensity is achieved.

The key component of this approach to training is intensity. It is the intensity of training rather than frequency or volume that is the major determinant of the improvements that take place. Based on this understanding, the following drills offer a variety of ways by which players can achieve desired training intensities, either training alone, with a colleague or even with the rest of the squad as part of pre-season training. The drills provide basic principles that can be applied to grassroots level as well as more professional teams. The progressions indicated are simply a guide as to what can be achieved over a period of months, depending on the initial training status of the players.

Figure 16 **Pitch widths (with and without ball)**

- One or more players
- Player runs across the pitch and returns within 30 seconds
- 30 seconds recovery, then repeat process
- Repeat ten times
- Progress to decreasing recovery (15, 10, 5, 0 seconds)
- Work as a 3 – 2 continuing repetitions/delivery (i.e. one minute on, 30 second recovery – repeat five times)
- Progress to five continuous repetitions, two minutes recovery (repeat two to three sets)

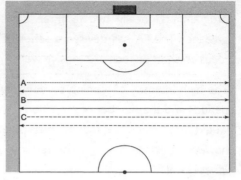

Increase intensity further by every second repetition being with a ball.

Figure 17 **Continuous varied pace group running**

- One or more players
- All players run at the same time but at a set pace
- Players complete each side of the rectangle in 15 seconds
- The long side (80–100 metres) covered in 15 seconds
- Across the box (40 metres) covered in 15 seconds
- One full lap completed in one minute (approximately 14–17 km per hour depending on dimensions)

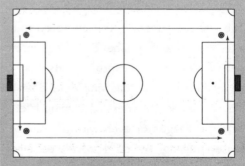

- Progress from two to three to four laps at one set with two to three minute recoveries. Build from one to four sets. Increase intensity by conducting alternate laps with a ball
- May have to vary distances for different ability levels.

Aerobic drills – various intensities

Figure 18 **Pitch circuit drill**

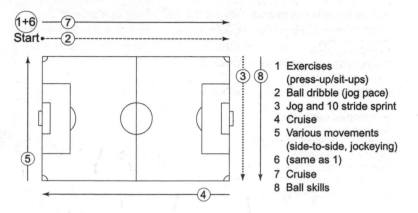

1 Exercises
   (press-up/sit-ups)
2 Ball dribble (jog pace)
3 Jog and 10 stride sprint
4 Cruise
5 Various movements
   (side-to-side, jockeying)
6 (same as 1)
7 Cruise
8 Ball skills

Pitch circuit

Purpose

Depending on the intensity of the session, the drill can be used to assist the recovery from previous exercise, maintain or improve cardiovascular fitness.

Procedure

The drill is performed in a continuous fashion alternating between various forms of activity. The intensity of the activities will depend on the aim of the session.

- **Start by performing 10–20 sit-ups and then run with the ball the length of the pitch.**

- **Jog the width of the pitch and perform one sprint in the middle (behind the goal area) incorporating ten strides.**

- **Cruise the length of the pitch and then conduct various movements (skipping, side-to-side, etc.), along the width of the pitch.**

- Back at the corner you started from perform 10–20 press-ups and cruise the length of the pitch to receive the ball, continuing behind the goal performing various ball skills.

- The cycle is continued moving the ball along one side of the pitch on each lap. You should aim to complete a 30–50 minute session. This may be gradual, performing ten-minute sets with four-minute recovery periods at first.

Aerobic drills – high intensity

Figure 19 **Box-to-box drill**

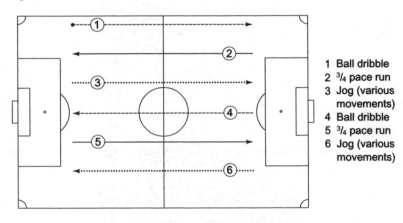

1 Ball dribble
2 ³/₄ pace run
3 Jog (various movements)
4 Ball dribble
5 ³/₄ pace run
6 Jog (various movements)

Box-to-box

Purpose

To develop the cardiovascular system and assist the recovery from high-intensity exercise.

Procedure

- Start by dribbling the ball from the edge of one box to the other. This should not be intense but serve to assist recovery.

- Leave the ball at the edge of the box and sprint ³/₄ pace across the pitch to the opposite box.

- Perform a recovery jog back across the pitch to the back and restart the cycle.

- Perform three to five minutes of continuous work, repeating three times with a two to three minute recovery between repetitions.
- Aim to have a heart rate response of 90–5% of your maximum heart rate.

Variations

During the dribbling phase perform different skills with the ball. During the recovery jog conduct various types of movements.

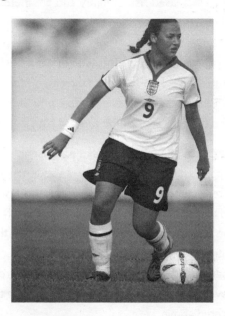

Developing strength

Strength and muscular endurance are important attributes for a football player. Although football is viewed as a multi-sprint sport that places demands on the various systems of energy delivery, there are situations throughout the game that require significant levels of strength and muscular endurance. If the strength of a player is poor, it is doubtful whether the player will be able to perform to his/her full potential.

Both upper and lower body strength needs to be addressed, the former not only being important for goalkeepers but also for outfield players. Lower body strength is required for many activities including tackling, jumping, kicking, changing direction and changing speed whereas upper body strength assists in resisting tackles, maintaining possession and a number of other activities.

Many people believe that the use of free weights or weightlifting exercises pose an increased risk of injury and are therefore reluctant to use these techniques. This is certainly not the case – the rate and prevalence of injuries caused by weight training are low among athletes as well as the general population. This type of work will in fact lead to an increase in the strength of bone and an increase in the strength of both the origin and insertion of the muscle tendon onto the bone, all of which contribute to the development of the football athlete.

Resistance exercise is any form of active exercise in which dynamic or static muscle contraction is resisted by an external force. Common examples of resistance equipment include the use of multi-gym equipment and traditional machines seen in most health clubs. Although these may have a role when isolating certain muscles, the better option is to utilize multi-joint exercises, utilizing free-weights equipment, pulley systems, clinibands and water, all of which allow a greater speed and freedom of movement which is important in enhancing the specificity of training highlighted above.

Designing a resistance training programme

The trainer has to consider a number of factors when designing a resistance training programme:

The specific needs of the player

The coach should assess the player to determine the present level of muscular strength. Furthermore, the strength needs of the player in terms of his/her position within a team, the players' health status (i.e. are they returning from injury?) etc., should also be determined.

Style of exercise to be performed

The exercise should incorporate movements that are similar to those incorporated in the game, for example, a squat is much more beneficial for the quadriceps than a leg extension exercise. The player/coach should remember that the same muscle, if exercised in different positions and with the muscle in differing degrees of lengthening, will produce different amounts of tension because of the length-tension relationship.

Resistance and number of repetitions

This depends on whether endurance, strength or power is to be developed. Various systems have been designed to develop these properties and all of them are based on the principle of using percentages of the repetition maximum (RM).

The RM is the greatest weight that the player can lift a specific number of times. The RM gives a useful indication of the work capacity of muscles at a particular time. When using a training regime to develop strength, the RM can be used to give an indication of strength improvement and can be tested on a regular basis.

The basic guidelines for the weight to be used can be determined by the number of repetitions that the player is required to perform.

Best Practice Always ensure you are supervised when lifting any weights.

An example of how to lift weights correctly

Figure 20 **Manipulation of the number of repetitions and weight for the development of strength, power, muscle endurance and muscle size**

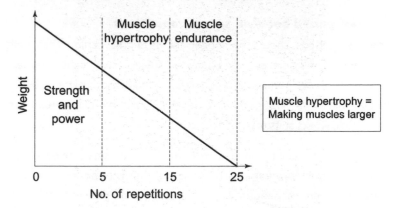

Strength

This usually involves the player being able to perform between one to ten repetitions of an exercise. It has been shown that a weight that allows a six RM seems to result in the greatest strength improvements.

With isometric muscle work it has been shown that a muscular contraction with about 40% of maximal strength is sufficient to give strength gains. This contraction should be held for six seconds.

Endurance

As the resistance decreases and the number of repetitions increases, strength gains diminish and the benefits of the exercise are biased more towards endurance. If the resistance is such that it allows 20 repetitions or more, gains are made primarily in muscle endurance.

The number of sets of repetitions

The performance of a single set of an exercise is less effective for increasing strength than performing two or three sets. Three sets are commonly used in the development of strength and endurance.

However, with advanced programme sets, repetitions and resistance are manipulated to achieve the desired aims.

The rest period between sets of repetitions

The rest periods should be longer for strength training than with endurance training since it is the quality of the exercise that is important rather than a large number of repetitions. Without appropriate recovery, fatigue will set in. When aiming to develop strength it is important that the muscle works at its maximum.

When strength training the ideal rest time between sets is two to three minutes. If the programme is designed for the development of endurance then rest periods of less than one minute are used. If weights are used to develop cardiovascular fitness then rest periods less than 30 seconds are used to sustain a relatively high heart rate.

The rest period between exercise sessions

The ideal weekly strength training regime should be three times a week, leaving a day to rest between exercise bouts, for example Monday, Wednesday and Friday, resting on the other days. This allows the muscle to recover from the intense bouts of exercise so that it can work maximally at the next exercise session.

However, for those that can't commit this much time to training, please be aware that rest is a crucial factor of training and that a number of continuous days strength/endurance exercise at any one time over a short period is not advisable.

■ Make a note of your typical training routine and decide if you have enough rest days.

The order and performance of the exercises

An important factor in the planning of an exercise regime is the sequence of the exercises to be performed. Care needs to be taken not to over exercise the same muscle group consecutively. As discussed previously, ensuring a variety of exercises will not only allow certain muscles time to rest (therefore reducing the chances of injury) but also maintain the interest levels of players.

Recommended resistance training regimes

The following table shows some of the commonly employed resistance training regimes. Ten repetitions are commonly used at the outset as this will provide both an endurance and strength stimulus.

Table 4 **Resistance training regimes**

Single set system	This is probably the oldest resistance training programme. It consists of using heavy weights and few repetitions with a five-minute rest between exercise. Research has shown that this system allows strength gains.
Multiple sets system	The multiple sets system consists of two or three warm-up sets of increasing resistance followed by several sets at the same weight. This system became popular in the 1940s and was the forerunner of the multiple sets and repetitions systems of today.
Light to heavy system	This system progresses from using light to heavy resistance. It became popular among Olympic lifters in the 1930s and 1940s. It consists of performing a set of three to five repetitions with a light weight. Add 2.5 kg and repeat. Add another 2.5 kg and repeat. Carry on with this until only one repetition can be performed.
Pyramid system	This consists of working light to heavy, heavy to light. It starts with 10–12 repetitions, working up to one repetition with heavy resistance then working in reverse. This system is popular with powerlifters.
Super set system	There are two distinct but similar types of programme. One programme consists of several sets of exercise for the same body part but for two groups of antagonistic muscles such as the front and back of the thigh. An example of this would be arm curls followed by tricep extensions. The second type of super setting uses one set of several exercises for the same body part; there is little rest between sets. This type of work is popular amongst body builders suggesting it helps muscle hypertrophy.
Circuit system	This consists of a series of resistance exercises performed one after the other. The exercises may be specific to the needs of the performer. The exercises should be performed as quickly as possible in good style. Local muscular endurance is the benefit from this type of training, with some effect on the respiratory system.

Developing speed

The critical elements for developing speed work are:

- **Effort** – players must be aware that exercises need to be performed at maximum effort.

- **Intensity** – quick and over short periods (no longer than ten seconds, which is relatively long considering the average sprint in a game is two seconds).

- **Volume** – short number of drills (maximum of four) with rest periods in between.

Speed is an essential component of the game today and it is therefore important that this area is thoroughly developed. Sprinting can be divided into three phases:

1 An acceleration phase (usually achieved over the first 10 m) giving an indication of power.

2 A maximum running speed phase (peak velocities are usually attained during the transition phase of 10–36 m).

3 A phase of deceleration or speed endurance (the extent to which high running velocities can be maintained).

The performance in each phase is very specific and relatively uncorrelated to those in the other phases of sprint performance and therefore need to be developed separately. For example, just because a player has an excellent ability to accelerate this does not mean his/her maximum speed is also excellent and therefore this may require specific training for it to be improved.

Speed is a major component in football, although its nature and function will vary. For example, the maximum possible speed is often essential during a race for the ball, but for goalkeepers speed of limb movement may be a critical factor rather than that of the whole body. In this case limb speed is important as well as reaction time.

One important aspect of speed work that should not be neglected is that of reaction time. So far as short distances are concerned, any variation in total movement time must be a major consideration for all players, whatever their position.

The term 'reaction time' refers to the time lapse between the stimulus (the moment at which the striker kicks the ball, or the moment the ball breaks loose after a tackle) and the first muscular contraction. Reaction time can be improved by practice, provided that practice conditions are similar to the actual requirements of the game.

Training for speed should involve maximal intensity work. Like other components of fitness, speed training should be made specific to the requirements of the game.

Examples of speed and agility drills
Maximal sprints (hollow)
Purpose
Improve ability to change pace and enhance ability to reach maximum speed.

Procedure
- Space five cones 20 yards apart.
- From the first cone gradually build up your speed towards the next cone and sprint maximally to the following cone. Slow down

Figure 21 **Maximal sprints**

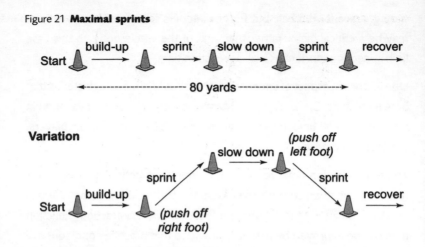

slightly up to the next cone and then accelerate into another maximal sprint. Slow down gradually and return to the start.

- During the recovery period light dribbling could be conducted if a ball is available.

- Ensure that you are fully recovered before you start the next sprint.

- The recovery period needs to be at least five times the duration of the drill.

- Repeat the drill four to eight times.

- A simple yet effective variation would be to push off at a 45° angle when each sprint is performed.

Speed/agility drills – line drills
20-yard shuttle
Purpose
Development of change of direction, footwork, and acceleration.

Figure 22 **20-yard shuttle**

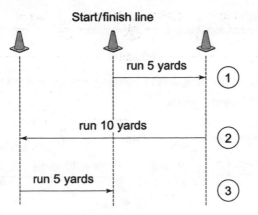

Procedure

- Start by performing small bouncing movements on the spot.
- Turn to the right, sprint, and touch a line 5 yards away with your right foot.
- Turn back to the left, sprint 10 yards, and touch the far line with your left foot.
- Turn back to the right, sprint 5 yards through the start line to the finish.
- During the recovery period dribble with the ball back and forth across the drill (three times) before leaving the ball at the opposite side and returning to the start.
- Ensure that you are fully recovered before you start the next sprint.
- The recovery period needs to be at least five times the duration of the drill.
- Repeat the drill five to ten times.

T-agility sprint

Purpose

Development of footwork and acceleration.

Procedure

- Start by performing small bouncing movements on the spot.
- Sprint forward 5 yards.

Figure 23 **T-agility sprint**

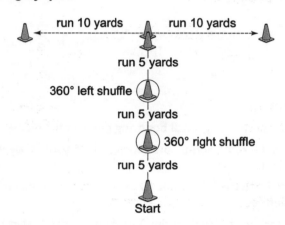

- Shuffle 360° around the cone while continually facing forwards, and sprint another 5 yards.
- Shuffle 360° around the next cone in the same manner, and sprint another 5 yards.
- Sprint right or left for 10 yards.
- During the recovery period dribble with the ball for three lengths (60 yards) at the top of the 'T' before returning to the start.
- Ensure that you are fully recovered before you start the next sprint.
- The recovery period needs to be at least five times the duration of the drill.
- Repeat the drill five to ten times.

Variation

Vary the movement to be incorporated at each cone (e.g. a step-over, throw a 'dummy').

Speed/agility drills – square drills
20-yard box drill
Purpose

Improve ability to change direction.

Figure 24 **20-yard box drill**

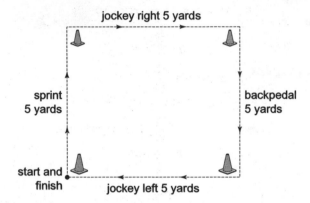

jockey right 5 yards

sprint
5 yards

backpedal
5 yards

start and
finish

jockey left 5 yards

Procedure

- Start by performing small bouncing movements on the spot.
- Sprint 5 yards to first cone, make sharp right cut.
- Jockey right 5 yards, make a sharp cut back.
- Backpedal 5 yards to next cone, make sharp left cut.
- Left jockey through finish.
- Jog and skip twice round the square to enable full recovery.
- Ensure that you are fully recovered before you start the next sprint.
- The recovery period needs to be at least five times the duration of the drill.
- Repeat the drill five to ten times.

Variation

- Start from different positions (e.g. lying, sideways facing, backwards facing, etc.).
- Cut with inside or outside leg.
- Shuffle around each cone.
- Introduce a ball during the recovery period and dribble around the square.

Speed/agility drills – cone drills

Zig-zag drill

Purpose

Improve cutting ability and acceleration.

Figure 25 **Zig-zag drill**

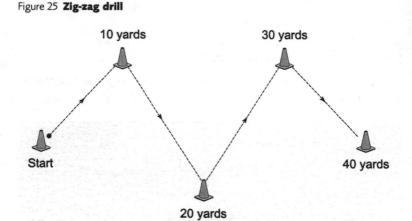

Procedure

- Place cones as indicated in Figure 25.
- Start by performing small bouncing movements on the spot.
- Sprint to the first cone, plant on outside leg and cut sharply towards the next cone.
- Continue through the course, decelerating sharply, cutting and accelerating from each cone.

- During the recovery period dribble a ball from the finish back through the course leaving the ball 10 yards behind the start, and then jog back to the finish from where the next repetition will begin.

- Ensure that you are fully recovered before you start the next sprint.

- The recovery period needs to be at least five times the duration of the drill.

- Repeat the drill five to ten times.

Variation

- Start from different positions (e.g. lying, facing backwards, etc.).

- Cut with inside or outside leg.

- Shuffle around the cones.

Developing suppleness

For techniques on increasing flexibility and stretching see Chapter 6, *Preparation and recovery*.

Structuring a training programme

Although all coaches have different styles, techniques and ways to structure a training programme, there are key basic elements that should always be covered in every training session.

Typical mid-season training session (approximately 120 minutes)

1   Warm-up – dynamic activity to increase body and muscle temperature, optimizing performance and reducing the potential for injury – 15–20 minutes.

2   Speed work – this should always be performed when the players are still fresh and not tired from training – 10–15 minutes.

3   Technical session – skills and practices (passing, shooting, heading etc.) – 30 minutes.

4   Small-sided game or 11 vs. 11 – crucial for enhancing endurance levels and for putting the skills into practice, but also an important fun element to keep players interested and motivated – 45–60 minutes.

5   Cool-down – gradual decrease in activity levels incorporating limb movements to assist blood flow and removal of waste products. Some stretching may be appropriate – ten minutes.

Typical pre-season training session (approximately 120 minutes)

1   Warm-up – see above – 15–20 minutes.

2   Speed work – see above – 10–15 minutes.

3   Technical session – skills and practices (passing, shooting, heading etc.) – 30 minutes.

4   Small-sided game or 11 vs. 11 – see above – 30 minutes.

5   Stamina work – as shown in the previous diagrams – 20–30 minutes.

6   Cool-down – see above – ten minutes.

Typical pre-pre-season training session (approximately 45–60 minutes)

1   Warm-up – see above – ten minutes.

2   Intensive workout – 30 minutes.

3   Cool-down – see above – ten minutes.

The sessions above only focus on on-field training. There are many other areas of training that also need to be incorporated in to training programmes if the full potential of the players is to be realized. Such sessions include strength and power development, flexibility and specific injury prevention sessions.

Summary

- All good training sessions will have specific aims and objectives, and must all begin with a sound warm-up.

- Maintain fitness levels throughout the close season so that pre-season becomes less of a shock to the body's systems.

- Strength, stamina and speed are essential elements of overall fitness and can all be improved through specifically-designed programmes.

Self testers
- What does FITT stand for?
- When do most football injuries happen and why?
- What are the three critical elements of speed training?

Action plan
Review your training sessions that take place at different times during the season and see if they follow a similar structure to our recommended one.

Chapter 6

Preparation and recovery

THIS CHAPTER WILL:

- Give an understanding of the importance of warming up.
- Provide an understanding of the importance of cooling down.
- Explain the correct way to stretch.

Player preparation and recovery have been neglected in the past. This is possibly due to the ill-fated beliefs that the recovery process will happen naturally and the preparation simply involves a few stretches. Consider the following factual pieces of information that have been generated from The Football Association's *Audit of injuries in professional football*:

- A total of more than 3,000 injuries are suffered each season by the 2,500 or so professionals in the Premier League and Football League.
- Each injury keeps a player out of action for an average of four games.
- Most players are injured at some stage every season.

- Injuries lead to players missing more than 55,000 training days and 10,000 competitive games each year.
- Roughly $\frac{1}{3}$ of injuries are sustained during training, while the remaining $\frac{2}{3}$ occur during competitive games.
- The largest single type of injury, by a long margin, is a muscle strain, which accounts for about $\frac{1}{3}$ of all injuries.
- About $\frac{1}{2}$ of all injuries are classified as minor, keeping players out for around one week (or one match).

Preparation and recovery strategies play important roles in optimizing player performance and consequently assist in the prevention of injuries. Effective preparation ensures that players are able to maximize their attributes while recovery strategies ensure that the appropriate adaptations to training and matches take place, assisting not only in the development of players but also the preparation of the next bout of activity.

Crucial to not only optimizing performance but also reducing the potential for injuries is the warm-up and cool-down procedures of the players.

The warm-up

Quote | 'A good warm-up is essential to the success of the session.'

The warm-up is designed to prepare the player for the ensuing physical activity, be it a training session or game, to enable players to perform optimally. There are several reasons why a warm-up period should be given as part of a training session and before games, and some of these reasons are also applicable at half-time in preparation for the second half of matches.

It has recently been shown that by performing warm-up exercises during the half-time period more distance can be covered by players at a high-intensity pace compared to what is normally achieved. This enhanced ability clearly has performance implications and consequently attention should be paid to this aspect of a player's/team's preparation.

Statistic

Every season, an estimated **50** professional players have to cut short their careers due to permanent disability.

In a body at rest, the blood flow to the muscles is comparatively low, and the majority of the small blood vessels (capillaries) supplying them are closed. When activity begins, the blood flow in the exercising muscles increases markedly as the capillaries open. To put this into perspective consider the fact that at rest 15–20% of the blood flow supplies muscles, while the corresponding figure after 10–12 minutes of all-round exercise is 70–5%. A muscle can only achieve maximum performance when all of its blood vessels are functional. Physical work increases the energy output and temperature of the muscle, this in turn leads to improved co-ordination with less likelihood of injury.

■ Think about how many times you have played football without spending time warming up.

A warm-up therefore prepares the body for a workout or competition by raising muscle temperature towards an optimum level for performance, enabling metabolic processes in cells to proceed at higher rates and nerve messages to travel faster. This in turn improves physical performance. A warm-up can be described as a process to increase awareness, improve co-ordination, elasticity and contractibility of muscles, and increase the efficiency of the respiratory and cardiovascular systems.

Reasons for conducting a thorough warm-up prior to training and matches include the following:

- To increase blood flow to muscular tissue.
- To increase muscle temperature.
- To reduce muscle tightness.
- To elevate body temperature.
- To stimulate reflex activity related to balance and co-ordination.
- To achieve full joint mobility in the specific joints involved in the activity.
- To achieve full soft tissue extensibility – muscles, tendons, ligaments.
- To enhance the functioning of the neuromuscular system.
- To prepare the cardiovascular and respiratory systems.
- To prepare the player psychologically for the coming activity.
- To familiarize players with the environmental conditions.

Warm-ups should be intense enough to increase the body temperature and resemble the activity that is going to be performed. The warm-up should begin with movements of the large muscle groups, as these are the main areas to which blood is redistributed. These include the following areas:

- Back lower leg: gastrocnemius and soleus,
- Front lower leg: peroneals (shin),
- Front thigh: quadriceps,
- Back thigh: hamstrings,
- Inner thigh: adductors,
- Back: erector spinae,
- Trunk: abdominal muscles,
- Shoulders and chest: deltoids and pectorials.

After the general warm-up players can begin more specialized exercises including mobilization of the joints and dynamic movements of muscles, particularly of the lower extremity. The final stage of a warm-up should concentrate on technique and/or practising a specific movement.

Statistic

The recommended time for warming up is between **15–20 minutes**.

Whether warm-ups are performed with or without a ball depends entirely upon the philosophy adopted by the coach. This part of the training session provides an opportunity to work on specific technical skills in conjunction with mobility work and may also provide a greater mental and neurological stimulus for the players. In sports generally, a lack or improper use of a warm-up and a cool-down can be a risk factor for lower extremity overuse muscular injuries, especially during running.

The cool-down

Following the end of vigorous physical activity it takes time for the body to return to its resting state. Large volumes of blood and waste products remain in the muscles that lead to a build-up of pressure within the muscle, which results in excess fluid accumulating in the tissues and muscles.

Best Practice Cool down after every training session.

Figure 26 highlights the importance of players performing a cool-down. When a player simply stops following a training session or game he/she is more likely to incur some form of muscle stiffness/soreness. By cooling down appropriately, the recovery process is accelerated, which diminishes subsequent discomfort and promotes the process of adaptation.

Figure 26 **Levels of lactic acid after activity (Bangsbo 1994)**
Source: *Fitness Training in Football – a Scientific Approach* Jens Bangsbo (Ho & Storm) (1994)

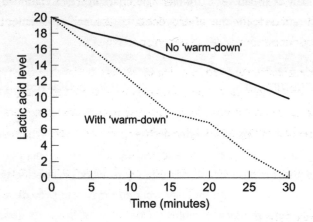

The aim of the cool-down is to encourage the gradual return of the heart, body metabolism and respiratory rate to normal, and to encourage effective reabsorption of the waste products from the muscles.

An active cool-down promotes the clearance of lactic acid, an exercise intensity of 65–70% of maximum heart rate being most beneficial. A gradual decrease in exercise intensity and the application of controlled rhythmical movements will also assist in cooling the body as the transfer of blood flow to the skin will be maintained, which allows further heat loss.

One of the major benefits of an active cool-down is that the ability to sleep is enhanced. This is crucial in ensuring that appropriate regeneration of the body can take place. From a performance perspective there is evidence to demonstrate an enhanced sprinting ability in subsequent training days and there is also a suggestion that the cool-down procedure partly offsets any depression in the immune system that commonly occurs after exercise.

A cool-down therefore helps the body to recover from a workout or competition and assists the process of regeneration. Good fluid and nutritional strategies (See Chapter 7) need to be adopted as failure to do so will compromise the effectiveness of the strategies adopted and subsequent performances in training and matches.

Stretching is often viewed as an important part of the cool-down process and is commonly discussed, however it should be recognized that conducted alone it is not a legitimate way to cool down and many of the proposed advantages highlighted above will be compromised.

■   Think about how often you cool down after training.

Stretching

Often, when stretching is discussed, the focus is on pre-game or training preparation. What is commonly overlooked is the significant importance of daily preventative stretching that is not linked to either the pre-game or post-game situation.

Researchers and practitioners continue to debate the best form of stretching in order to enhance flexibility. However, generally speaking, static stretches of 20–30 seconds repeated two or three times, three per week have been shown to enhance flexibility in many individuals. For this reason we will focus on static stretches in the following diagrams.

Quote	'Exercises that involve the stretching of muscles can be beneficial for maintenance or even the enhancement of flexibility. Such exercises include many of the movements adopted when utilizing free weights.'

One of the most common injuries in football is the muscle strain. In many cases these strains will be sustained by so called 'two-joint muscles' – muscles that work over two joints such as the hamstring muscles or the rectus femoris at the front of the thigh. It is important that a sufficient range of motion is allowed around the joints through which these muscles pass. However, it is equally important that muscle strength is developed and maintained throughout this range of motion.

In the young and adolescent player bone grows faster than soft tissue such as muscle. Therefore, during growth the muscles become anatomically shorter than the bones they attach to. This 'tightening' leaves the young player particularly vulnerable not only to muscle injuries but also to injuries to the soft bony attachments on the skeleton.

A progressive daily stretching programme in conjunction with other forms of training will assist in reducing the chances of injury and improve the general mobility of the player.

The easiest and safest way to perform stretches involves the following steps:

- Warm up the muscle to optimal temperature prior to stretching.
- Slowly take up the stretch of the muscle to the point of tension and minimal discomfort (stretching should not be painful). It is a sustained stretch. Adjust the position to achieve a stretch in different areas.
- Do not bounce into the stretch. The muscle will contract to protect itself and the muscle will not be stretched properly.
- Sustain the stretch at the point of minimal discomfort for a period of 20–30 seconds. A minimum of six seconds is required to remove the 'muscle stretch reflex' which is a contraction of the muscle in response to the stretch.
- Slowly release the stretch.
- Repeat the stretch three to four times for each muscle group.
- Have a systematic approach to stretching so that a muscle group is not omitted.

The following are examples of stretches that can be performed on the major muscle groups of the body presented in Chapter 1.

Quadriceps (rectus femoris)

Figure 27

1 The leg is moved into a position of hip extension at the commencement of the stretch.

2   The leg is then flexed at the knee to afford a stable grip of the ankle by the hand.

3   Maintaining pressure of the ankle onto the hand, bring the hip towards an extended position until a mild stretch is felt on the anterior aspect of the thigh.

4   This represents the process of 'phasic stretch' of the quadriceps muscles representing the 'kicking action' in football.

Gastrocnemius

Figure 28

1   The player adopts a 'walk forward' stance.

2   The heel of the rear foot remains in contact with the ground/floor throughout the stretch.

3   The bodyweight is slowly transferred forwards until a mild stretch is felt in the calf region of the rear leg with the knee held in the extended position.

Soleus

1   The player adopts a 'walk forward' stance.

2   The heel of the forward foot remains in contact with the ground/floor throughout the stretch.

3   The forward leg is flexed at the knee throughout the stretch.

Figure 29

4   The bodyweight is slowly transferred forwards until a mild stretch is felt in the calf region of the forward leg.

5   An alternative method is shown on the previous page where the soleus muscle of the rear leg is being stretched by flexion of the knee with the heel on the ground. A supporting surface (wall) may be used to assist with balance.

Hamstrings

1   The subject is lying on his/her back with the hip and knee flexed to 90°.

Figure 30

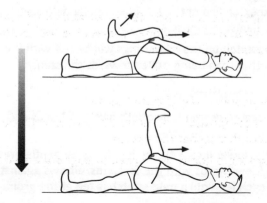

2   The arms may assist the hip into flexion.

3   The hamstring muscles of the leg are put into stretch and under tension by this position being held and the knee joint being carefully extended until a mild stretch can be felt in the hamstring muscles.

Figure 31

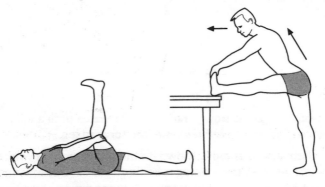

An alternative method of stretching the hamstrings:

1   Place the leg on a table.

2   The heel is supported on the table with the knee joint in some degree of flexion.

3   The hamstring muscles of the leg are put under stretch and tension by the forward flexion of the hips, together with the controlled extension of the left knee until a mild stretch can be felt in the hamstring muscles.

4   A greater stretch on the hamstrings will be felt with the toes pointed rather than being pulled towards the shin.

Adductors (groin/hip)

1   From the seated position, flex both hips and knees and place the soles of the feet together.

2   Holding the lower legs with the hands, apply gentle pressure outwards/downwards with the forearms/elbows against the inside of each leg until a mild stretch is felt at the groin.

Figure 32

Alternatively:

1　The player takes a 'sideways lunge' position as shown above.

2　The player slowly and carefully bends the leading knee, which puts the groin adductor muscles of the other leg under tension and stretch.

3　This continues until a mild but effective stretch is achieved.

4　The knee of the flexed leg should not pass beyond the position of the foot.

Back extensors

Figure 33

1   In the back lying position, flex the hips and the knees until the knees are in contact with the chest.

2   Placing the hands onto the knees, gently pull the knees towards the chest and slowly raise the pelvis off the ground/floor.

3   The head may be lifted gradually off the ground/floor until a mild stretch is felt in the back.

Alternatively:

1   The player can adopt a 'lax stoop' standing position with the knees in some degree of flexion (please see Figure 33).

2   The player holds the lower leg near the ankles and forces the head and spine as far as possible in a curling manner until a mild, but effective stretch can be felt in the back extensor muscles of the spine.

3   By having the knees in some degree of flexion the hamstring muscles are not put under tension and a more effective stretch of the back extensors can be achieved.

The need for flexibility

Flexibility work is all too often viewed by players as being a necessary evil prior to 'proper' training. Developing and maintaining flexibility through stretching is therefore constantly overlooked by many and used ineffectively by others within the game of football.

The majority of training sessions exhibit a tendency to focus on developing skill, strength, speed and endurance. These are all exciting qualities of football, the end results of which are easily seen in performance. However, the qualities of flexibility are not always so obvious and, as such, flexibility is not always perceived as being an important element of good performance in football.

Clearly, however, in light of the research evidence, flexibility training is a fundamental and integral aspect of a football player's development. By improving flexibility, the ability of a player to produce an effective movement in a game is significantly enhanced. Flexibility training is the crucial unifying factor that facilitates the other aspects of training – skill, strength, speed and endurance – leading to improved performances.

In addition to improving performance, flexibility training can help reduce the risk of unnecessary injury and thus allow players to reach their individual optimum level of performance more consistently and safely and, ultimately, sustain it for longer.

Summary

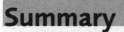

- **Many injuries are caused by not warming up before training and playing.**

- **Warming up and cooling down should be incorporated into all training programmes.**

- **Stretching is important to maximizing performance and reducing the risk of injury.**

Self testers

- Name five reasons for warming up.
- What is the aim of the cool-down?
- Describe the 'back extensor' stretches.

Action plan

Review your training sessions and ensure that they include both a warm-up and cool-down session.

Chapter 7

The FA

LEARNING

Nutrition for the footballer

THIS CHAPTER WILL:
- Examine the importance of a healthy balanced diet.
- Explain the need for carbohydrate.
- Give an understanding of what to eat and when.

Without the correct nutritional support the player will not be able to sustain an intensive training programme over a long period of time, and improvement will therefore be limited.

An understanding of nutrition is also necessary to ensure optimum performance in competition, with manipulation of the diet leading to substantial improvements in performance. The difference between the skills and fitness characteristics of the winning and losing team can often be small and, where other things are equal, attention to diet can be the difference between the team at the top of the league and the others.

It is consistently shown in surveys that the importance of attention to diet is recognized by coaches and athletes from all sports, and a large majority believe that nutrition is an important part of the preparation for competition.

This recognition of the importance of nutrition is not, however, matched by knowledge of the principles on which good nutritional support is based and how, practically, this is best achieved.

Nutrients and foods

It is important that the components of nutrition are known, mainly:

- **Carbohydrates,**
- **Fats,**
- **Proteins,**
- **Vitamins,**
- **Minerals,**
- **Fibre,**
- **Water,**
- **Alcohol.**

The food and drink that we consume contain a variety of these nutrients, and it is essential that the right balance is achieved on a daily basis in order to optimize performance.

░░ Think about what you ate yesterday and try to categorize each food according to the list above.

The foods that we consume play three major roles within our bodies:

1 **Providing energy** – almost all our bodily functions rely on the energy contained within the foods we eat and drink.
2 **Assisting in growth and repair** – body tissues are constantly being broken down and regenerated. This is achieved by utilizing the foods we eat and is especially important when players are injured.
3 **Maintaining general body function** – as well as providing energy to train and compete, the daily needs of individuals must be

met in order to maintain the function of our biological systems, for example, the heart, lungs and stomach.

For the footballer, ensuring the diet contains sufficient energy to meet the daily requirements is most critical. When considering whether a player's diet is 'healthy' or 'balanced', many nutritionists believe that if the correct amount of fuel is provided by the right proportion of nutrients, then enough of the other essential nutrients will also be provided.

No one food contains all the nutrients we need, therefore, it is important that a wide variety of foods are consumed. Figure 34 shows a number of foods from the major food groups and indicates what proportion should be consumed on a daily basis.

Figure 34 **The major food groups and proportional daily requirements**

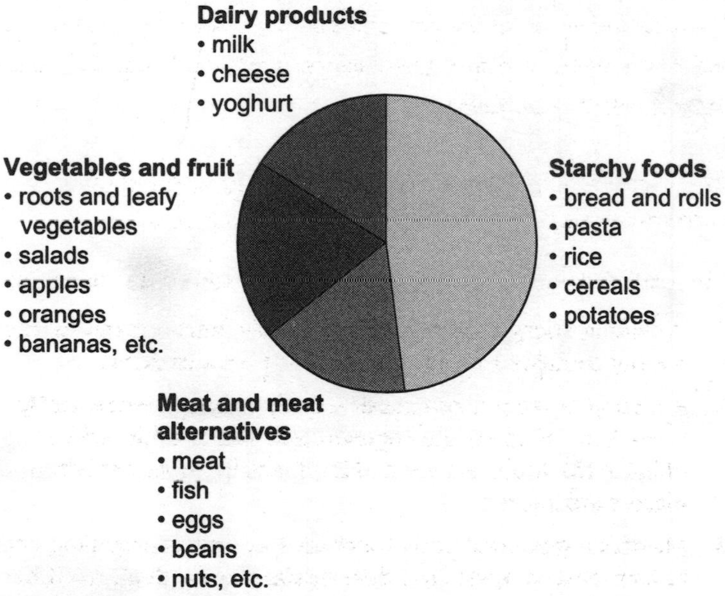

Dairy products
• milk
• cheese
• yoghurt

Vegetables and fruit
• roots and leafy
  vegetables
• salads
• apples
• oranges
• bananas, etc.

Starchy foods
• bread and rolls
• pasta
• rice
• cereals
• potatoes

Meat and meat alternatives
• meat
• fish
• eggs
• beans
• nuts, etc.

Table 5 **Sources of nutrients and their major roles**

Nutrient	Major roles	Sources
Carbohydrates Foods high in carbohydrate are commonly divided into two types: • Simple carbohydrates, which tend to be found in highly refined foods. • Complex carbohydrates, which tend to exist in their natural unrefined state.	Carbohydrates in either form are broken down to glucose in the body and stored as glycogen. The majority is stored in muscles; some is stored in the liver, which is used to raise the level of blood glucose when required and supply the brain and muscles. Great demands are placed on carbohydrate stores during heavy exercise (see Figure 37, page 128).	Simple (sugars): confectionery, cakes, preserves, soft drinks. Complex (starches): rice, bread, pasta, potatoes, cereals, fruit.
Fats Fats can be split into two types: • Saturated fatty acids, which are mainly found in animal fats and are usually solid at room temperature. • Unsaturated fatty acids, which mainly come from vegetable or fish sources and are liquid or soft at room temperature.	Fats are stored mainly in adipose tissues and some are stored in muscle cells. They contribute to the general health of individuals, their metabolism playing an important role in the production of energy. Some essential fatty acids must form part of any diet.	Butter, margarine, lard, oils, oily fish (mackerel, pilchards, salmon), pasties, cheese, whole milk, nuts, fresh food.
Proteins	Proteins are composed of amino acids, and form an essential component of any diet. They are required for the growth and repair of body tissues, the building blocks of hormones and enzymes. They are also important in the functioning of the immune system.	Milk, cheese, meat, yoghurt, poultry, fish, eggs, nuts, pulses.

Vitamins and minerals	Vitamins and minerals play an important role in energy metabolism; deficiency of one or more of these micronutrients can impair exercise capacity. Deficiencies, however, are rare in sportspeople. Excessive amounts of some micronutrients may be harmful.	Fruit, vegetables, nuts, fish, meat, eggs, dairy products, cereals.
Fibre (non-digestible vegetables, carbohydrate)	Dietary fibre is a mixture of mainly indigestible substances which are found in plant cells. In the digestive system dietary fibre assists the body to absorb and use nutrients. Deficiencies can result in constipation and gallstones.	Seeds, peas, beans, vegetables, fruits, wholegrain cereals.
Water	Water performs numerous functions and is one of the body's most important nutrients. It acts as the major transport medium in the body and is crucial in the regulation of body temperature and preventing dehydration.	Foods, drinks, formulated sports drinks.
Alcohol	Alcohol may make a major contribution to the total energy intake of a person's diet. However, this energy source cannot be utilized by muscles; it is slowly metabolized by the liver at a constant rate. Excessive amounts are stored as fats.	Alcoholic drinks: beers, wines, etc.

Energy, energy sources and requirements for football

The adequacy of a diet is often expressed by referring to the percentage of energy supplied by the three nutrients (carbohydrate, fat and protein). Before we can assess this, the energy content of these nutrients must be understood.

A healthy diet is one in which the energy intake matches a person's daily demands and over half is provided by carbohydrate-containing foods, less than a third from fat and the remainder from protein (Figure 35).

Figures 35 and 36 **The major food groups and proportional daily requirements**

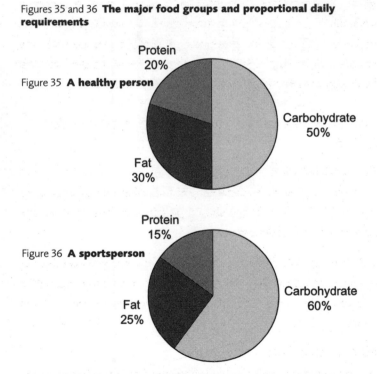

Figure 35 **A healthy person**

Protein 20%
Carbohydrate 50%
Fat 30%

Figure 36 **A sportsperson**

Protein 15%
Carbohydrate 60%
Fat 25%

The recommended composition of a sportsperson's diet is slightly different (Figure 36), with the energy requirements being greater in the case of footballers. This is determined by three components:

1 **Basal metabolic rate (BMR) which is the minimum rate of metabolism for an individual (approximately ²/₃ of our daily energy expenditure).**

2 **The energy expended on the digestion, absorption and storage of food (approximately 10% of our daily energy expenditure).**

3 **The energy cost of exercise, including daily activities and training/playing.**

It is recommended that players should get as much as 60–70% of their daily energy requirements in the form of carbohydrate. Tables 6 and 7 on pages 126–7 (Diet 1 and Diet 2) represent hypothetical daily diets. It should be apparent that although Diet 1 would meet the energy requirements of an active 75 kg male player, it would not fulfill his requirements in terms of the proportion of nutrients required. On the other hand, Diet 2 is the reverse – the proportions of the diet are ideal but the energy requirements of the player would not be met.

■ Use Tables 6 and 7 as a template and track your daily food intake.

Energy metabolism

Everyone should have an understanding of how different energy sources are used by the body, but this should definitely be the case for any footballer involved in regular participation.

Figure 37 on page 128 illustrates the effect the intensity of exercise has on the relative contributions of fat and carbohydrate form the muscle and blood towards the production of energy, providing you with a brief overview of this area.

Aerobic metabolism

Energy is provided mainly by carbohydrate and fat. During low-intensity exercise the body uses oxygen to burn up both carbohydrate and fat to

Table 6 **Hypothetical daily food intake (Diet 1)**

Food	Weight (g)	Energy (kcal)	Protein (g)	Fat (g)	Carbohydrate (g)	Fibre (g)
Breakfast						
Sausage (fried)	60	222.1	6.4	19.3	5.7	0
Bacon (fried)	60	268.5	14.7	23.3	0	0
Eggs (fried)	45	66.1	5.5	4.9	0	0
Bread (fried)	30	73.3	2.3	0.5	14.9	0.8
Lard	30	270	0	30	0	0
Coffee	5	4.8	0.7	0	0.5	0
Milk	30	19.5	1.0	1.1	1.4	0
Sugar	30	128	0	0	32.0	0
Lunch						
Mars bar	45	205.7	2.4	8.5	29.9	0
Cheese	20	405.5	26.0	33.5	0	0
Butter	100	150.8	0.8	16.4	0	0
White roll	80	196.6	6.2	1.4	39.8	2.2
Crisps	30	164	1.9	10.8	14.8	3.6
Cola drink	285	119.6	0	0	29.9	0
Dinner						
Cod in batter	200	402.2	39.2	20.6	15.0	0
Chips	250	655.6	9.5	27.2	93.2	6.3
Two pints beer	1,140	269	2.4	0	26.2	0
Totals		**3,621**	119	197.5	303.3	12.9
% energy			13%	46.4%	34.0%	

+ 6.6% alcohol

Table 7 **Hypothetical daily food intake (Diet 2)**

Food	Weight (g)	Energy (kcal)	Protein (g)	Fat (g)	Carbohydrate (g)	Fibre (g)
Breakfast						
Muesli	100	385.2	13.0	7.6	66.2	7.4
Skimmed milk	250	86.7	8.5	0.3	12.5	0
Wholemeal toast	100	226.7	8.8	2.7	41.8	8.5
Low-fat spread	20	72.9	0	8.1	0	0
Honey	50	153.6	0.2	0	38.2	0
Fresh orange juice	150	53.2	0.6	0	12.7	0
Tea	3	0	0	0	0	0
Skimmed milk	30	10	1	0	1.5	0
Lunch						
Wholemeal bread	100	226.7	8.8	2.7	41.8	8.5
Low-fat spread	20	72.9	0	8.1	0	0
Lean ham	50	135.1	12.4	9.5	0	0
Tomato	25	3.6	0.2	0	0.7	0.4
Lettuce	15	1.2	0.1	0	0.2	0.2
Apple	150	73.6	0.5	0	17.9	2.3
Dinner						
Roast chicken	120	170.4	31.8	4.8	0	0
Jacket potato	200	267.6	5.2	5.2	50	5
Sweetcorn	60	48.3	1.7	0.3	9.7	3.4
Runner beans	60	14.8	1.4	0	2.3	2
Cauliflower	80	10.8	1.5	0	1.2	1.4
Tinned peaches	120	139.6	0.6	0	34.3	3
Ice cream	150	257.5	5.2	11.1	34.2	0
Totals		**2,410**	101.5	60.4	365.2	42.1
% energy			**16.8%**	**22.6%**	**60.6%**	

provide energy for the muscles to work (Figure 37). This method of energy production is known as aerobic metabolism. At this intensity fat accounts for more than half of energy production.

Anaerobic metabolism

As exercise becomes more intense, the body utilizes mainly carbohydrates, and relies less on aerobic metabolism. This is known as anaerobic metabolism. Most anaerobic energy comes from converting carbohydrate to lactic acid, which can only continue for a limited period of time because of the fatiguing effects of lactic acid.

A player's carbohydrate stores are limited, and when the exercise intensity requires energy to be produced anaerobically the carbohydrate stores are used up quickly. The lactic acid produced is a waste product of this energy system and is known to be linked with muscular fatigue.

As a player becomes better trained, his or her capacity to produce energy aerobically, and therefore decreasing the production of lactic acid, increases. Also, a player's capacity to store carbohydrate in the

Figure 37 **Effect of exercise intensity on the relative contribution of blood glucose, muscle glycogen and fat towards energy production**

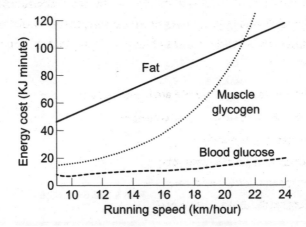

working muscles increases. One of the aims of nutrition for footballers is to utilize this capacity and maximize a player's potential, eliminating any likelihood of a player depleting his or her carbohydrate energy stores during a competitive match.

Dietary habits of football players

There has been very little research undertaken to investigate the nutritional habits of football players. Whilst evidence of nutritional habits is scarce, what evidence there is, combined with anecdotal evidence from those who have worked with football players, suggests that there is considerable scope for improvement in the nutritional habits of football players, which will in turn lead to improvements in playing performance.

Whilst the amount of work undertaken to analyse the diets of football players has been limited, the results of the studies that have been made clearly suggest that there is considerable potential for footballers at all levels to increase their carbohydrate intake.

Understanding carbohydrates

Carbohydrate and fluid intake should be the main consideration for football players as glycogen (stored carbohydrate) depletion and dehydration are two major causes of fatigue during football training and matches.

Foods that contain carbohydrate are listed below:

- **Breads, pizza bases, and crispbreads,**
- **Rice, pasta and noodles,**
- **Potatoes and potato products,**
- **Peas, beans, lentils and corn,**
- **Fruits (fresh, dried and tinned),**

- Sugar, jams, honey and fruit spreads,
- Biscuits, cakes and buns,
- Confectionery and muesli bars,
- Fruit yoghurts and other puddings,
- Soft drinks and commercial sports drinks,
- Glucose polymer powders.

Carbohydrate can be divided into two main categories: complex (starchy) carbohydrate found in foods such as rice, pasta, bread and potatoes, and simple (sugary) carbohydrate found in fruits, jams, honey and confectionery. In reality, most of the foods we eat contain a mixture of simple and complex carbohydrate e.g. cakes, buns, biscuits, breakfast cereals and puddings.

To ensure that a footballer's diet is high in carbohydrate and is also 'balanced' a mixture of carbohydrate-rich foods and drinks should be consumed. This variety will help the player to consume adequate quantities of other nutrients such as protein, vitamins, minerals and fibre, which are also found in foods such as breads, rice, pasta, breakfast cereals, pizza, potatoes and fruits.

During training a player may need as much as 5–7 g of carbohydrate per kg of body mass per day, with a little more during intense training periods and in the 24-hour period after matches.

The immediate recovery period post training and matches is a crucial period during which the depleted muscle carbohydrate stores can be replenished at a faster rate than normal. It is recommended that immediately post training players consume 1–2 g of carbohydrate/kg and then the same again two hours later.

In conjunction with the fluids that players should be consuming, 1–2 g of carbohydrate per kg of body mass is not substantial and is therefore not unrealistic to achieve. As a guide, the following food portions contain 50 g of carbohydrate:

- **Four to five slices bread/1½ bread rolls/3½ crumpets/1 banana sandwich,**
- **Large bowl cereal/four Weetabix,**
- **170 g jacket potato/60g (½ packet) instant mashed potato,**
- **170–225 g cooked pasta/rice,**
- **450 g can baked beans,**
- **Three bananas/four to five pieces fruit (apples, oranges, pears),**
- **Just over one bar chocolate or 60–100 g sugar confectionery.**
- **Seven teaspoons honey/ten teaspoons sugar,**
- **Just under 1 l 'isotonic' sports drink.**

■   Read the labels on food packaging so that you can see the carbohydrate content of each food item.

It is difficult to achieve the recommended intake of carbohydrate from only three meals a day. Therefore, snacking should play a crucial role in a footballer's nutrition programme. The size and timing of these snacks and whether they are in fluid or solid form will depend upon individual preference. For example, some players may have difficulty eating solid foods immediately after exercise, therefore, for these individuals, a sports drink should be consumed which will meet both fluid and carbohydrate requirements.

Best Practice Maintain carbohydrate levels by eating sensibly at meal times and snacking sensibly throughout the day.

The following snacks are popular amongst athletes. They are high in carbohydrate and relatively low in fat:

- Banana/jam/honey/chocolate spread or peanut butter sandwiches,
- Muesli bars or sweetened popcorn,
- Fruit cake, currant buns, scones, American muffins,
- Crumpets, bagels, English muffins, scotch pancakes,
- Pop Tarts, rusks and cereal,
- Jelly cubes and confectionery,
- Low-fat rice pudding, bread pudding.

What to eat and when

The competitive year for the football player can be divided into three main phases: the close season, the pre-season and the playing season. We will briefly consider the nutritional habits of football players during each of these phases:

Close season

During the close season, it is suggested that the energy intake of a football player tends to greatly exceed energy expenditure. Activity levels decrease, and there is little attempt to modify eating habits accordingly. Total energy intake is not reduced to match the decrease in

There are three key phases of development. Coaches will need to be aware of each phase and the types of training they should focus on in order to maximize player potential, enjoyment and reduce the risk of injury.

A the fundamental phase, 6–11 years old

B training to train phase, 11–14 years old

C training to compete phase, 14–20 years old

To decrease the risk of injury always ensure that each training session begins with a thorough warm-up.

Be aware that rest is a crucial factor of training. Continuous days of strength or endurance exercises over a long period is not advisable.

Well-planned training sessions will have predetermined aims and objectives.

Cooling down is an essential part of every training session.

Flexibility work is often overlooked and viewed as a necessary evil. By improving flexibility the ability of a player to produce an effective movement in a game is significantly enhanced.

energy expenditure and during this phase there tends to be significant increases in the body-fat percentages of many football players.

Pre-season

During the pre-season phase, energy expenditure increases significantly as players enter a period of intense conditioning and fitness work. However, many players often severely restrict their energy intake during this phase in order to reduce the body fat which has been gained during the close season.

This restriction in energy intake is likely to adversely affect a player's ability to train and play, and would not be necessary if energy intake had more closely matched energy expenditure during the close season. During the close season, players should therefore be encouraged to reduce their total energy intake to match their lower level of energy expenditure, although these will not be significant reductions if appropriate conditioning is adopted out of season.

Playing season

Throughout the playing season, energy intake generally appears to equal energy expenditure for the majority of football players. However, the contribution of the macronutrients, protein, fat, carbohydrate and alcohol to total energy intake could be changed to facilitate improved recovery and to support improved training and playing performances.

Many football players are not aware of the vital role of carbohydrate in supporting intensive training and playing. When travelling to away fixtures that involve extensive journey times players may miss breakfast and have to grab a quick snack on the road which will often have a high fat content. This will delay the process of digestion, and coupled with the lack of breakfast the low carbohydrate intake will contribute to an earlier onset of fatigue during the game.

After the match, energy consumption is often high in both fat and alcohol, which will not facilitate a rapid rate of recovery. It is suggested that high carbohydrate 'snacks' should be made available to players travelling to and from away matches. Players should also be encouraged to eat foods with a high carbohydrate content after training sessions, and to ensure that their diet consistently contains a high proportion of carbohydrate foods.

During periods of injury, energy expenditure generally decreases, whilst energy intake often remains the same, or even increases. Since energy intake will, therefore, exceed energy expenditure, the majority of players with medium to long-term injuries experience significant increases in their body-fat levels. This decreases the rate of recovery and, if not corrected, increases the risk of further injury occurring. Injured players should be encouraged to pay particular attention to their nutritional habits during a period of injury by attempting to match their energy intake with energy expenditure.

During the close and pre-season phases (and periods of injury) there should be fundamental changes in the balance between energy intake and expenditure. Throughout the playing season there should be more subtle changes in the percentage contribution of fat, carbohydrate, protein and alcohol to energy intake, with the emphasis placed on increased carbohydrate consumption. These changes can be achieved through a combination of self-discipline and sensible rather than radical changes in nutritional habits.

█ Review your dietary habits at various points throughout the season and compare this to the recommendations above.

Consuming a diet which is low in fat

It is not necessary to totally eliminate fat from the diet. In fact, a certain amount of dietary fat is essential to ensure good health. However, many footballers are consuming large quantities of fat at the expense of their carbohydrate intake.

The following recommendations are designed to help a player to achieve a low intake of fat as well as a high intake of carbohydrate:

- **Base every meal and snack around a carbohydrate-rich food and make sure that these items are the main food on the plate.**

- **Meats and sauces should be accompaniments to the breads, pasta, rice, potatoes, etc.**

- **Use some reduced fat alternative foods such as reduced-fat milk, spreads, cheeses and yoghurts and choose lean cuts of meat.**

- **Grill, poach, bake or microwave food rather than frying or roasting.**

- **Choose 'plain' cakes, buns and biscuits. These tend to contain less fat than the fancy versions.**

Consuming adequate quantities of fluid

During training and competition it is vital to monitor a player's state of hydration. The following checks will help you:

- **Weight** – 1 kg of weight lost over a training session is equivalent to the loss of 1 l of fluid. Players should aim to drink 1–1½ l of decaffeinated fluid for every 1 kg of weight loss during training and matches.

- **The 'pee' test** – Small volumes of dark coloured, smelly urine generally indicate the need to drink. Regular visits to the toilet producing copious quantities of relatively clear-coloured urine indicates sufficient hydration.

- **Thirst** – Thirst is an unreliable indicator of the need to drink. By the time you are thirsty you are already partly dehydrated.

If you finish a training session and you are thirsty then you have not taken enough fluid on board during the session. Whenever you become thirsty start to drink immediately. Preferably, drink before you are thirsty.

Best Practice Always look to maintain fluid levels throughout the day by drinking little and often.

The best fluid to drink (i.e. one which has a rapid gastric emptying rate and is quickly absorbed) is a diluted carbohydrate/electrolyte solution. Generally, commercial sports drinks are formulated to try to meet these recommendations. It is difficult to ensure that home-made alternatives contain the correct mix of carbohydrates, fluid and electrolytes.

The recommendation is to drink before, during and after training as well as drinking as frequently as possible during a match. Practise drinking a little and often. Gastro-intestinal distress is usually associated with drinking too much too quickly and is often noted in individuals who are already dehydrated.

Quote | 'Optimal nutrition is fundamental to a player's success.'

Key hydration points

* Rehydration is a major part of the recovery process after exercise, but little attention has been placed by players and coaches on the need to adequately rehydrate in order to optimally perform during subsequent exercise bouts.

* It is well established that exercise performance is severely impaired in a dehydrated state ($\approx$2% decrease in body weight can lead to a greater than 30% fall in performance) and that both high-intensity and endurance activities are affected. There is also an increased risk of heat illness in individuals who begin exercise in a dehydrated state.

* Rehydration requires replacement of body water loss, but ingestion of plain water is not an effective way to achieve a positive state of hydration. Drinks should contain moderately high levels of sodium and possibly some potassium.

* To surmount ongoing urine losses, the volume consumed should be greater than the volume of sweat lost. Palatability of beverages is an important factor in stimulating drinking.

Traditionally, sports nutrition research has focused on running and cycling performance because of the ease by which research studies either on a treadmill or bike can be controlled. However, the critical influence that nutrition can have on football training and competition has now been recognized. A diet that is high in carbohydrate and adequate in its fluid content will ensure that the footballer can support consistent and intensive training, ultimately affecting performance.

LEARNING

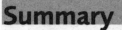
Summary

- **Nutrition is a key aspect in the overall performance of footballers and should be taken seriously.**

- **Ensuring adequate quantities of carbohydrate are consumed is critical for maintaining the quality of training.**

- **Consuming adequate quantities of fluid is critical to the well-being of all footballers.**

Self testers

- Name five foods that are high in carbohydrate.
- Approximately how many grams of carbohydrate are contained in four to five slices of bread?
- A 1 kg loss in weight after a training session is the equivalent to how many litres of lost fluid?

Action plan

Review your diet and ensure you're meeting the correct levels of carbohydrate and fluid intake.

Chapter 8

Monitoring progress

> THIS CHAPTER WILL:
> - Explain how to record your fitness progress.
> - Demonstrate how to monitor your dietary habits.
> - Show how to perform simple tests to measure your physical capabilities.

Now that you have an understanding of all the different aspects that combine to make up the overall fitness of players it is crucial that you are able to monitor your progress.

How to record your progress – general training and fitness

Diaries play a key role in the monitoring process. The following details two different components of the diary that can be used, namely the training diary and the lifestyle diary.

All players should keep a training diary so that they can monitor their responses to training. A training diary is one of the most important tools to help a player recognize whether or not he/she is coping with training.

Learning to listen to and recognize the body's signs and cues is the most important skill that you can acquire. Every day, you should record four essential markers:

- **The details of your training,**
- **The quality of your sleep,**
- **Your morning resting heart rate,**
- **A daily rating of energy levels.**

Although some of the measures require specialist equipment that you may not have, complete all the sections that you are able to. The overall aim is not necessarily to complete all the requirements but to encourage players to begin to monitor aspects that make up their overall fitness.

Training diary

For each individual training session completed, it is worth recording the type of session, duration and approximate intensity, with heart rate information if possible. Try to be as accurate as possible when outlining the type of sessions that you have completed, especially if this is a session with your club.

Also, ensure that you list all of the sessions and matches you have completed (including duration of the match played and your position).

Before completing your diary, please read the following notes and keep referring back to them. This should serve as a basis for the development of your fitness and should form part of your good practice in ensuring that you complete it accurately and honestly. Your diary will also serve as a reference point when analysing changes in your fitness over the forthcoming months.

- **Date and day** – Make sure that you indicate clearly the day and date that you are referring to and ideally you should complete an entry even if you are not training as a record of other feelings should be made – just indicate that it is your rest day. If you complete any kind of recovery or relaxation sessions (for example, pool, spa, sauna) then make sure that you indicate this and always start a new page for each new day and training session.

- **Time of session** – Make sure that you state clearly what time of day you completed each session. If you do more than one session in a day then you should complete two separate pages. For all sessions, you need to give a clear outline of the content of the session, including club training. For example, if it was a speed session, try to give an estimation of the number of sprints, distance of each sprint, etc. If it was a technical session, indicate whether it was 11 vs. 11 or a rehearsal of set plays, etc.

- **Duration** – Clearly indicate how long the session lasted. If possible, try to break the session down, for example 20 minutes warm-up, 20 minutes speed training and 20 minutes of 11 vs. 11.

- **Intensity** – Estimate how intense the session was, on a scale of 1–5 with 1 being an extremely light and easy session (i.e.

recovery) and 5 being an extremely intense session, at the end of which you were shattered.

- Heart rate – If you have access to a heart-rate monitor, you should wear it for every session and should be familiar with its operation. For every session, you need to write down the minimum, maximum and average heart rate for each session. You can access this information by scrolling through the file option on your watch.

- Final heart rate – At the end of every session, and prior to the cool-down, you should make a note of your final heart rate. You should then monitor your recovery heart rate for the next three minutes, making a note of the reading every minute. Make sure that you do the same activity when analysing this, i.e. stand still, walk or jog slowly.

- Energy used – You should have your watch set in the kcals mode, and this will give you an 'estimate' of the number of kcals that you have used during each session. Again you need to write this information down for every session completed.

Table 8 opposite gives an example of how you should keep a record of your daily training.

Lifestyle diary

It is important not only to monitor the amount of training that is conducted but also how an individual responds to different training loads, i.e. how he or she feels. By recording this together with some lifestyle components it is possible to get an indication of how an individual is coping with the demands of training. This information assists in making decisions on whether the training load should be decreased or even increased. The lifestyle diary includes the following components:

- Hours of training – For each day of training, indicate accurately the number of hours trained on that day.

- Hours of sleep – For each day of training, indicate accurately the number of hours you have slept during the previous night.

Table 8 **A sample diary entry**

Date 18/02/04   **Day** Wednesday

Description of session completed

Time of session	11.30 a.m.
Type of session	Warm-up (20 minutes)
	Speed (2 sets, 6 reps of 8–10 m sprints)
	Agility (2 sets, 5 reps of T-agility drill)
	Endurance run (High intensity 4 × 4 minutes)
	Cool-down
Duration	1 hour 10 minutes
Intensity (1–5)	1 2 3 ④ 5
Resting heart rate	63
Maximum heart rate	181
Average heart rate	166
Minimum heart rate	88
Final heart rate	178
1 min heart rate	123
2 min heart rate	110
3 min heart rate	94
Kcals	458

For the next nine parameters, you need to indicate on a scale of 1–5 how you feel each day, (1 = awful and 5 = excellent). Be as accurate as possible.

- **Quality of sleep – How good was your night of sleep? Did you wake up many times throughout the night, did it take you long to get to sleep or did you go straight to sleep? Did you wake up feeling refreshed or did you struggle to get out of bed?**

- Energy levels – How energetic do you feel today? Do you feel bright and breezy or are you tired and lethargic?

- Muscle soreness – Do your muscles ache, perhaps from a match or from a strength session? Is it your whole body or just certain muscles?

- Motivation – Were you keen to do your training session, or was it difficult to get to your training venue and put in maximal effort throughout the session? How does this compare to how you normally feel?

- Attitude to work – Are you motivated at work or are you more restless than usual and struggling to finish tasks that you have started? Are you less tolerant with colleagues, or customers? Have you got exams or assignment deadlines?

- Health – Do you feel vibrant and full of energy at the moment or have you suffered from sore throats, colds, niggling injuries or lethargy? Do you struggle to get out of bed?

- General tiredness – Do you feel energetic and vibrant during work and at training, or do you feel generally lethargic and is it a real effort to go to work, school, college or training? Does training make you feel more vibrant, or does it make you feel even more tired?

- Diet – What has your diet been like today? Have you just snacked all day, or have you eaten sensibly throughout the day, with a majority of carbohydrate foods?

- Comments – Anything which you feel would affect your training should be highlighted in this section.

If you are under more pressure at work, or having to work longer hours and therefore feel more tired when training, then you should highlight this. If you are currently sitting exams at school or college, then this will be placing extra demands on you. Also, if you have any personal problems that are worrying you, or causing you not to sleep, then again you should make a note of this. This diary will serve as a reference over the coming months, and eventually years when analysing your training routine and changes in fitness levels. Hence, you should provide as much information as possible in this diary.

Table 9 is an example of this section of the training diary and shows how scores should be marked.

Table 9 **A sample training diary entry**

Subjective feelings and lifestyle

Hours of training today   2 hours
Approximate number of hours sleep   9 hours

For the following eight parameters, please CIRCLE on a scale of 1–5, where 1 = awful and 5 = excellent

Quality of sleep	1	2	3	(4)	5
Energy levels	1	2	3	(4)	5
Muscle soreness	1	2	(3)	4	5
Motivation	1	(2)	3	4	5
Attitude to work	1	(2)	3	4	5
Health	1	2	(3)	4	5
General tiredness	1	2	(3)	4	5
Diet	1	2	(3)	4	5

Comments   Day off work, was still a bit tired from the game on Sunday. Had a cold last week, still recovering from that and still feel a little bit lethargic with that. Lots of things on at work, and lots of deadlines to meet, having to work longer hours than usual.

Date   Day

How to record your progress – eating and drinking habits

As described in the training diary, it is crucial that players begin to track their eating and drinking habits. We have already highlighted how important nutrition and fluid intake are and in order to follow progress and improvements in eating and drinking habits we recommend that a nutritional diary is kept.

On the following pages we have provided an example of a diet diary that we recommend you use as a guide to record your eating habits.

For each item recorded, state an approximate portion size (i.e. small, medium, large) and where appropriate, state the method used to cook items, i.e. deep fried, grilled, oven baked, etc.

Before completion, it is advisable that you read the following notes and refer to them throughout the completion of the diary.

Description of food and drink items

It is important to give an accurate description of each food item and remember to record the method of cooking, for example, cornflakes with semi-skimmed milk and sugar.

- Milk – Full-fat, semi-skimmed, skimmed, etc.
- Cheese – Cheddar, cottage cheese, processed cheese slices, etc.
- Yoghurt – Low fat, full fat, Greek style, etc.
- Eggs – Specify size and whether boiled, poached, fried or scrambled, etc.
- Meat/Fish – Cut of meat, whether lean or fatty meat, raw or cooked and cooking method. Type of fish and cooking method.
- Bread and rolls – Wholemeal, white, brown, granary, buttery rolls, etc. Also indicate whether thin or thick sliced, and number of slices.

- Biscuits – Savoury, sweet, chocolate or cream, etc.

- Fruit – Fresh fruit (specify type), canned fruit (specify if in syrup or in juice), cooked fruit (specify if stewed with sugar or sweetener).

- Vegetables – Raw, boiled, baked, fried, frozen or canned, etc.

- Butter/Margarine – Butter, low-fat spread, cooking oil, lard, etc.

- Beverages – Tea, coffee (specify if decaffeinated, instant or ground), fizzy drinks (specify if diet or decaffeinated), pure fruit juice and squash (specify if sweetened, unsweetened or sugar free, etc).

- Alcohol – Be honest! Spirits (specify type and record as pub measures), mixers (specify if normal or diet), wine (specify if red, white or rosé, dry, medium or sweet), beer, lager and alco pops (specify type – if draught, bottled, canned, etc.).

Table 10 **Example of a diet diary**

Date	Day			
Meal	**Description of food/drink consumed**	**Portion, size or quantity**	**Cooking method**	

Monitoring your fitness – fitness tests

In order to monitor your progress in terms of the four S's discussed earlier we recommend that on a regular basis (at least once every four to six weeks during the season) players use the following tests.

The following tests have been chosen as they are relatively simple to complete but will still provide the player with a reliable measure of any improvements following the changes made to his/her training programme.

Vertical jumps

The vertical jump has frequently been used as a test of anaerobic power. Jumping height is a key component of performance in football, although there is considerable variability in the manner in which jumps are performed.

For example, a centre back may execute jumps from a single or double leg take-off, a standing position or from various length run-ups, and even whilst running backwards.

The following jumping tests take into consideration the specific requirements of football and will give all those performing the test an excellent benchmark to measure their own performance.

In previous studies of vertical jumps the averages achieved by professional footballers has ranged from 50–65 cm.

Vertical jump (Sargent jump)
Aim/Objective
To assess a player's standing vertical jump.

Equipment
- Chalk,
- Wall,
- Ruler,
- Stepladder.

Location
Inside or outside.

Procedure
- Chalk the fingertips of the player's preferred hand.
- The player stands side-on, with the preferred hand nearest the wall.
- The player reaches as high as possible with their feet flat on floor and makes a chalk mark on the wall.
- From standing, the player performs a counter-movement jump, taking both feet and makes a second chalk mark as high as possible.
- The distance between the two chalk marks is then measured.

Scoring
- Distances should be measured to the nearest centimetre.

Step 1

Step 2

Step 3

The sequence of movements involved in the vertical jump

- The player performs three jumps – one practice followed by two trials. The best of the two trials is recorded. The assessor must ensure that the players are given adequate time for a full recovery between trials.

Standing long jump

Aim/Objective

To assess a player's standing long jump.

Equipment

- Measuring tape.

Location

A football pitch.

Procedure

- The player begins with feet approximately shoulder-width apart on a designated starting line.
- The player performs a counter-movement jump, leaping forward as far as possible, taking off and landing on both feet.
- The distance jumped is then measured.

Scoring

- Distances should be measured and recorded to the nearest centimetre.
- The player performs three jumps – one practice followed by two trials. The best of the two trials is recorded. The assessor must ensure that the players are given adequate time for a full recovery between attempts.

Cooper run

This is simply a 12-minute run when the player covers as much distance as possible.

Equipment

- Stopwatch.

Location

A football pitch as this makes measuring the distance easier, although the player can run on the road.

Scoring

Distance is recorded to the nearest ¼ of a pitch and is recorded after the 12-minute run has been completed.

Summary

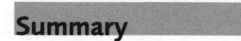

- Keeping both a training and diet diary are useful exercises for keeping a historical record and for measuring progress.

- The more often you can record the events and the more detailed the information the greater the potential benefit.

- Measuring physical capabilities through simple tests assists in measuring progress and analysing the effectiveness of the individual's training programme.

Self testers

- When measuring fitness and general well-being what are the four markers that should be recorded?
- Ideally, how often should you complete the diaries?
- What is the Cooper run?

Action plan

Complete the training and diet diaries.

Conclusion

The philosophy of fitness training should be based upon sound scientific knowledge and experience of what does and does not work. This guide can play a role in laying down the foundations upon which both football theory and practice can develop. A range of topics have been discussed with practical strategies and action plans being suggested along the way, which will serve to enhance your understanding of the various elements of fitness.

The guide has provided a brief overview of the respiratory, cardiovascular and muscular systems together with the various methods utilized by the body to produce energy for work, either with or without oxygen. The responses of these systems to exercise begin to show the role each system plays when exercising, and the analysis of the game demands has demonstrated the need for footballers to possess some of the attributes displayed by sprinters and some of those displayed by athletes. The four S's of fitness were identified with some practical guidelines given, the structure of each component being determined by FITT. The importance of the training principles of individuality, specificity, progressive overload, reversibility and recovery have also been stressed.

A fitness programme that works will depend upon adhering to the principles covered in this guide. Chapter 8 discussed the concept of monitoring, which is the first step towards players taking on some form of self-management. This is a strategy that our youngsters should take on board from an early age.

As the fitness industry continues to boom there still remains a battle throughout the football industry to change tradition, especially in the area related to fitness training. As mentioned in the introduction to this guide, fitness does not develop by chance. There is a desire by many practitioners to enhance the understanding of those around them and to create a positive fitness culture where players themselves take more of an interest in their own bodies and how best to develop them.

Fitness is indeed a complex area; the careful manipulation of conditioning methods and their integration with football training is required at the highest level. This introductory guide provides an overview of the basic areas of fitness that impact on performance, and the relevance of each area with respect to the demands of football has been highlighted along the way. Whether your aim is to gain an insight into the world of conditioning to provide some direction for yourself, your son or your daughter, or to embrace the whole area and go in pursuit of further knowledge by gaining appropriate qualifications, a simple overview has been provided. Although at times the whole area of fitness may appear daunting, especially when all the other factors related to football performance are considered, just remember there are no secrets; train smart, eat well and pay attention to the detail. Ultimately enjoy the game, whatever role you play.

Contacts

**Fédération Internationale de
Football Association (FIFA)**
FIFA House
Hitzigweg 11
PO Box 85
8030 Zurich
Switzerland
Tel: +41-43/222 7777
Fax: +41-43/222 7878
Internet: http://www.fifa.com

Confederations

Asian Football Confederation (AFC)
AFC House, Jalan 1/155B
Bukit Jalil
Kuala Lumpur 57000
Malaysia
Tel: +60-3/8994 3388
Fax: +60-3/8994 2689
Internet: http://www.footballasia.com

**Confédération Africaine de
Football (CAF)**
3 Abdel Khalek Sarwat Street
El Hay El Motamayez
PO Box 23
6th October City
Egypt
Tel: +20-2/837 1000
Fax: +20-2/837 0006
Internet: http://www.cafonline.com

**Confederation of North, Central
American and Caribbean
Association Football
(CONCACAF)**
Central American and Caribbean
Association Football
725 Fifth Avenue, 17th Floor
New York, NY 10022
USA
Tel: +1-212/308 0044
Fax: +1-212/308 1851
Internet: http://www.concacaf.net

Confederación Sudamericana de Fútbol (CONMEBOL)
Autopista Aeropuerto Internacional y
Leonismo Luqueño
Luque (Gran Asunción)
Paraguay
Tel: +595-21/645 781
Fax: +595-21/645 791
Internet: http://www.conmebol.com

Oceania Football Confederation (OFC)
Ericsson Stadium
12 Maurice Road
PO Box 62 586
Penrose
Auckland
New Zealand
Tel: +64-9/525 8161
Fax: +64-9/525 8164
Internet: http://www.oceaniafootball
.com

Union European Football Association (UEFA)
Route de Genève 46
Nyon 1260
Switzerland
Tel: +41-22/994 4444
Fax: +41-22/994 4488
Internet: http://www.uefa.com

Associations
Argentina
Asociación del Fútbol Argentino (AFA)
Viamonte 1366/76
Buenos Aires 1053
Tel: ++54-11/4372 7900
Fax: ++54-11/4375 4410
Internet: http://www.afa.org.ar

Australia
Soccer Australia Limited (ASF)
Level 3
East Stand, Stadium Australia
Edwin Flack Avenue
Homebush NSW 2127
Tel: ++61-2/9739 5555
Fax: ++61-2/9739 5590
Internet: http://www.socceraustralia
.com.au

Belgium
Union Royale Belge des Sociétés de Football Assocation (URBSFA/KBV)
145 Avenue Houba de Strooper
Bruxelles 1020
Tel: ++32-2/477 1211
Fax: ++32-2/478 2391
Internet: http://www.footbel.com

Brazil
Confederação Brasileira de Futebol (CBF)
Rua Victor Civita 66
Bloco 1 – Edifício 5 – 5 Andar
Barra da Tijuca
Rio de Janeiro 22775-040
Tel: ++55-21/3870 3610
Fax: ++55-21/3870 3612
Internet: http://www.cbfnews.com

Cameroon
Fédération Camerounaise de Football (FECAFOOT)
Case postale 1116
Yaoundé
Tel: ++237/221 0012
Fax: ++237/221 6662
Internet: http://www.cameroon.fifa.com

Canada
The Canadian Soccer Association (CSA)
Place Soccer Canada
237 Metcalfe Street
Ottawa ONT K2P 1R2
Tel: ++1-613/237 7678
Fax: ++1-613/237 1516
Internet: http://www.canadasoccer.com

Costa Rica
Federación Costarricense de Fútbol (FEDEFUTBOL)
Costado Norte Estatua León Cortés
San José 670-1000
Tel: ++506/222 1544
Fax: ++506/255 2674
Internet: http://www.fedefutbol.com

Croatia
Croatian Football Federation (HNS)
Rusanova 13
Zagreb 10 000
Tel: ++385-1/236 1555
Fax: ++385-1/244 1501
Internet: http://www.hns-cff.hr

Czech Republic
Football Association of Czech Republic (CMFS)
Diskarska 100
Praha 6 16017
Tel: ++420-2/3302 9111
Fax: ++420-2/3335 3107
Internet: http://www.fotbal.cz

Denmark
Danish Football Association (DBU)
Idrættens Hus
Brøndby Stadion 20
Brøndby 2605
Tel: ++45-43/262 222
Fax: ++45-43/262 245
Internet: http://www.dbu.dk

England
The Football Association (The FA)
25 Soho Square
London W1D 4FA
Tel: ++44-207/745 4545
Fax: ++44-207/745 4546
Internet: http://www.TheFA.com

Finland
Suomen Palloliitto (SPL/FBF)
Urheilukatu 5
PO Box 191
Helsinki 00251
Tel: ++358-9/7421 51
Fax: ++358-9/7421 5200
Internet: http://www.palloliitto.fi

France
Fédération Française de Football (FFF)
60 Bis Avenue d'Iéna
Paris 75116
Tel: ++33-1/4431 7300
Fax: ++33-1/4720 8296
Internet: http://www.fff.fr

Germany
Deutscher Fussball-Bund (DFB)
Otto-Fleck-Schneise 6
Postfach 71 02 65
Frankfurt Am Main 60492
Tel: ++49-69/678 80
Fax: ++49-69/678 8266
Internet: http://www.dfb.de

Greece
Hellenic Football Federation (HFF)
137 Singrou Avenue
Nea Smirni
Athens 17121
Tel: ++30-210/930 6000
Fax: ++30-210/935 9666
Internet: http://www.epo.gr

Ireland Republic
The Football Association of Ireland (FAI)
80 Merrion Square, South
Dublin 2
Tel: ++353-1/676 6864
Fax: ++353-1/661 0931
Internet: http://www.fai.ie

Italy
Federazione Italiana Giuoco Calcio (FIGC)
Via Gregorio Allegri, 14
Roma 00198
Tel: ++39-06/84 911
Fax: ++39-06/84 912 526
Internet: http://www.figc.it

Japan
Japan Football Association (JFA)
JFA House
3-10-15, Hongo
Bunkyo-ku
Tokyo 113-0033
Tel: ++81-3/3830 2004
Fax: ++81-3/3830 2005
Internet: http://www.jfa.or.jp

Kenya
Kenya Football Federation (KFF)
PO Box 40234
Nairobi
Tel: ++254-2/608 422
Fax: ++254-2/249 855
Email: kff@todays.co.ke

Korea Republic
Korea Football Association (KFA)
1-131 Sinmunno, 2-ga
Jongno-Gu
Seoul 110-062
Tel: ++82-2/733 6764
Fax: ++82-2/735 2755
Internet: http://www.kfa.or.kr

Mexico
Federación Mexicana de Fútbol Asociación, A.C. (FMF)
Colima No. 373
Colonia Roma
Mexico, D.F. 06700
Tel: ++52-55/5241 0190
Fax: ++52-55/5241 0191
Internet: http://www.femexfut.org.mx

Netherlands
Koninklijke Nederlandse Voetbalbond (KNVB)
Woudenbergseweg 56–58
PO Box 515
Am Zeist 3700 AM
Tel: ++31-343/499 201
Fax: ++31-343/499 189
Internet: http://www.knvb.nl

Nigeria
Nigeria Football Association (NFA)
Plot 2033, Olusegun
Obasanjo Way, Zone 7, Wuse Abuja
PO Box 5101 Garki
Abuja
Tel: ++234-9/523 7326
Fax: ++234-9/523 7327
Email: nfa@microaccess.com

Northern Ireland
**Irish Football Association Ltd.
(IFA)**
20 Windsor Avenue
Belfast BT9 6EE
Tel: ++44-28/9066 9458
Fax: ++44-28/9066 7620
Internet: http://www.irishfa.com

Paraguay
**Asociación Paraguaya de Fútbol
(APF)**
Estadio de los Defensores del Chaco
Calle Mayor Martinez 1393
Asunción
Tel: ++595-21/480 120
Fax: ++595-21/480 124
Internet: http://www.apf.org.py

Poland
Polish Football Association (PZPN)
Polski Zwiazek Pilki Noznej
Miodowa 1
Warsaw 00-080
Tel: ++48-22/827 0914
Fax: ++48-22/827 0704
Internet: http://www.pzpn.pl

Portugal
**Federação Portuguesa de Futebol
(FPF)**
Praça de Alegria, N. 25
PO Box 21.100
Lisbon 1250-004
Tel: ++351-21/325 2700
Fax: ++351-21/325 2780
Internet: http://www.fpf.pt

Romania
**Romanian Football Federation
(FRF)**
House of Football
Str. Serg. Serbanica Vasile 12
Bucharest 73412
Tel: ++40-21/325 0678
Fax: ++40-21/325 0679
Internet: http://www.frf.ro

Russia
Football Union of Russia (RFU)
8 Luzhnetskaya Naberezhnaja
Moscow 119 992
Tel: ++7-095/201 1637
Fax: ++7-502/220 2037
Internet: http://www.rfs.ru

Scotland
**The Scottish Football Association
(SFA)**
Hampden Park
Glasgow G42 9AY
Tel: ++44-141/616 6000
Fax: ++44-141/616 6001
Internet: http://www.scottishfa.co.uk

South Africa
**South African Football
Association (SAFA)**
First National Bank Stadium
PO Box 910
Johannesburg 2000
Tel: ++27-11/494 3522
Fax: ++27-11/494 3013
Internet: http://www.safa.net

Spain
Real Federación Española de Fútbol (RFEF)
Ramon y Cajal, s/n
Apartado postale 385
Madrid 28230
Tel: ++34-91/495 9800
Fax: ++34-91/495 9801
Internet: http://www.rfef.es

Sweden
Svenska Fotbollförbundet (SVFF)
PO Box 1216
Solna 17 123
Tel: ++46-8/735 0900
Fax: ++46-8/735 0901
Internet: http://www.svenskfotboll.se

Switzerland
Schweizerischer Fussball-Verband (SFV/ASF)
Postfach
Bern 15 3000
Tel: ++41-31/950 8111
Fax: ++41-31/950 8181
Internet: http://www.football.ch

Tunisia
Fédération Tunisienne de Football (FTF)
Maison des Fédérations Sportives
Cité Olympique
Tunis 1003
Tel: ++216-71/233 303
Fax: ++216-71/767 929
Internet: http://www.ftf.org.tn

Turkey
Türkiye Futbol Federasyonu (TFF)
Konaklar Mah. Ihlamurlu Sok. 9
4. Levent
Istanbul 80620
Tel: ++90-212/282 7020
Fax: ++90-212/282 7015
Internet: http://www.tff.org

United States of America
US Soccer Federation (USSF)
US Soccer House
1801 S. Prairie Avenue
Chicago IL 60616
Tel: ++1-312/808 1300
Fax: ++1-312/808 1301
Internet: http://www.ussoccer.com

Uruguay
Asociación Uruguaya de Fútbol (AUF)
Guayabo 1531
Montevideo 11200
Tel: ++59-82/400 4814
Fax: ++59-82/409 0550
Internet: http://www.auf.org.uy

Wales
The Football Association of Wales, Ltd (FAW)
Plymouth Chambers
3 Westgate Street
Cardiff CF10 1DP
Tel: ++44-29/2037 2325
Fax: ++44-29/2034 3961
Internet: http://www.faw.org.uk

For details of County FAs please see **www.TheFA.com**/Grassroots

LEARNING

Index

All about FA Learning

FA Learning is the Educational Division of The FA and is responsible for the delivery, co-ordination and promotion of its extensive range of educational products and services. This includes all courses and resources for coaching, refereeing, psychology, sports science, medical exercise, child protection, crowd safety and teacher training.

The diverse interests of those involved in football ensures that FA Learning remains committed to providing resources and activities suitable for all individuals whatever their interests, experience or level of expertise.

Whether you're a Premier League Manager, sports psychologist or interested parent, our aim is to have courses and resources available that will improve your knowledge and understanding.

If you've enjoyed reading this book and found the content useful then why not take a look at FA Learning's website to find out the types of courses and additional resources available to help you continue your football development.

The website contains information on all the national courses and events managed by The FA as well as information on a number of online resources:

- **Psychology for Soccer Level 1 – Our first online qualification.**
- **Soccer Star – Free online coaching tool for young players.**
- **Soccer Parent – Free online course for parents.**

All these resources can be accessed at home from your own PC and are currently used by thousands of people across the world.

Psychology for Soccer Level 1

Enrol today and join hundreds of others around the world taking part in FA Learning's first ever online qualification.

This pioneering project is the first of its kind to be provided by any Football Governing Body and is available to anyone with access to the internet. There are no additional qualifications required to take part other than an interest in learning more about the needs of young players and an email address!

The course is aimed at coaches, parents and teachers of 7–12 year olds looking to gain an introduction to psychology and features modules based on 'true to life' player, coach and parent scenarios.

Psychology for Soccer Level 1 is a completely interactive, multimedia learning experience. Don't just take our word for it, read some of the comments from those that have already completed the course:

'Wow what a wonderful course! Thank you for the time and effort to make this possible.' **Tracy Scott**

'Just passed the final assessment ... it was a good experience to learn this way and hopefully more qualifications will become available in this format. Thanks.' **Shayne Hall**

'I am a professional football coach working in schools and clubs and have travelled all around the world. I have really enjoyed the literature in this course and it has made me think about how I should address my coaching sessions. I want to progress in the field of sport psychology and this course has whetted my appetite for this subject.' **Chris Rafael Sabater**

The course modules are:

- Psychology and Soccer
- Motivation
- Learning and Acquiring skills
- Psychological Development
- Environment and Social Influences

In addition to the five course modules, learners also have access to a number of further benefits included as part of the course fee. The benefits include:

- **Three months support from qualified FA tutors**
- **Classroom specific online discussion forums**
- **A global online discussion forum**
- **All successful students receive a FA Qualification in psychology**

- **An exclusive resource area containing over 100 articles and web links relating to coaching 7–12 year olds.**

Within the five modules, there are over 20 sessions totaling over eight hours worth of content. Including the use of discussion forums, resource area and the course tasks, we anticipate the course will take on average 20 hours to complete.

For more information and to enroll on the course visit www.**TheFA.com**/FALearning.

THE OFFICIAL FA GUIDE

A PARENT'S GUIDE TO FOOTBALL

Be a part of the game

The Official FA Guide: A Parent's Guide to Football is essential reading for any parent of a young footballer, who wants to get involved and help their child to do their very best.

This book includes:
- **choosing a club and being involved in it**
- **sharing the football interest**
- **being a 'garden coach'.**

Packed with practical exercises, information and expert advice, this book will improve your understanding and enhance your ability and enjoyment of the world's greatest game.

The author, **Les Howie**, is responsible for the development of all clubs in the non-professional national game for The Football Association.

FA Learning
'learning through football'

TheFA.com/FALearning

Visit the website for information on all FA Learning's educational activities.

THE OFFICIAL FA GUIDE TO
PSYCHOLOGY FOR FOOTBALL

Be a part of the game

The Official FA Guide to Psychology for Football is an
introductory guide for anyone who wants to understand the
needs of young players.

This book includes:
- **understanding the motivation, learning and
  development of players**
- **the affect of a player's environment**
- **how to develop individual strategies.**

Packed with practical exercises, information and expert advice,
this book will improve your understanding and enhance your
ability and enjoyment of the world's greatest game.

The author, **Dr Andy Cale**, is The Football Association's
Education Advisor and was previously a lecturer in Sports
Psychology at Loughborough University.

FA Learning
'learning through football'

TheFA.com/FALearning

Visit the website for information on all FA
Learning's educational activities.

THE OFFICIAL FA GUIDE TO
BASIC TEAM COACHING

Be a part of the game

The Official FA Guide to Basic Team Coaching covers all the
essential aspects of coaching and is vital for those who coach
amateur football, or who are considering becoming a coach.

This book includes:
- **team strategies and tactics**
- **leadership and management**
- **match analysis.**

Packed with practical exercises, information and expert advice,
this book will improve your understanding and enhance your
ability and enjoyment of the world's greatest game.

The author, **Les Reed**, is The FA's Acting Technical Director and
was formerly the Assistant Manager at Charlton Athletic. Les has
coached England players at every level from youth to senior teams.

FA Learning
'learning through football'

TheFA.com/FALearning

Visit the website for information on all FA
Learning's educational activities.

THE OFFICIAL FA GUIDE TO
BASIC REFEREEING

Be a part of the game

The Official FA Guide to Basic Refereeing is essential reading for all referees and those in training, and also provides vital knowledge for anyone involved in the game.

This book includes:
- **the laws of the game and how to apply them**
- **recognising free kick and offside offences**
- **important advice about managing players.**

Packed with practical exercises, information and expert advice, this book will improve your understanding and enhance your ability and enjoyment of the world's greatest game.

The author, **John Baker**, is Head of Refereeing at The Football Association, responsible for the 30,000 registered referees in England.

FA Learning
'learning through football'

TheFA.com/FALearning

Visit the website for information on all FA Learning's educational activities.

THE OFFICIAL FA GUIDE TO
RUNNING A TEAM

Be a part of the game

The Official FA Guide to Running a Team is written for anyone involved in the administration side of the game.

This book includes:
- **advice on how to start and run a team**
- **who to turn to for help**
- **how to deal with any problems that may occur**
- **finance, administration, PR and marketing.**

Packed with practical exercises, information and expert advice, this book will improve your understanding and enhance your ability and enjoyment of the world's greatest game.

The author, **Les Howie**, is responsible for the development of all clubs in the non-professional national game for The Football Association

FA Learning
'learning through football'

TheFA.com/FALearning

Visit the website for information on all FA Learning's educational activities.